Written & Illustrated by
# RONALD WIMBERLY

Letters by Jared K. Fletcher ♠ Logotype & Design Assist by Jorden Haley

IMAGE COMICS, INC. • Todd McFarlane: President • Jim Valentino: Vice President • Marc Silvestri: Chief Executive Officer • Erik Larsen: Chief Financial Officer • Robert Kirkman: Chief Operating Officer • Eric Stephenson: Publisher / Chief Creative Officer • Shanna Matuszak: Editorial Coordinator • Marla Eizik: Talent Liaison • Nicole Lapalme: Controller • Leanna Caunter: Accounting Analyst • Sue Korpela: Accounting & HR Manager • Jeff Boison: Director of Sales & Publishing Planning • Dirk Wood: Director of International Sales & Licensing • Alex Cox: Director of Direct Market & Specialty Sales • Chloe Ramos-Peterson: Book Market & Library Sales Manager • Emilio Bautista: Digital Sales Coordinator • Kat Salazar: Director of PR & Marketing • Drew Fitzgerald: Marketing Content Associate • Heather Doornink: Production Director • Drew Gill: Art Director • Hilary DiLoreto: Print Manager • Tricia Ramos: Traffic Manager • Erika Schnatz: Senior Production Artist • Ryan Brewer: Production Artist • Deanna Phelps: Production Artist • IMAGECOMICS.COM

# FOREWORD

I love Hip Hop.

I know. A lot of people do.

However, I came up poor, black, and unseen in rural Mississippi in a supposedly post-integration-post-Civil Rights South. Little did I know how much the culture would affect the way I made art, the way I did research, and the way I live my life. Hip Hop, to borrow from John Berger, is a "way of seeing". It's an epistemology through which one can move through the world.

Fast forward a few decades and I am writing a piece for a book called *Design Studies* that posits a traditional studio design course fused with tenets from Hip Hop culture. The next semester I was teaching a class at the University of Illinois at Urbana-Champaign that was, as far as I can tell, the first course of its kind to successfully translate Hip Hop culture into a traditional college classroom studio setting. My mission was to create "see-jays". Yeah. It's a word I made up but that's what we do in the Academy. So, sue me. Essentially, the way I see it, a SeeJay visually "samples" information and translates what he or she takes in from their visual built environment into narratives, graphic art, etc. To me, Ron Wimberly's PRINCE OF CATS is the type of artifact that I have encouraged my students to have the foresight to produce in my classes. It's a prime example of the type of work that I have based my career upon. That's heavy right?

Wimberly's narrative isn't just a mish-mash of thing he digs. Yes it's *Romeo and Juliet* meets Kurosawa meets *The Warriors* meets "Planet Rock." However, what makes PRINCE OF CATS so innovative is the fact that it acts as a reified index of what Hip Hop culture would manifest itself as visually. That is, it's a pure cultural expression, straight from the source. The genius of Hip Hop culture is the method of production called the remix. The deliberate juxtaposition of seemingly unlike artifacts, assets, beats, what have you, into a cohesive re-mediated cultural expression. The brilliance of Hip Hop, and this story, isn't the formal aspects of it. Those are amazing, to be sure. What makes Wimberly a master of this medium is his visual and intellectual acumen to project equivalence onto myriad types of productions from various cultural sources. To a SeeJay, or whatever you want to call it, one thing is equal to the other. Therefore, one thing can stand in for the other. This syncretic attitude is the backbone of Hip Hop and it's fueled generations of cultural expressions throughout the African Diaspora.

PRINCE OF CATS cleverly deals with notions of class, race, and gender through this unlikely courtship of comics, Hip Hop, and the work of Shakespeare. Wimberly creates a black speculative space that explores the constructions of black masculinity, notions of good and evil, and the nuanced storytelling methods that are totally part of the affordances of the comics medium. Tybalt is meant to die. That's the script. However, when the script is flipped, a black Tybalt is even more cursed and doomed. Or is he? When the curtain falls on this imaginative tale of star-crossed lovers and samurai swords we see a crossroads in the cross swords and a space that might have been. Even Erwin Schrodinger couldn't postulate such a conclusion.

As a child of the Hip Hop generation and a black American man who "wasn't supposed to make it past 25", I see an alternate self reflected into those angry katanas. I see a life that could have been, if the mix had commanded the universe to spin so. PRINCE OF CATS is a visual love-letter to a culture, not stolen, but sold away freely and more's the pity.

To be or not be? Black is and Black ain't? It's the same question but the lips have supposedly opposing shapes.

JOHN JENNINGS is a Professor of Media and Cultural Studies at the University of California at Riverside. His work centers around intersectional narratives regarding identity politics and popular media. Jennings is co-editor of the Eisner Award-winning collection *The Blacker the Ink: Constructions of Black Identity in Comics and Sequential Art* and co-founder/organizer of The Schomburg Center's Black Comic Book Festival in Harlem. He is co-founder and organizer of the MLK NorCal's Black Comix Arts Festival in San Francisco and also SOL-CON: The Brown and Black Comix Expo at the Ohio State University. Jennings is currently a Nasir Jones Hip Hop Studies Fellow with the Hutchins Center at Harvard University. Jennings' current comics projects include the Hip Hop adventure comic *Kid Code: Channel Zero*, the supernatural crime noir story *Blue Hand Mojo*, and the upcoming graphic novel adaptation of Octavia Butler's classic dark fantasy novel *Kindred*.

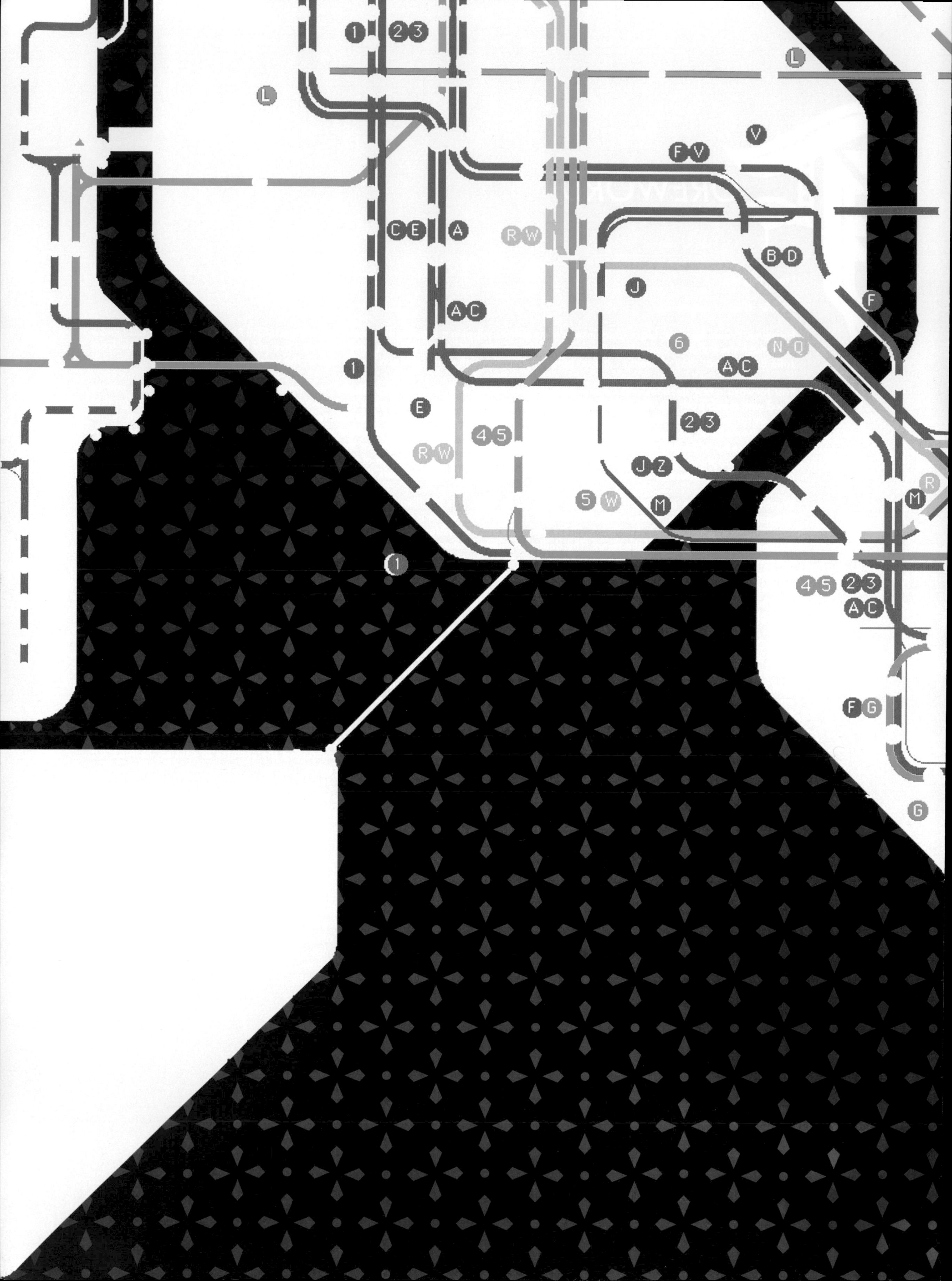
1 2 3
L
L
V
F V
C E
A
R W
B D
J
F
A C
6
N Q
1
A C
E
2 3
4 5
R W
J Z
5 W
M
R
M
1
4 5
2 3
A C
F G
G

Remember back in the day,
niggas wore waves,
Gazell-e shades, corn braids, dueled aplenty,
But never ended deadly, they wore dull blades
And kept it friendly, even though enemy.
Fast forward from nineteen hundred eighty-three
To whet steel corners, with new mutiny.
In Brooklyn Babel, where we lay our scene,
Here hood born youth, adolescence addled,
Spill civil blood, make civil hands unclean;
Traded rattles for father's swords and battled.
Saddled with their parents spiteful legacy
Love, it's collateral casualty.
A thin line is blurred, a child interred
To redeem American dreams deferred...

# Dramatis Personae

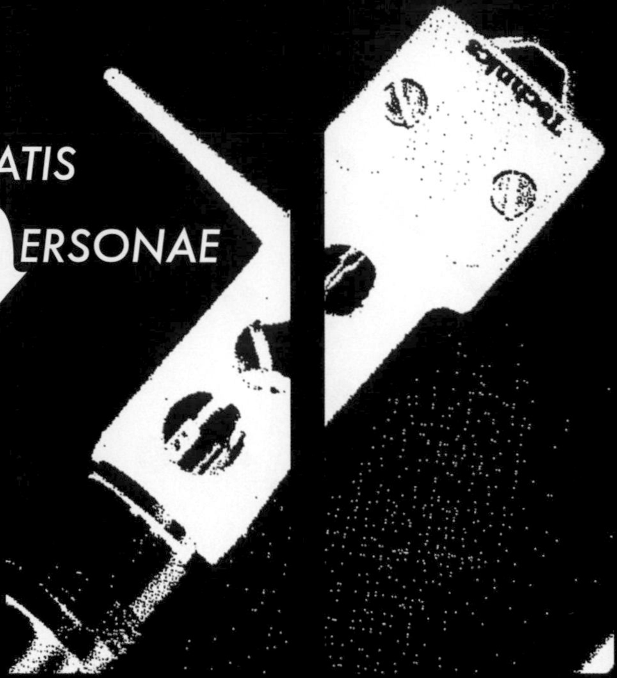

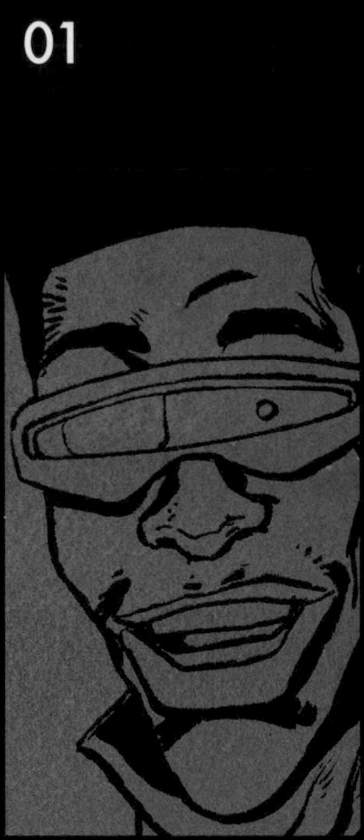
01

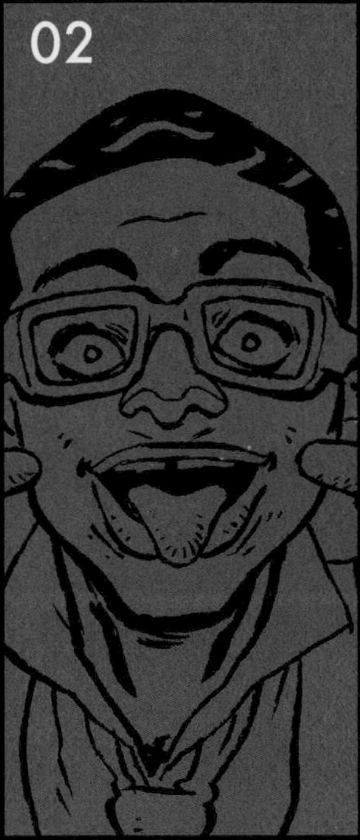
02

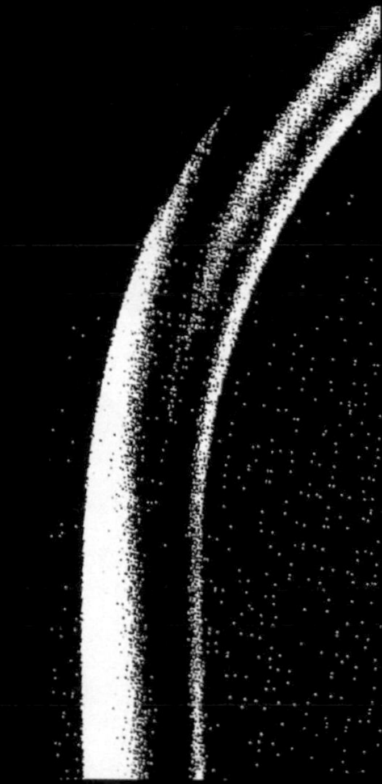

01. Sampson
02. Gregory
03. Tybalt
04. Ibrahim
05. Saul
06. Balthazar
07. Romeo
08. Friar Lawrence
09. Petruchio
10. Petruchio's Grandmother

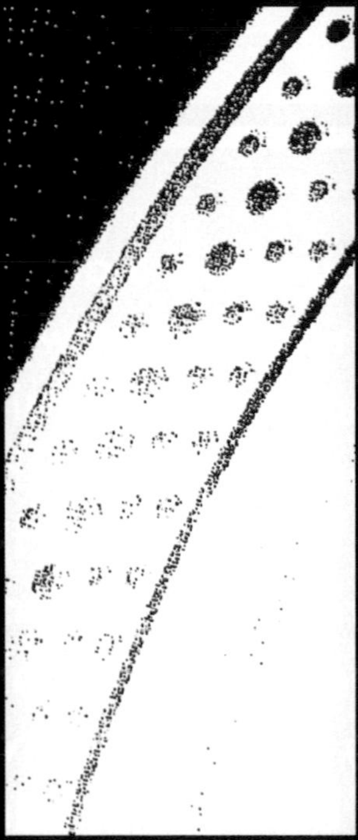

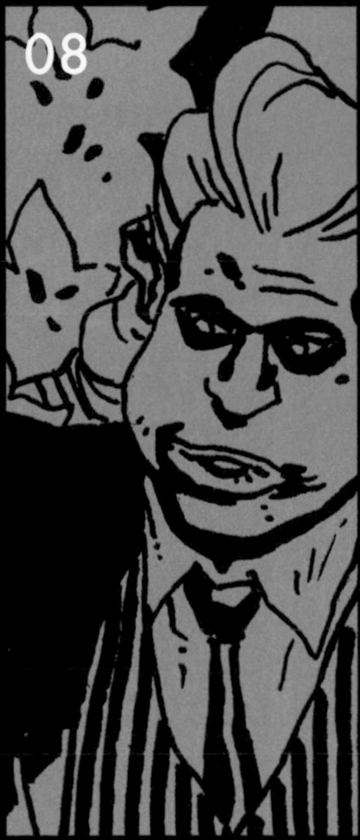
08

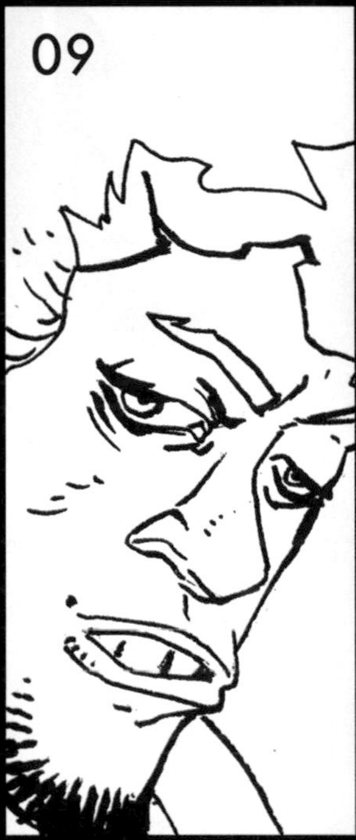
09

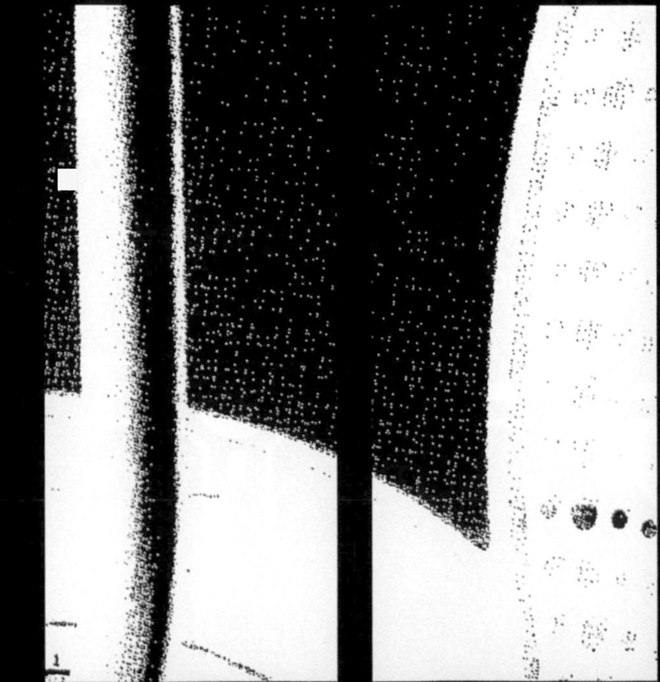

11. Luciano Canolio
12. Donatello Canolio
13. Rosalyn
14. Juliet
15. Jaquelyn
16. Roxanne
17. Mercutio
18. Barabus
19. Benvolio
20. Noh Mercy Killers
21. Tybalt's Mother

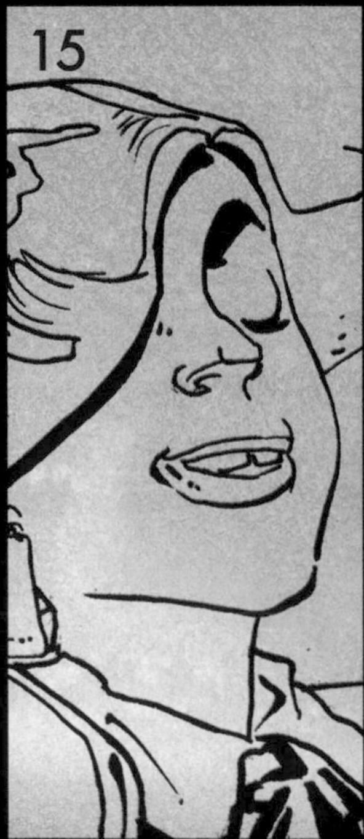
15

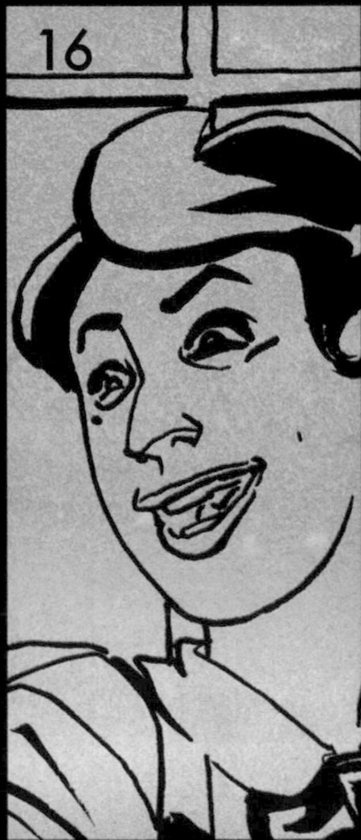
16

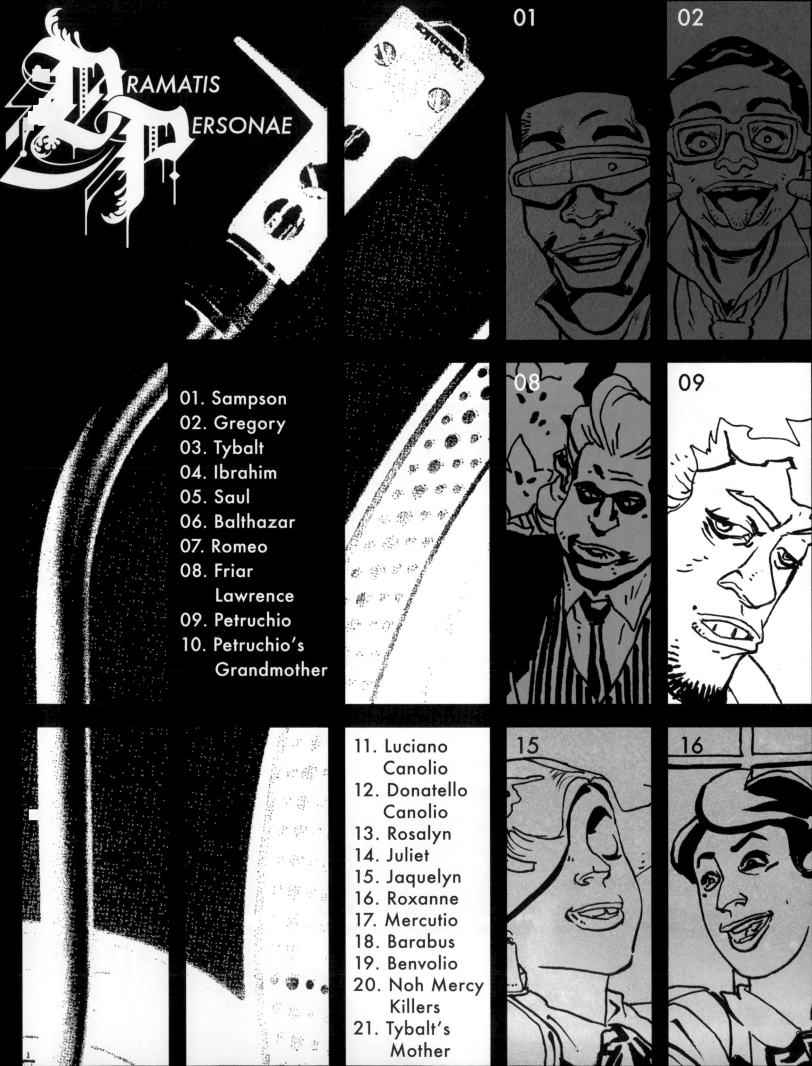

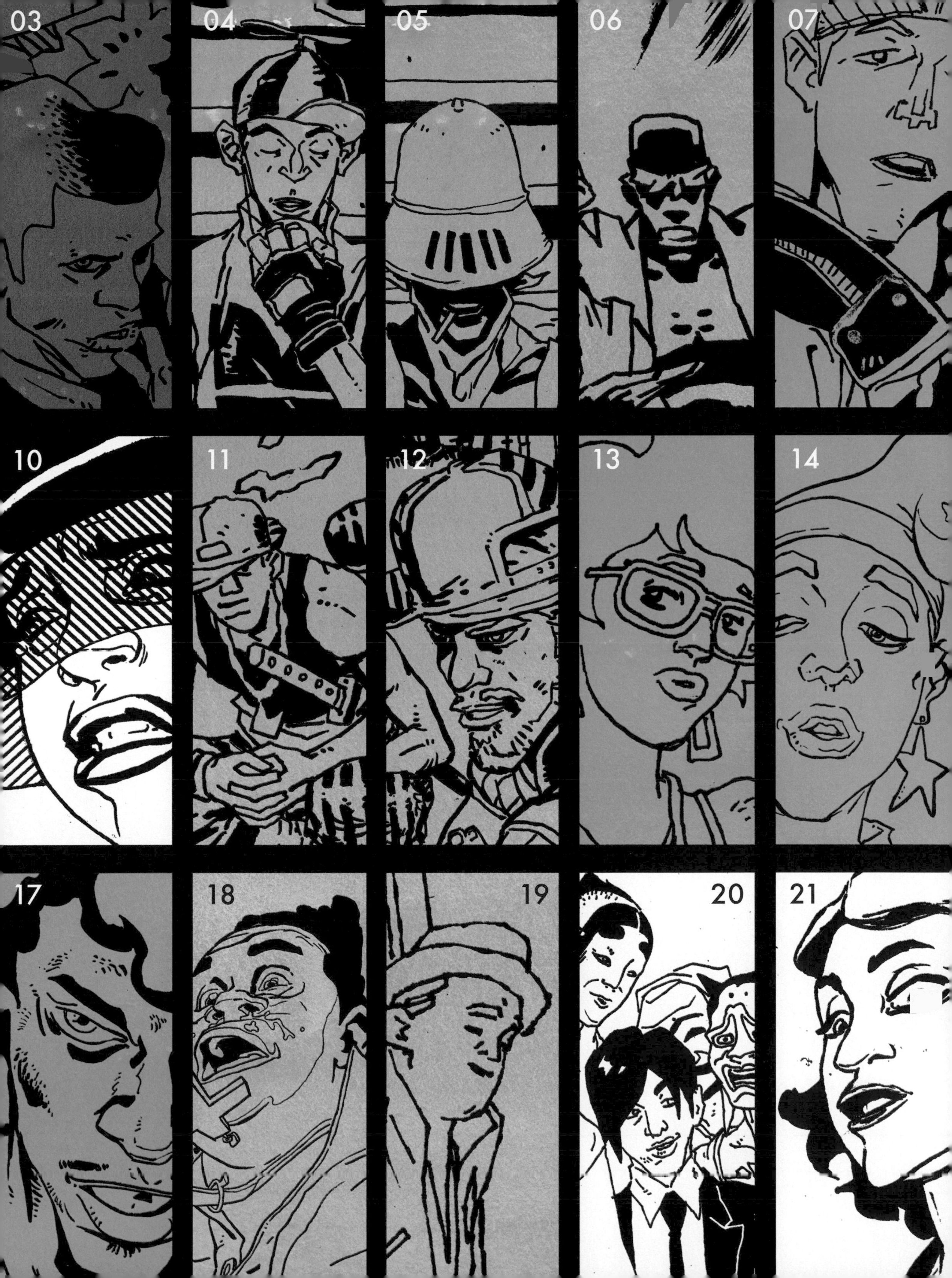

03
04
05
06
07
10
11
12
13
14
17
18
19
20
21

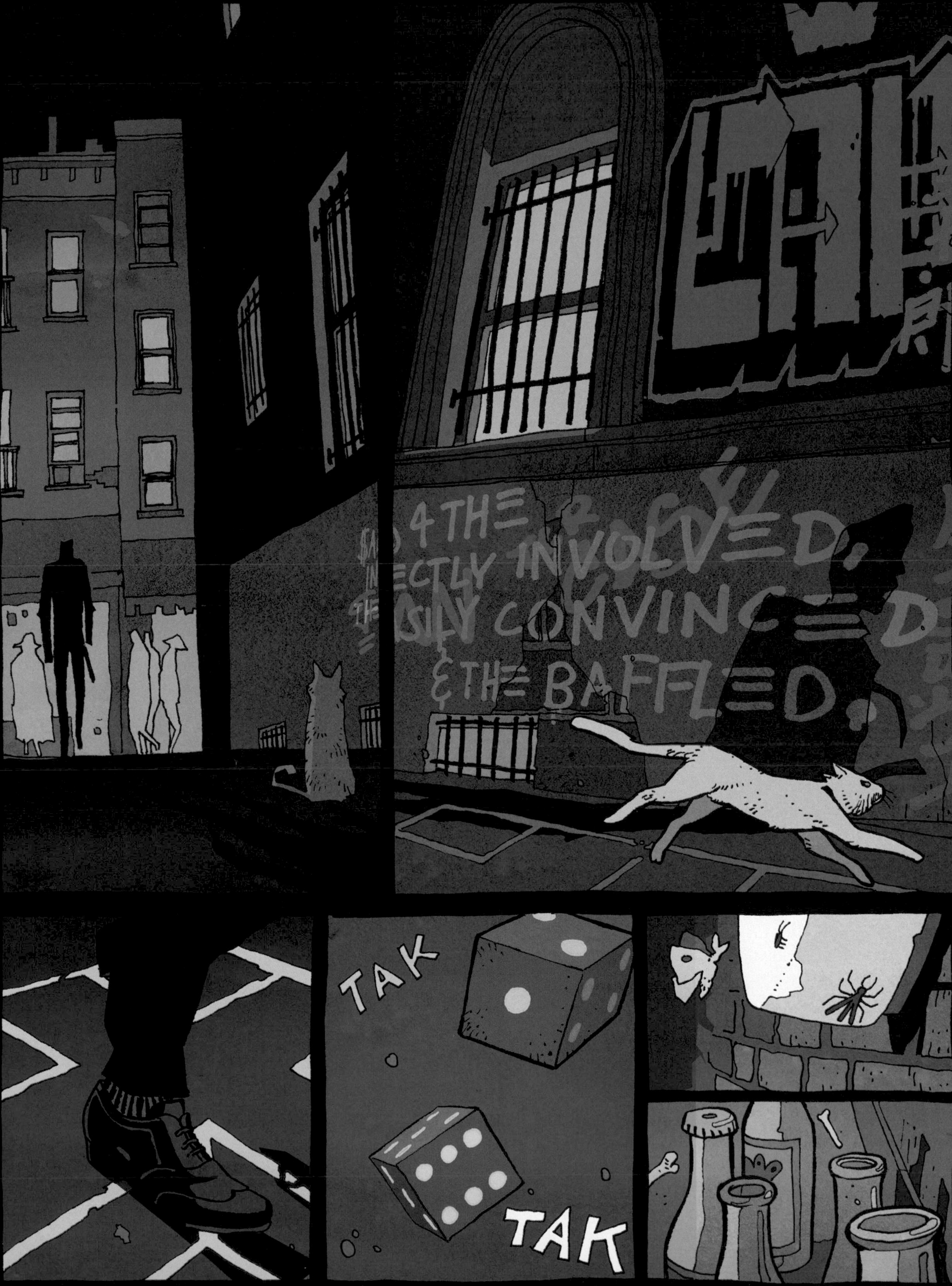

4 THE
INVOLVED.
CONVINCED
& THE BAFFLED.
TAK
TAK

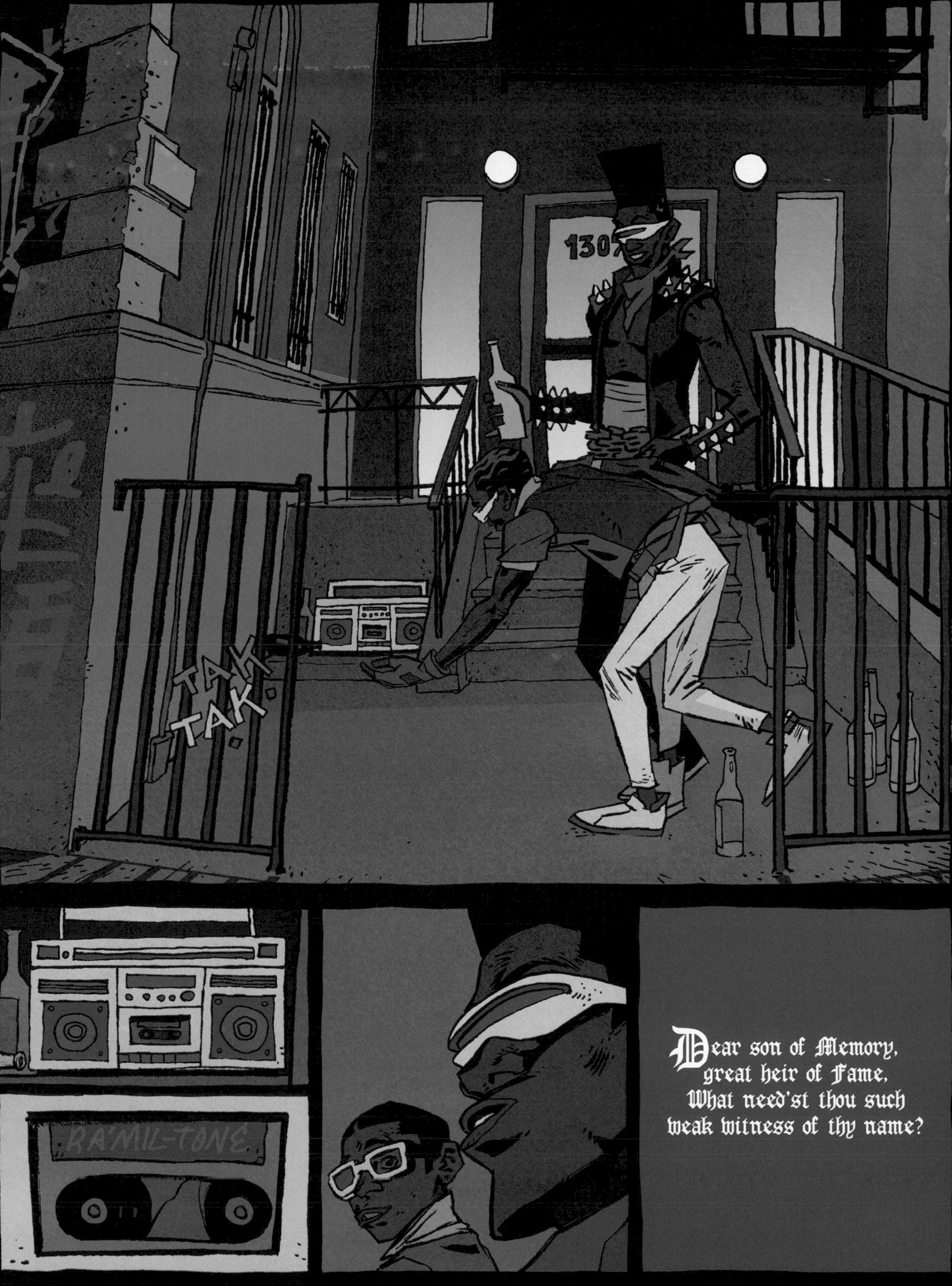
TAK TAK.
RA'MIL-TONE
Dear son of Memory,
great heir of Fame,
What need'st thou such
weak witness of thy name?

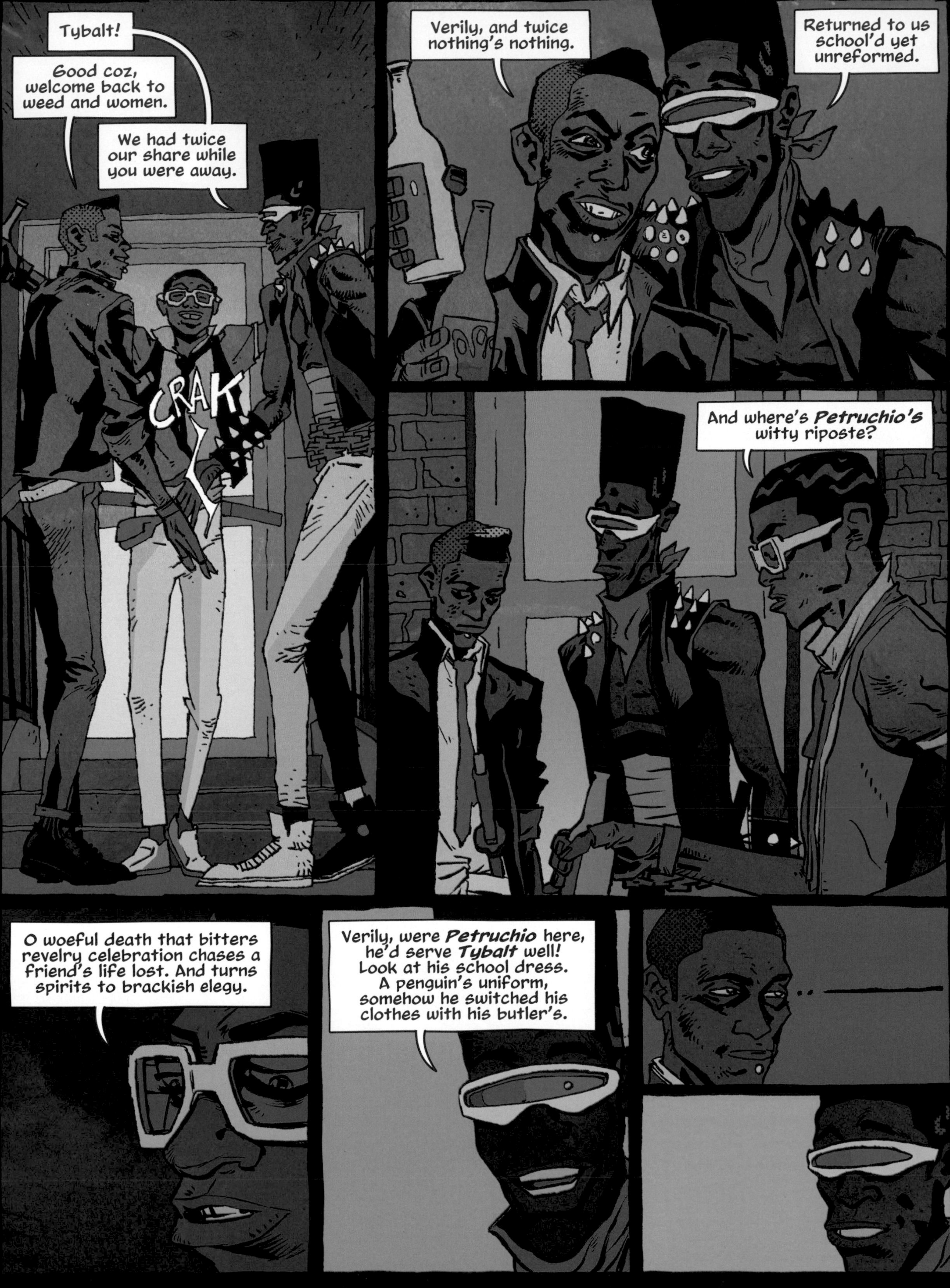
Tybalt!
Good coz, welcome back to weed and women.
We had twice our share while you were away.
CRAK
Verily, and twice nothing's nothing.
Returned to us school'd yet unreformed.
And where's Petruchio's witty riposte?
O woeful death that bitters revelry celebration chases a friend's life lost. And turns spirits to brackish elegy.
Verily, were Petruchio here, he'd serve Tybalt well! Look at his school dress. A penguin's uniform, somehow he switched his clothes with his butler's.
...

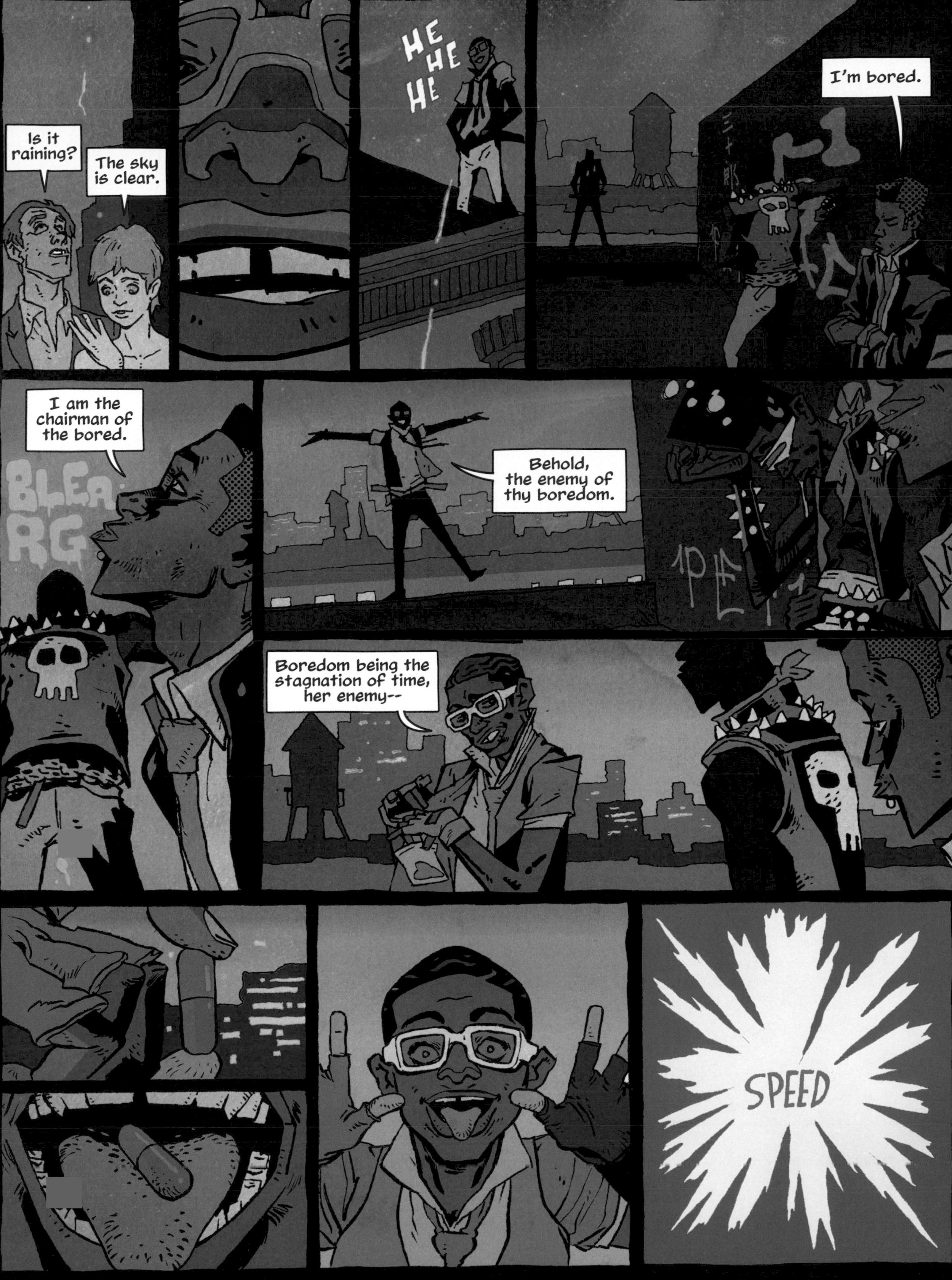
Is it raining?
The sky is clear.
HE HE HE
I'm bored.
BLEARG
I am the chairman of the bored.
Behold, the enemy of thy boredom.
Boredom being the stagnation of time, her enemy--
SPEED

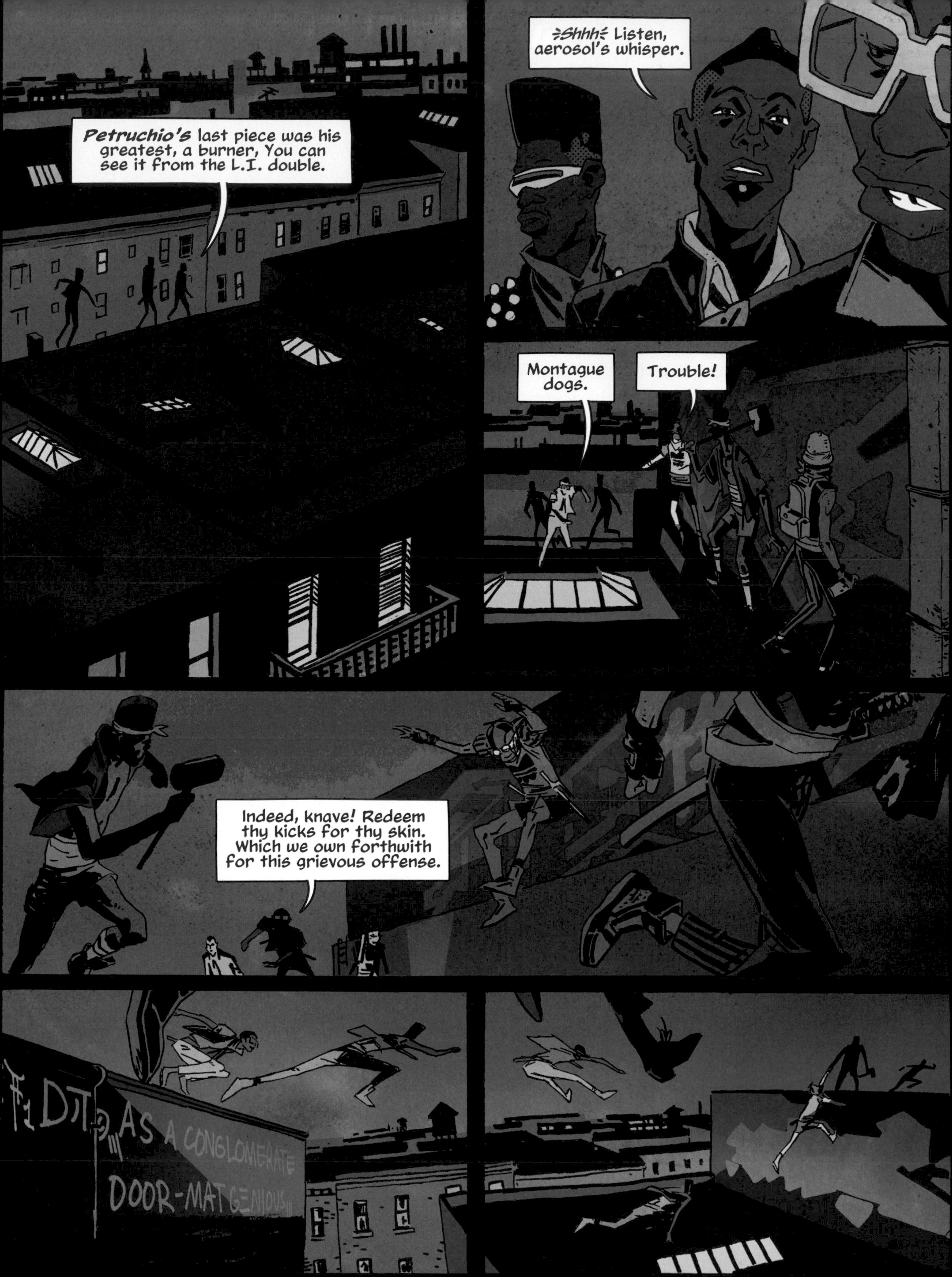

*Petruchio's* last piece was his greatest, a burner, You can see it from the L.I. double.
Shhh Listen, aerosol's whisper.
Montague dogs.
Trouble!
Indeed, knave! Redeem thy kicks for thy skin. Which we own forthwith for this grievous offense.
AS A CONGLOMERATE
DOOR-MAT GENIOUS

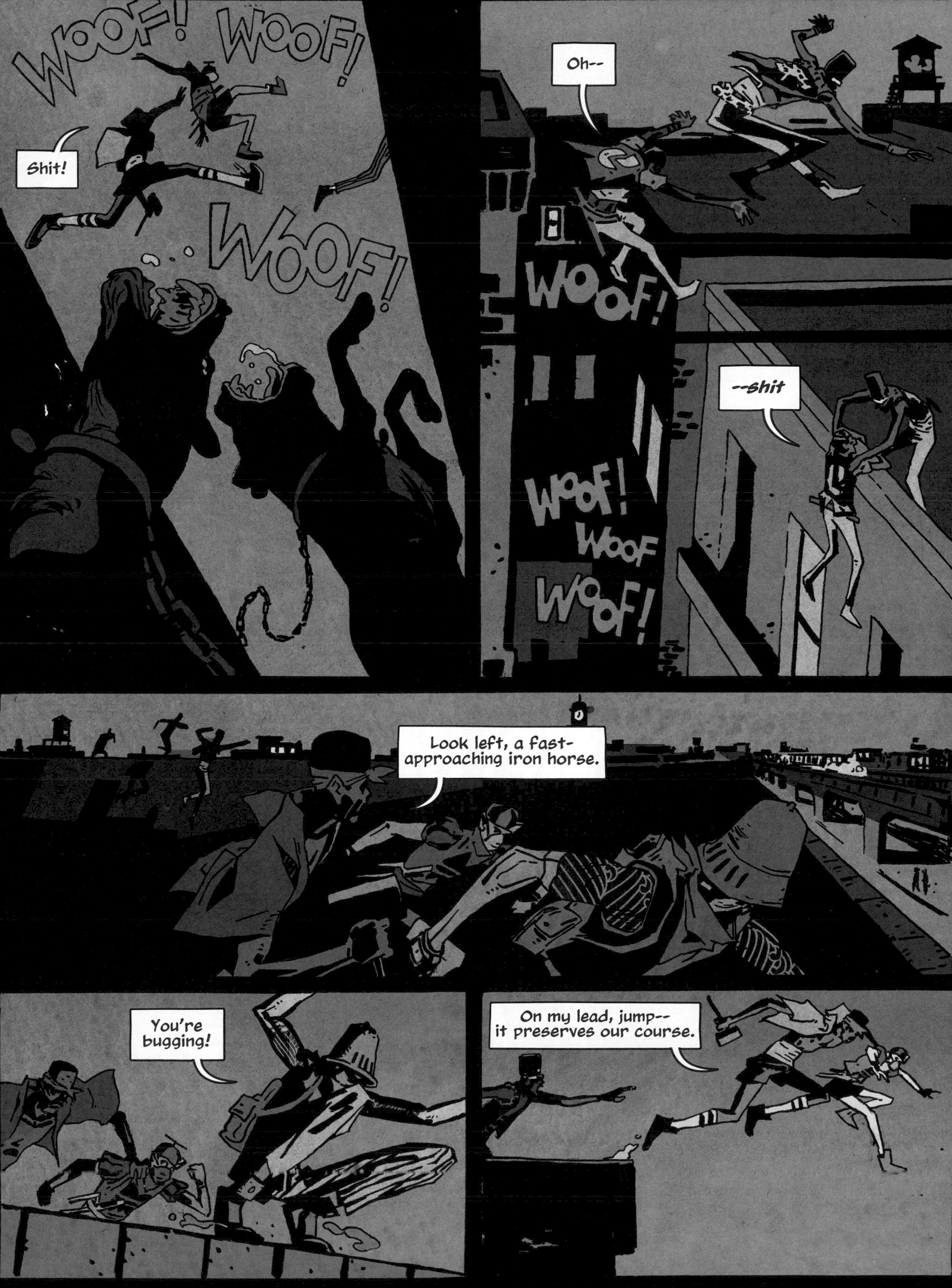
WOOF! WOOF!
Shit!
WOOF!
Oh--
WOOF!
--shit
WOOF!
WOOF
WOOF!
Look left, a fast-approaching iron horse.
You're bugging!
On my lead, jump--it preserves our course.

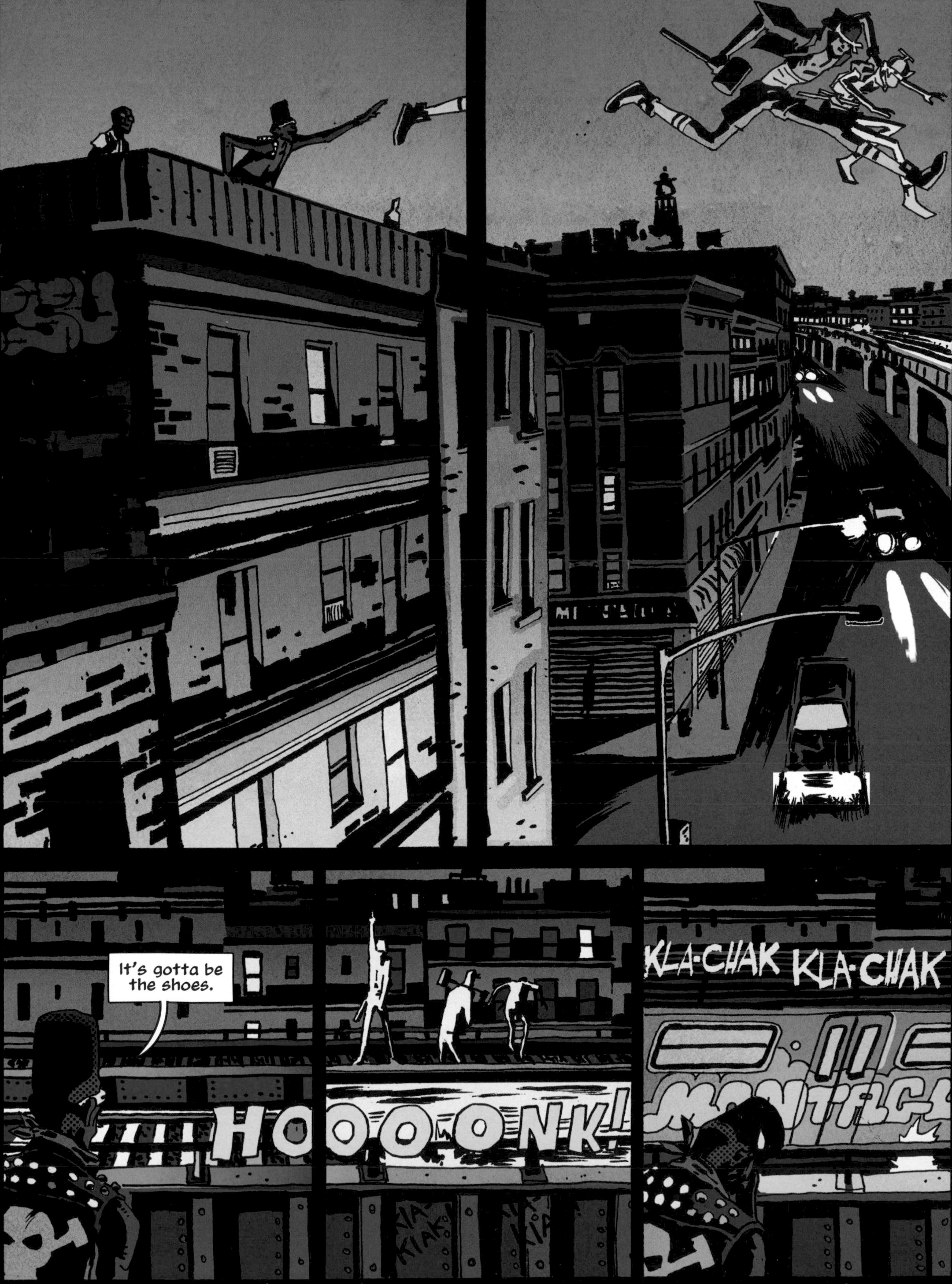
It's gotta be the shoes.
HOOOONK!
KLA-CHAK KLA-CHAK

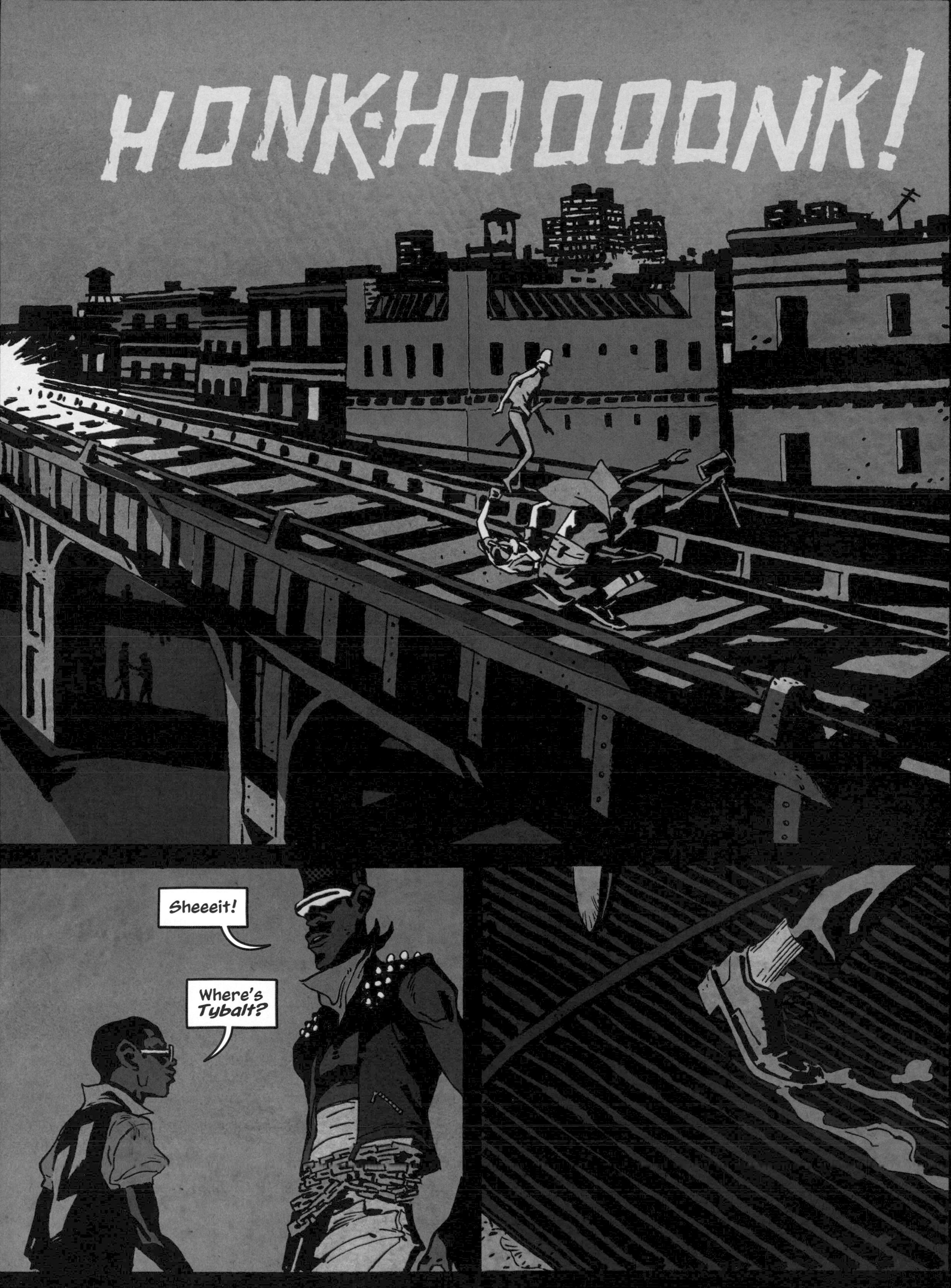
HONK-HOOOONK!
Sheeeit!
Where's *Tybalt?*

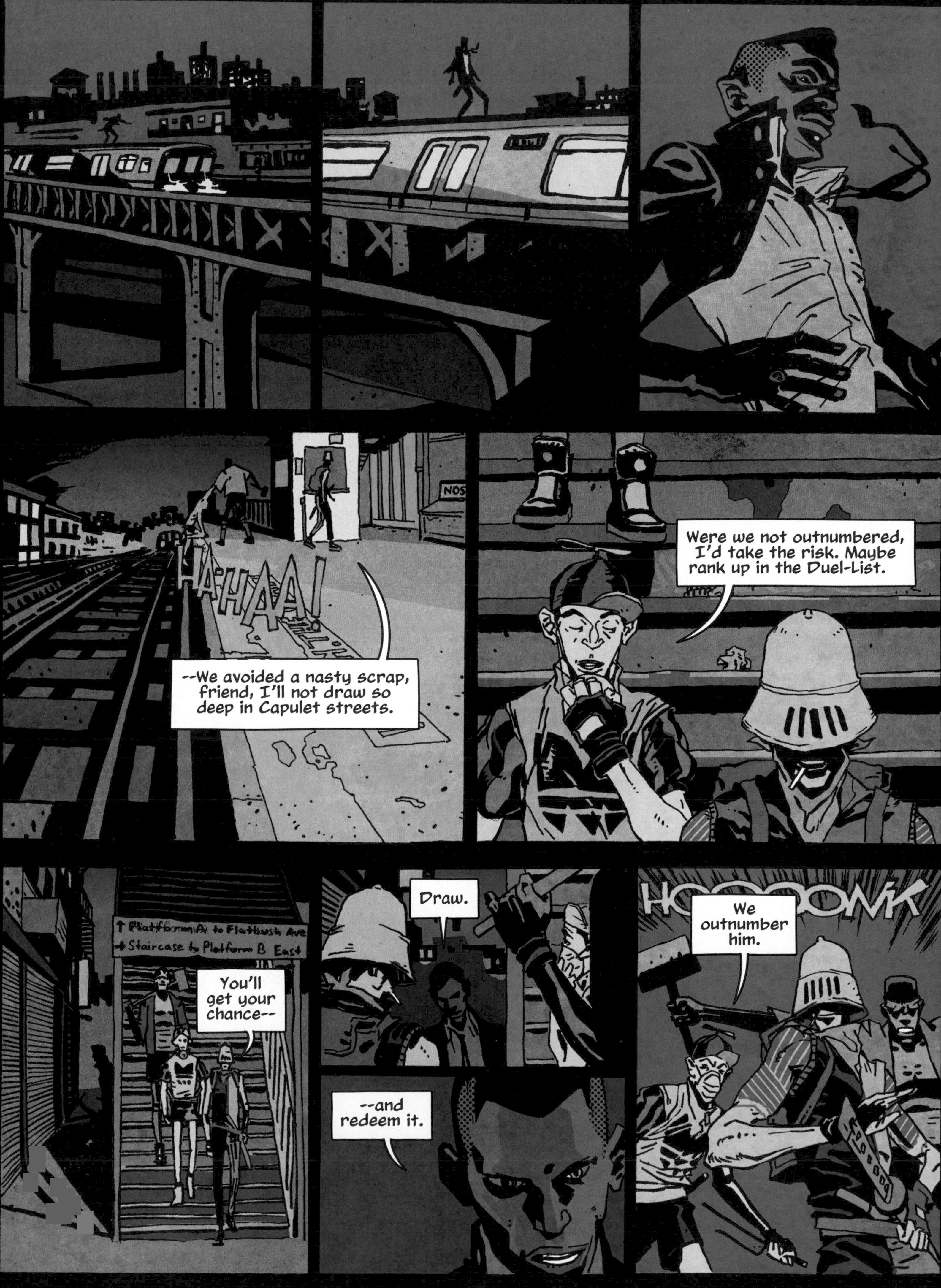
HAHAAA!
--We avoided a nasty scrap, friend, I'll not draw so deep in Capulet streets.
Were we not outnumbered, I'd take the risk. Maybe rank up in the Duel-List.
Platform A to Flatbush Ave
Staircase to Platform B East
You'll get your chance--
Draw.
--and redeem it.
HOOOONK
We outnumber him.

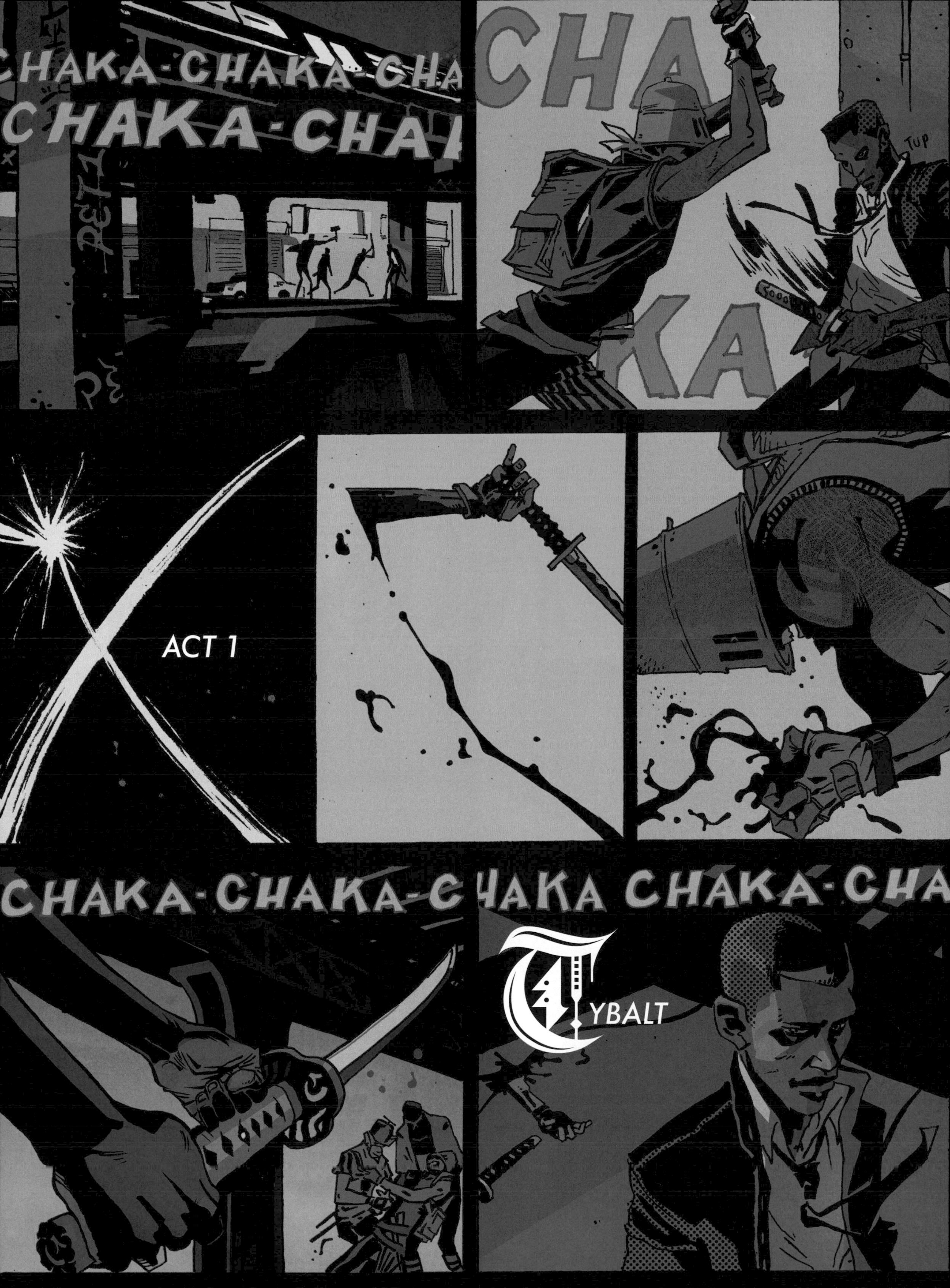
CHAKA-CHAKA-CHA
CHAKA-CHA
CHA
TUP
KA
ACT 1
CHAKA-CHAKA-CHAKA CHAKA-CHA
TYBALT

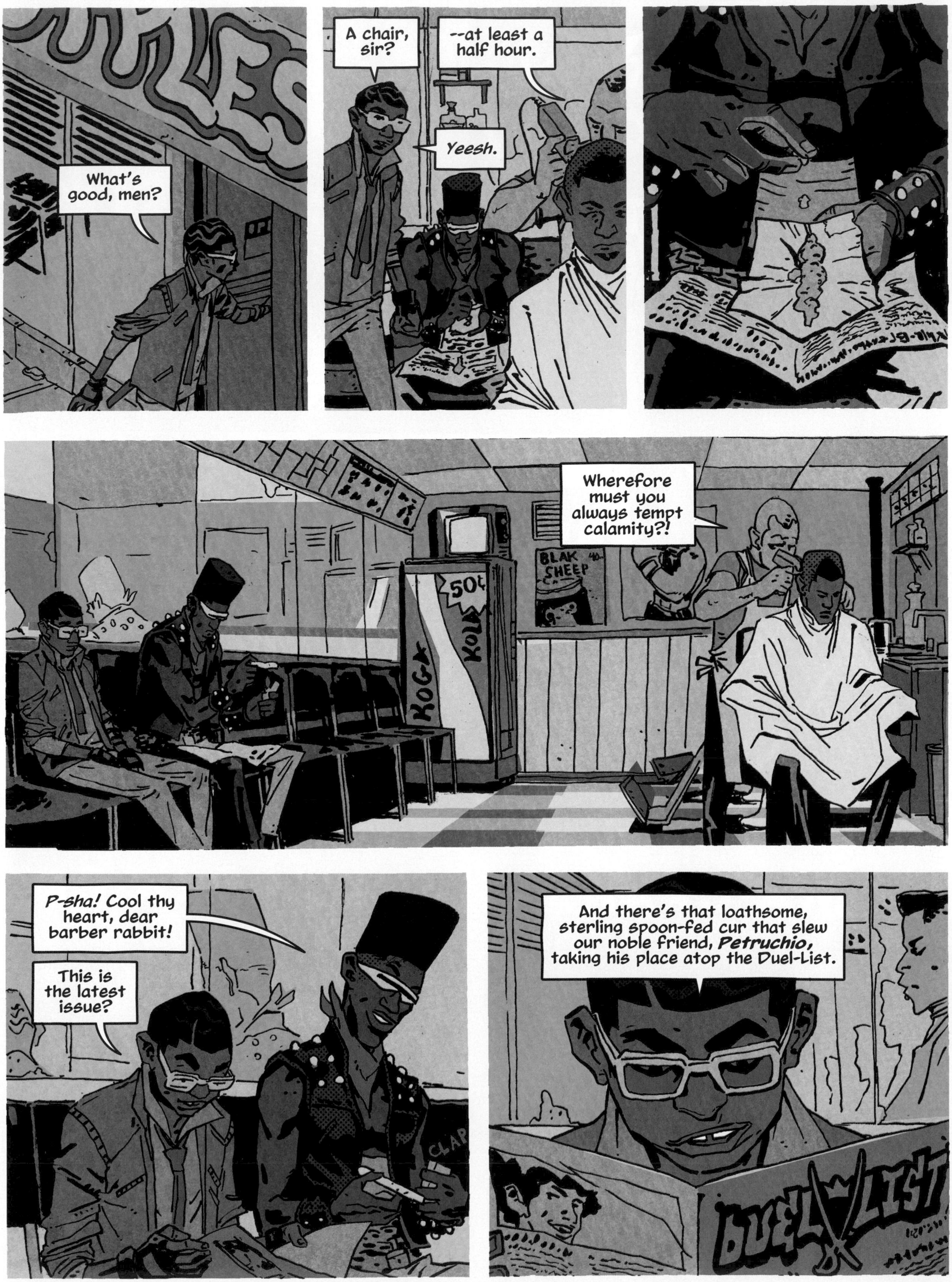
What's good, men?
A chair, sir?
--at least a half hour.
Yeesh.
BLAK SHEEP
50¢
KOLA
Wherefore must you always tempt calamity?!
P-sha! Cool thy heart, dear barber rabbit!
This is the latest issue?
And there's that loathsome, sterling spoon-fed cur that slew our noble friend, *Petruchio*, taking his place atop the Duel-List.
DUEL LIST

# Milk-Breathed Montague Makes Moves

***Robert Greene***

This issue, Newly crowning the duel-list
Is Montague progeny, Romeo,
Whose deft Tsubame Gaeshi dismissed
The one-armed defense of Petruchio.
Ye may have yet to hear young Romeo's name
No doubt ye heard his father's, Lord Montague
Who made it known through slum-glorious game,
the weight he moved, the foes he fought and slew.
Much has been made of Romeo's pedigree
Yet with this touché his reputation bought.
He's proven apples fall not far from trees,
He's of his brazen father's mettle wrought.
Though none made witness of the Title duel
Petruchio's ranking paper was retrieved.
As is the official duel-list rule
Its captor, Romeo, its ranking received.
Petruchio did not survive the match.

**-For memorial details see 'the dispatch'**

## Duel List

01. Romeo Montague
02. Benvolio Montague
03. Luciano Canolio
04. Donatello Canolio
05. "Notorious" Barabus

...

06. Tybalt Capulet
07. Jaquelyn
08. Malachi
09. Metatron
10. Moiritsuke

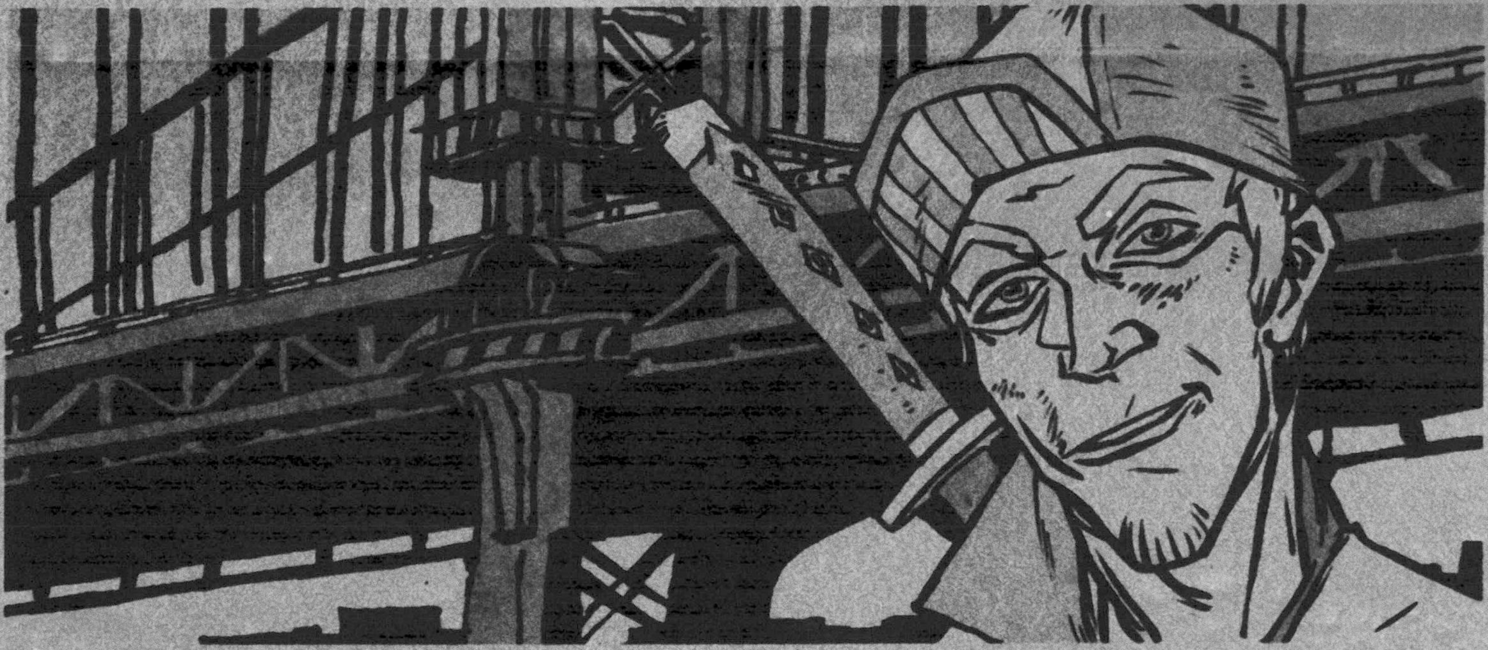

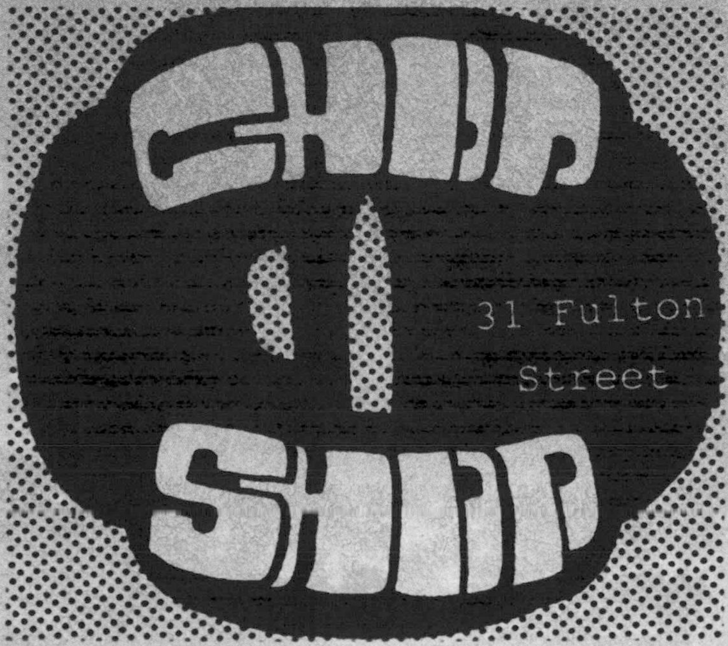
CHOP
SHOP
31 Fulton
Street

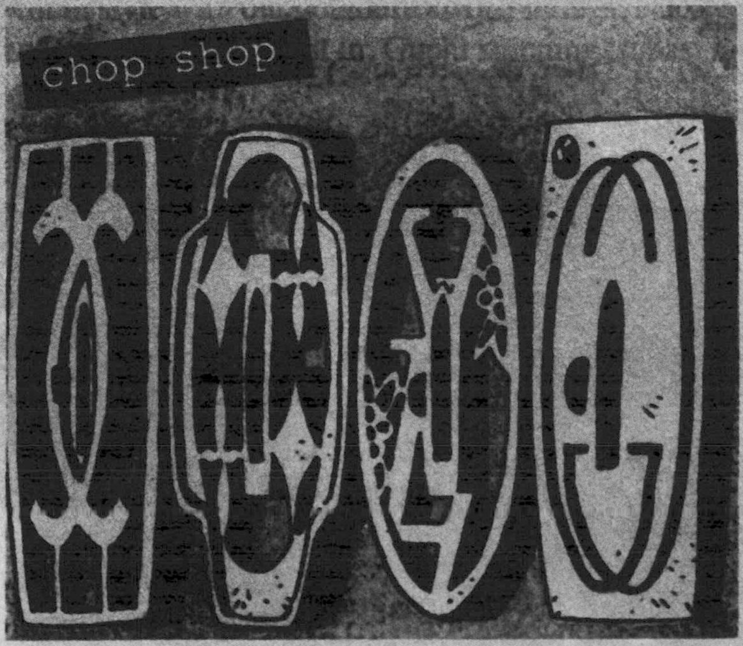
chop shop

So what it read, coz?

Ha! think it you so easy to rank, Coz? Thou'lt not find the answer to the street's tests In thy professor's book of formulas.
You get an "F", toe tagged in death.

Thy deeds went unreported, cousin. No doubt, the duelist you disarmed was unranked ...The top four is flush with clan Montague.

--More children pierced over childish bullshit.

Not bullshit, Barber, but the beef of our lord.

Verily, cousin! For our lord, I'd cut beef.

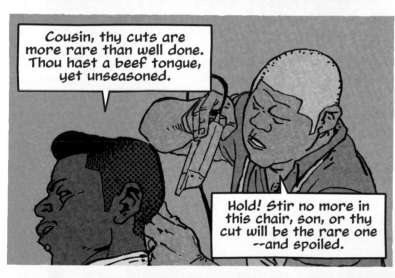

Cousin, thy cuts are more rare than well done. Thou hast a beef tongue, yet unseasoned.

Hold! Stir no more in this chair, son, or thy cut will be the rare one --and spoiled.

Well, *Romeo's* technique was a prime cut, and with it, Petrucio's youth consumed.

22

God rest his sword... But...I'd love to see the *Tsubame Gaeshi.*

Hehe... Verily, And rap with Charon on the subject, Whilst thou ride with him across the Styx.

*Petruchio's* sword game was gutter born, Top form, yet *Romeo* delivered his fall. And while you starched and pressed your school uniform, *Petruchio* uniformly pressed Montague to the wall.

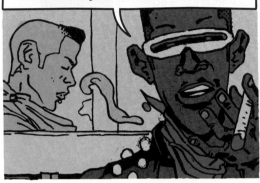
...And thy blade's edge ain't the only thing softened In private school. The lessons may not be cheap but street tuition is steep, and often students graduate to a coffin--

KSHT KSHT

23

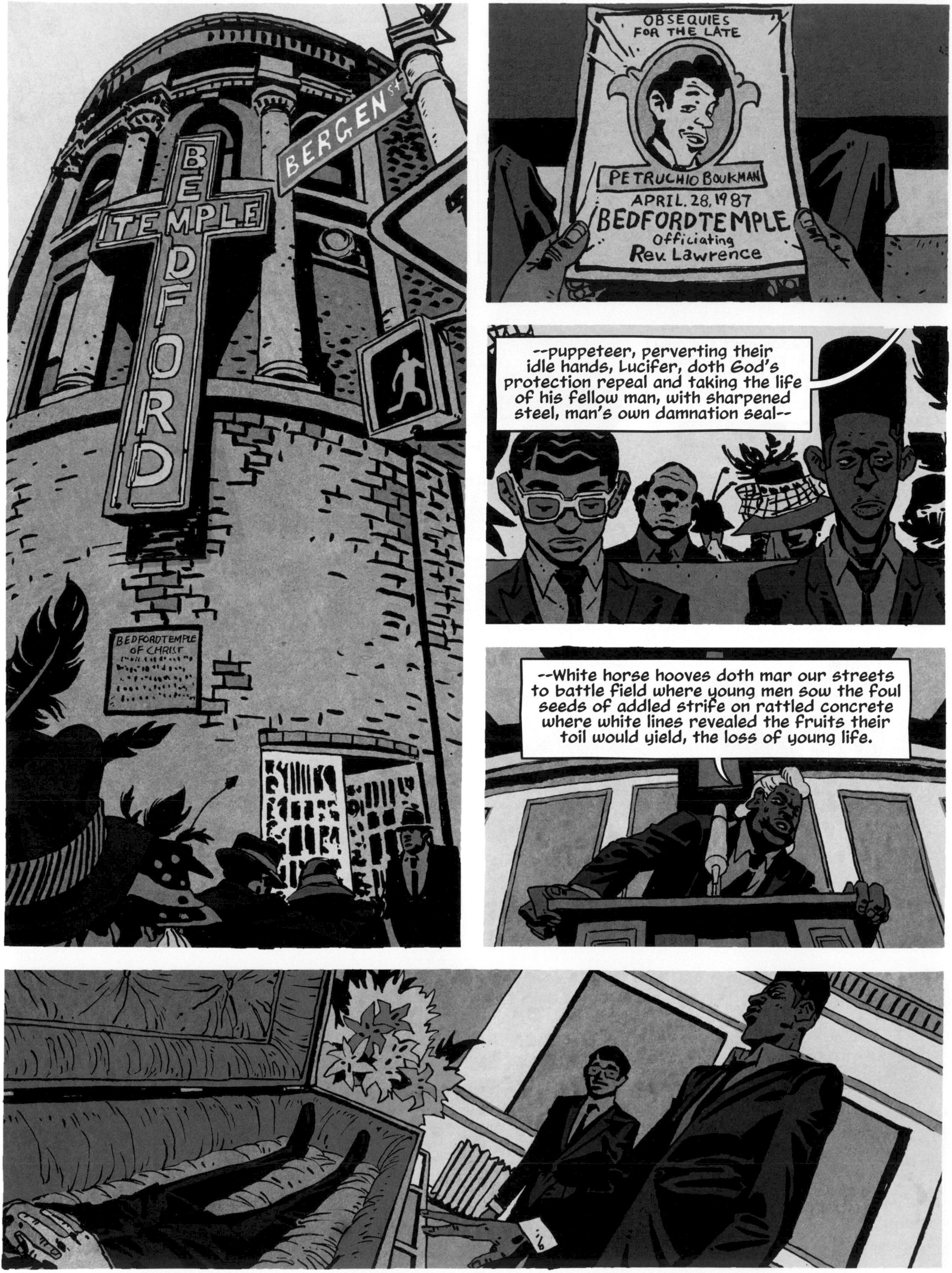
BERGEN St
BEDFORD TEMPLE
BEDFORDTEMPLE OF CHRIST
OBSEQUIES FOR THE LATE
PETRUCHIO BOUKMAN
APRIL. 28, 1987
BEDFORDTEMPLE
Officiating
Rev. Lawrence
--puppeteer, perverting their idle hands, Lucifer, doth God's protection repeal and taking the life of his fellow man, with sharpened steel, man's own damnation seal--
--White horse hooves doth mar our streets to battle field where young men sow the foul seeds of addled strife on rattled concrete where white lines revealed the fruits their toil would yield, the loss of young life.

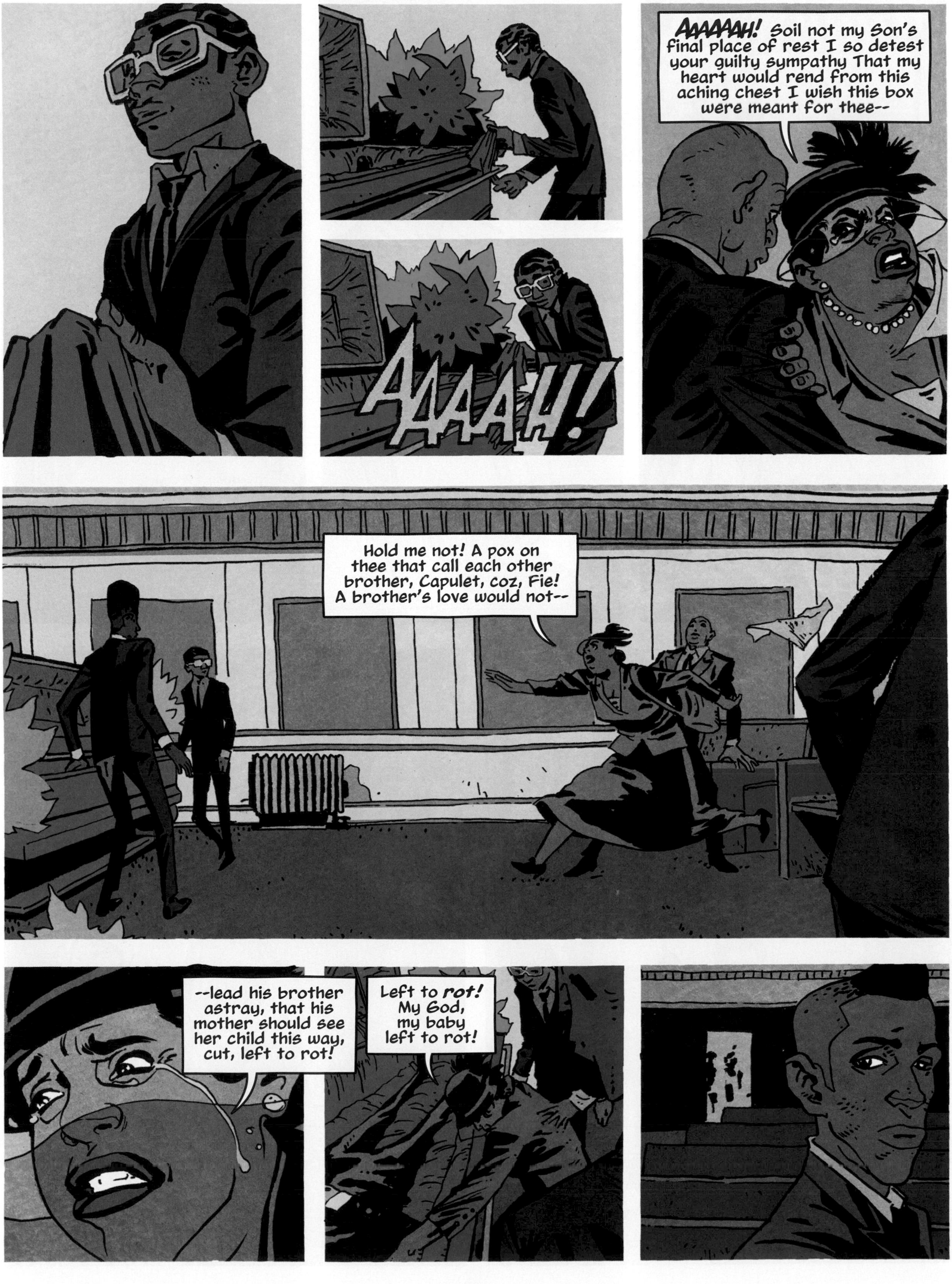
AAAAH!
AAAAAH! Soil not my Son's final place of rest I so detest your guilty sympathy That my heart would rend from this aching chest I wish this box were meant for thee--
Hold me not! A pox on thee that call each other brother, Capulet, coz, Fie! A brother's love would not--
--lead his brother astray, that his mother should see her child this way, cut, left to rot!
Left to rot! My God, my baby left to rot!

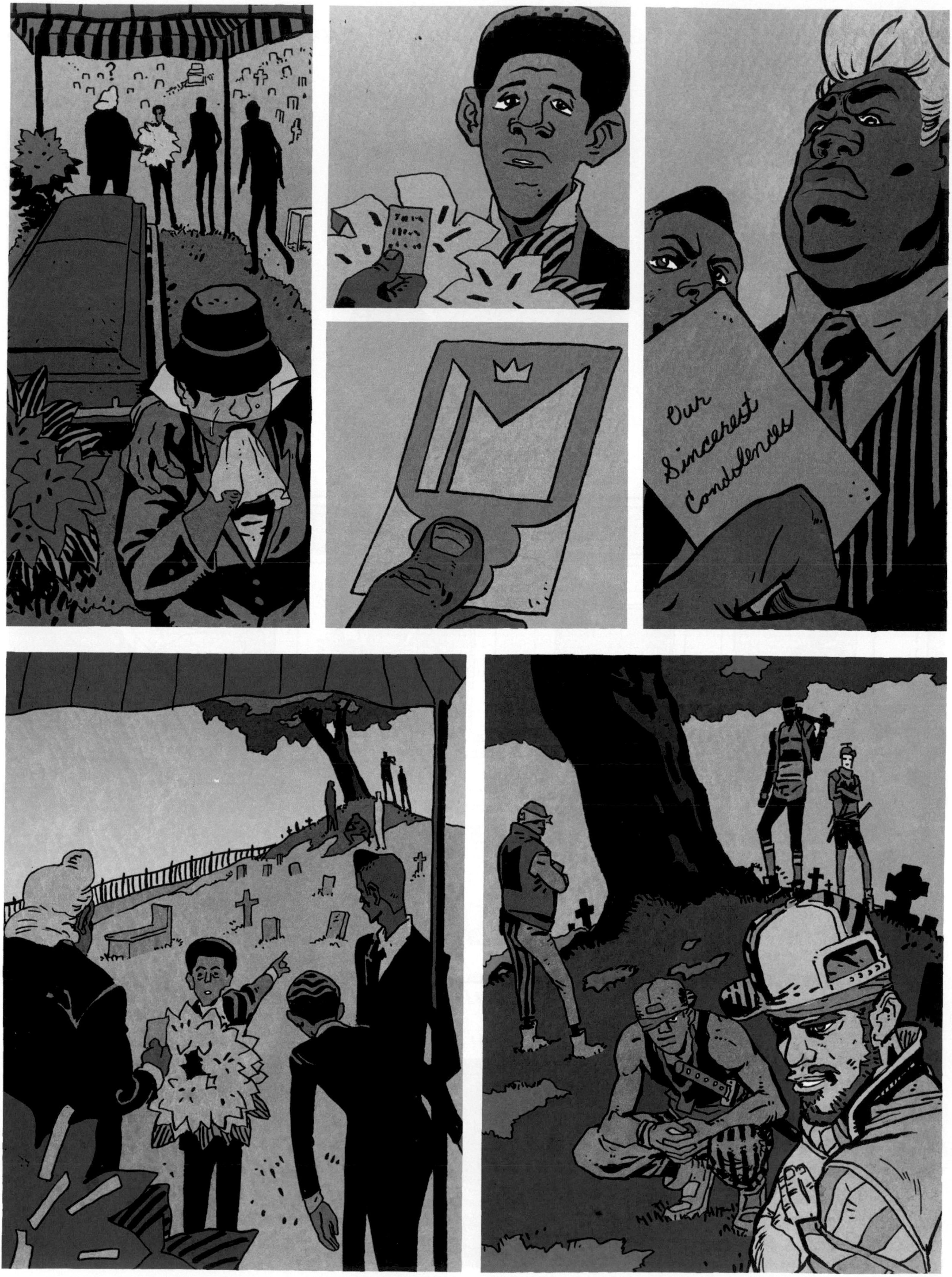
Our Sincerest Condolences

...as the Lord revealed them to Matthew twenty-six, verse fifty-one--

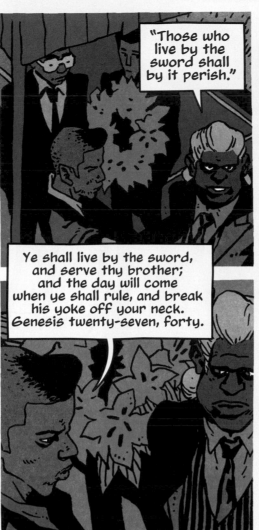

"Those who live by the sword shall by it perish."

Ye shall live by the sword, and serve thy brother; and the day will come when ye shall rule, and break his yoke off your neck. Genesis twenty-seven, forty.

Impressive. Though ye may misunderstand the text, maybe ye would better serve thy brethren from the pulpit.

I'd rather serve my brother's vengeance to a Montague dog and usher him into thy care, Friar.

Business looks good.

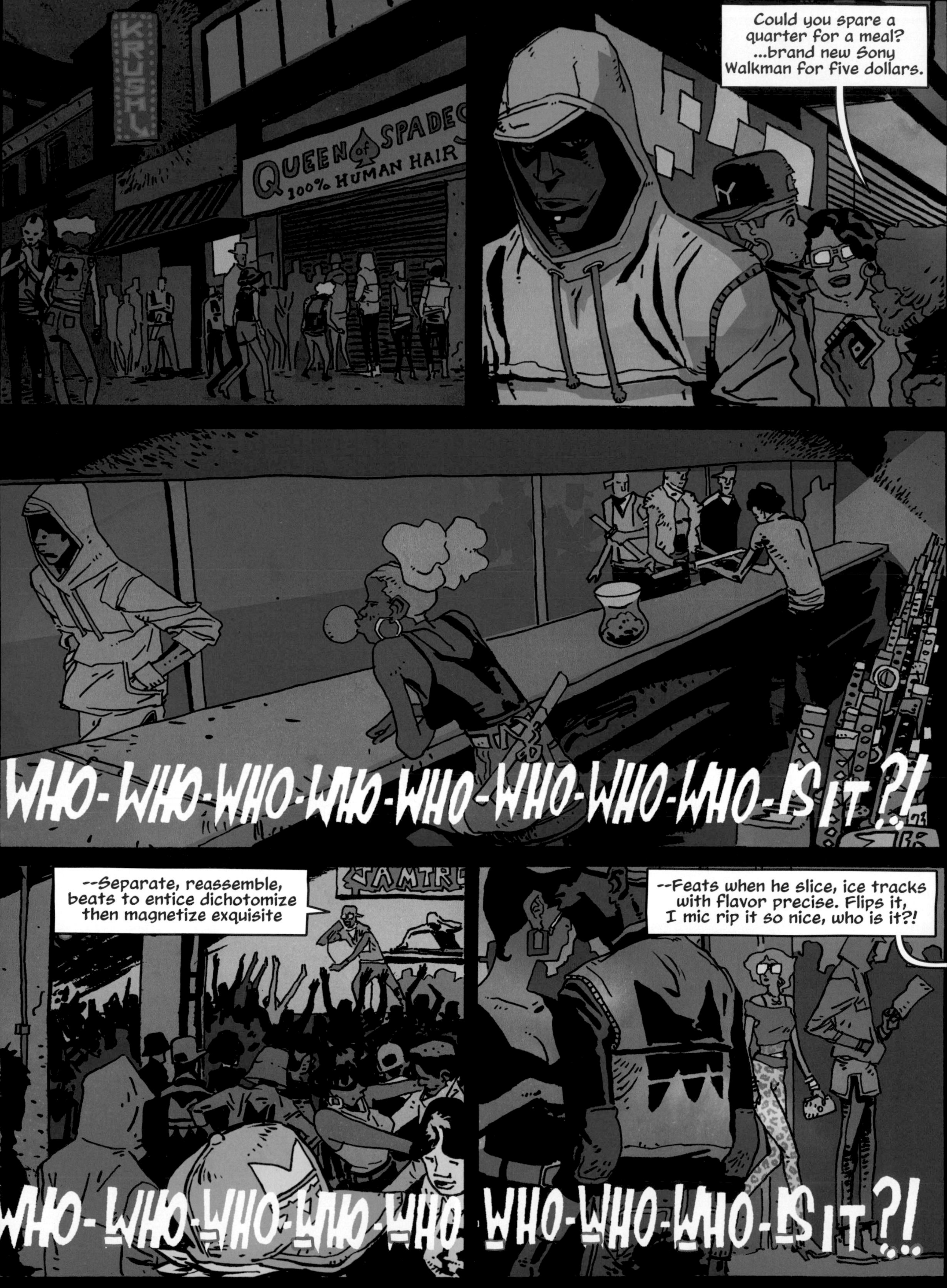

KRUSH
QUEEN of SPADES
100% HUMAN HAIR
Could you spare a quarter for a meal? ...brand new Sony Walkman for five dollars.
WHO-WHO-WHO-WHO-WHO-WHO-WHO-WHO-IS IT?!
--Separate, reassemble, beats to entice dichotomize then magnetize exquisite
--Feats when he slice, ice tracks with flavor precise. Flips it, I mic rip it so nice, who is it?!
WHO-WHO-WHO-WHO-WHO WHO-WHO-WHO-IS IT?!

League Makes Moves

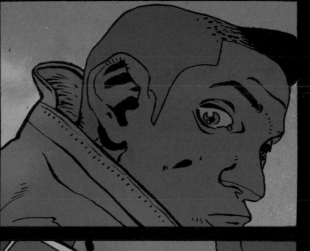

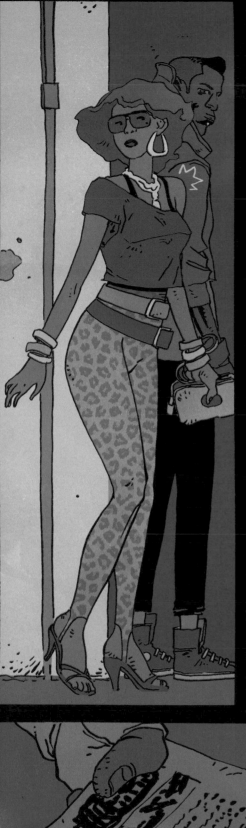

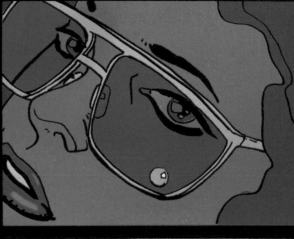

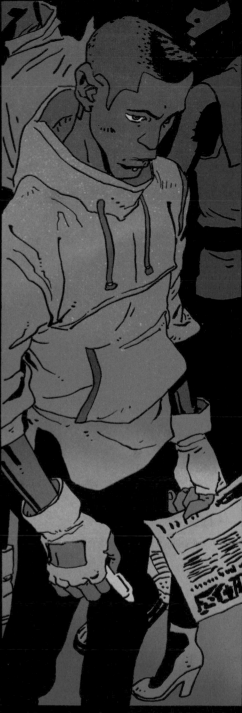

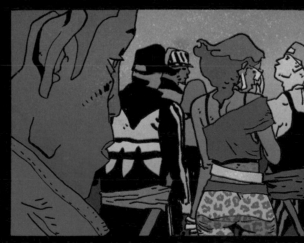

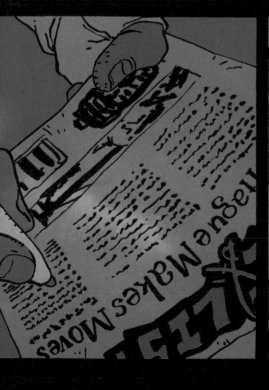

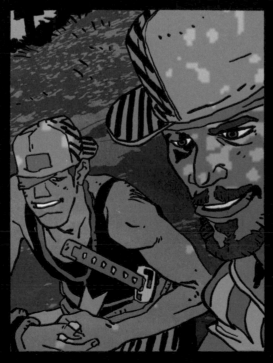

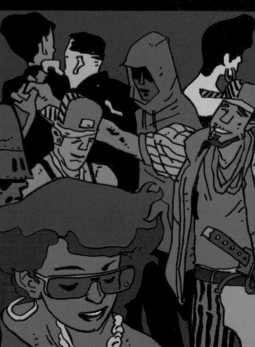

# Romeo Remains, Canolios are Slain

**Robert Greene**

Romeo remains, Canolios are slain.
A ruddy new blade debuts at rank four.
That merked the smartly dressed duo and did stain
With Montague blood the new rub dance floor

Tybalt, nephew of the Capulet Lord
Did swordless, enter the Montague den
Brandishing boxcutter, defied a horde
of Montague men and still did defend

His life against the Montague's attempts.
When he, on accident scuffed Lu's New Kicks
Lu drew quick yet caught Tybalt's Coup de temps
in open eye, and then Tybalt, through Trick

Did cleverly disarm the one brother,
And after hewing through three Montague men,
dispatched efficiently the other,
Young Donatello, quickly after his Kin.
In all, five Montague did lose their lives.
See memorial details on page five.

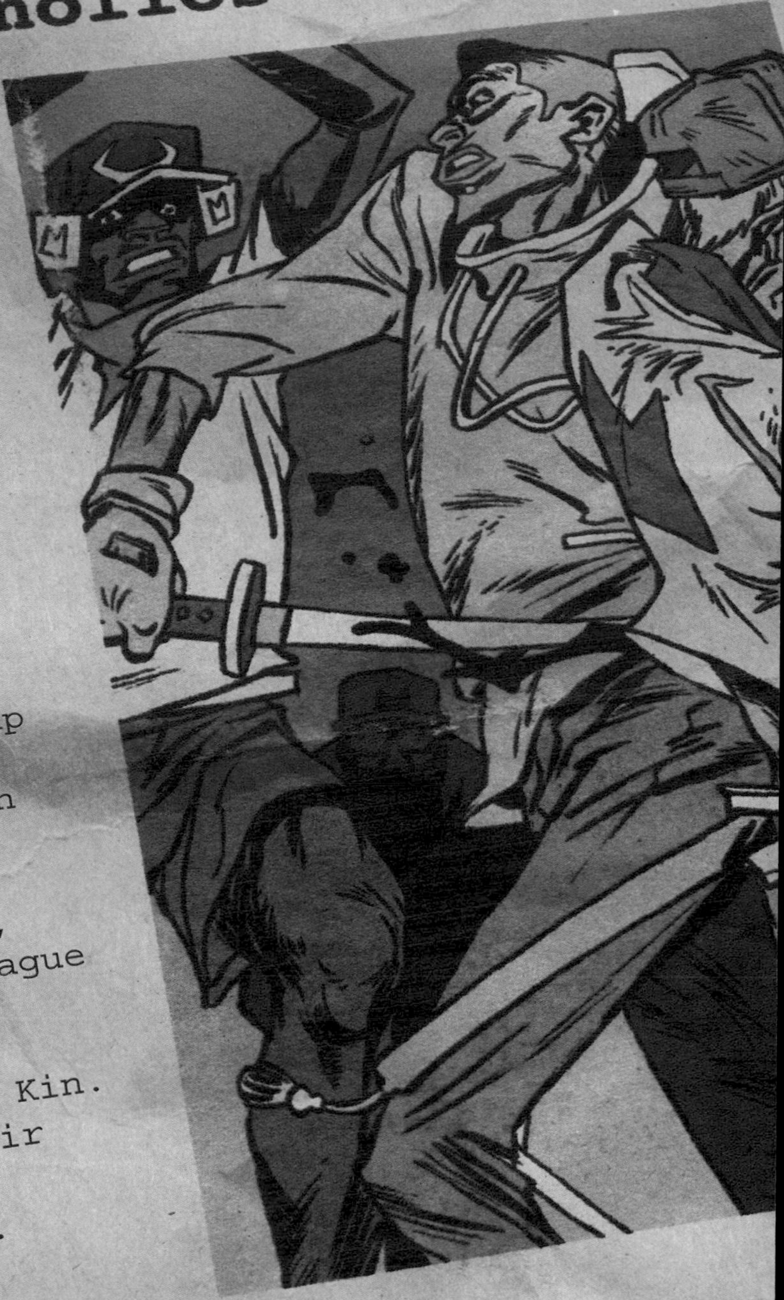

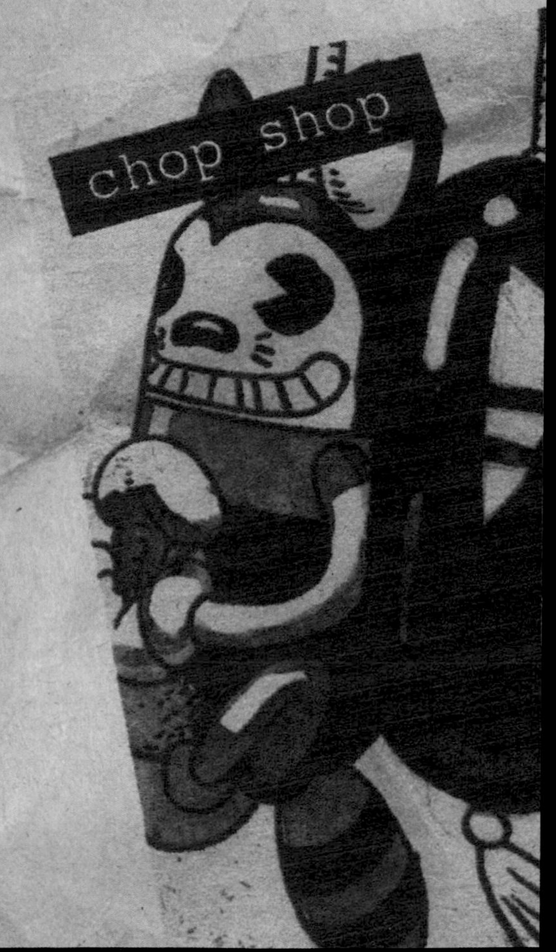
chop shop

## Duel List

01. Romeo Montague
02. Benvolio Montague
03. "Notorious" Barabus
04. Tybalt Capulet
05. Jacquelyn
...
06. Malachi
07. Murder Maeve
08. Moiritsuke
09. Little Julius
10. Dipi Ittosai

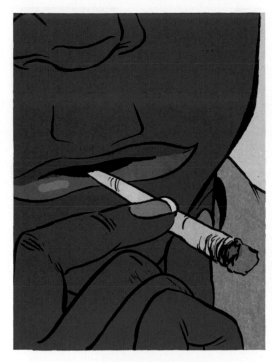

--Verily, he's cute, *Juliet*, admit.

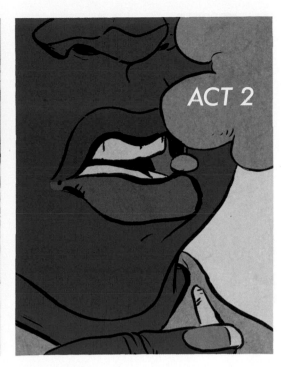

ACT 2

Yuck! He's my cousin, *Roxie!*

*JULIET*

...And a Capulet, unfortunately.

Hey!

--but look at this picture.

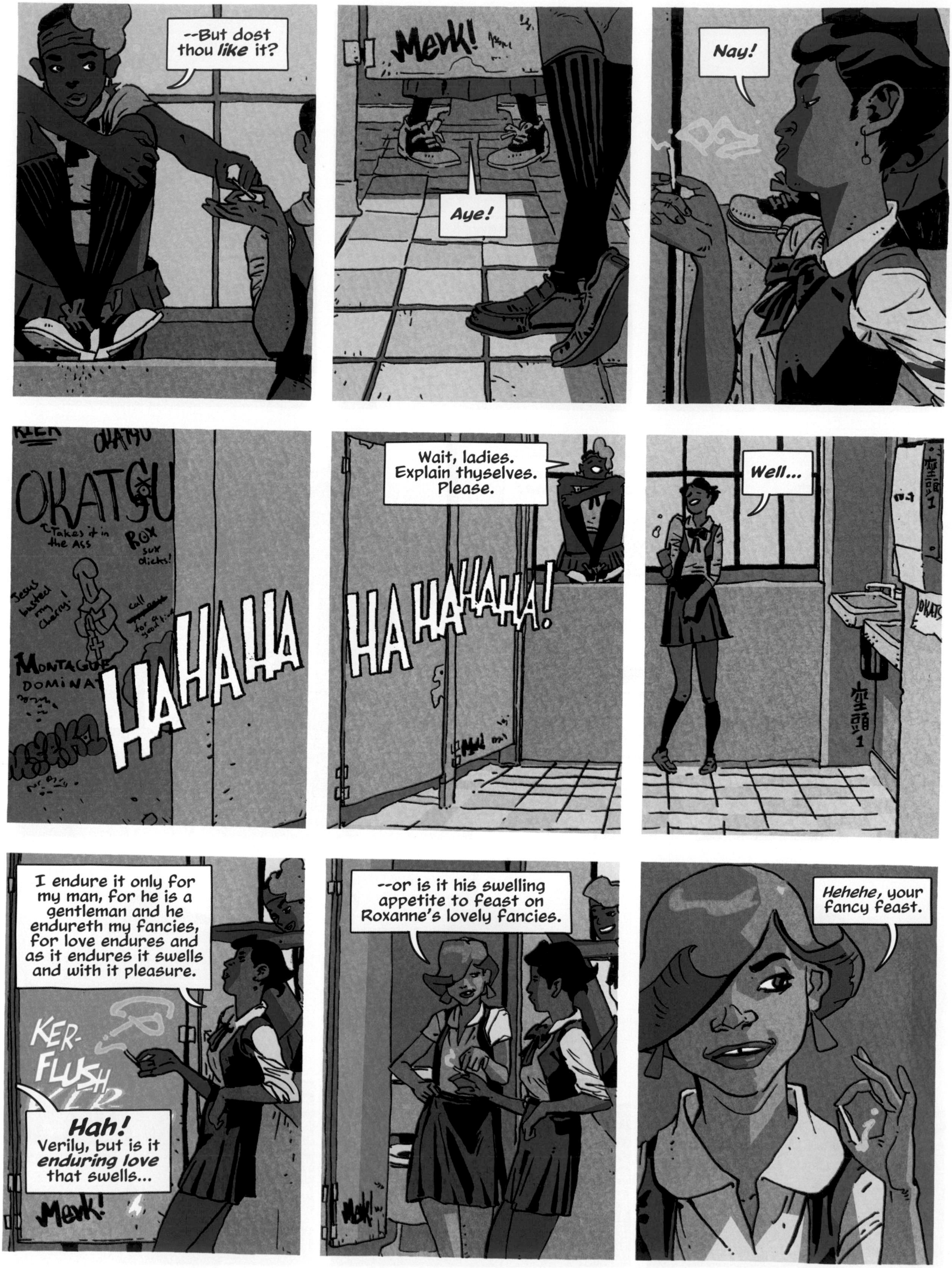
--But dost thou *like* it?
Merk!
Aye!
Nay!
HAHAHA
HAHAHAHA!
Wait, ladies. Explain thyselves. Please.
Well...
I endure it only for my man, for he is a gentleman and he endureth my fancies, for love endures and as it endures it swells and with it pleasure.
KER-FLUSH
**Hah!** Verily, but is it ***enduring love*** that swells...
--or is it his swelling appetite to feast on Roxanne's lovely fancies.
*Hehehe*, your fancy feast.

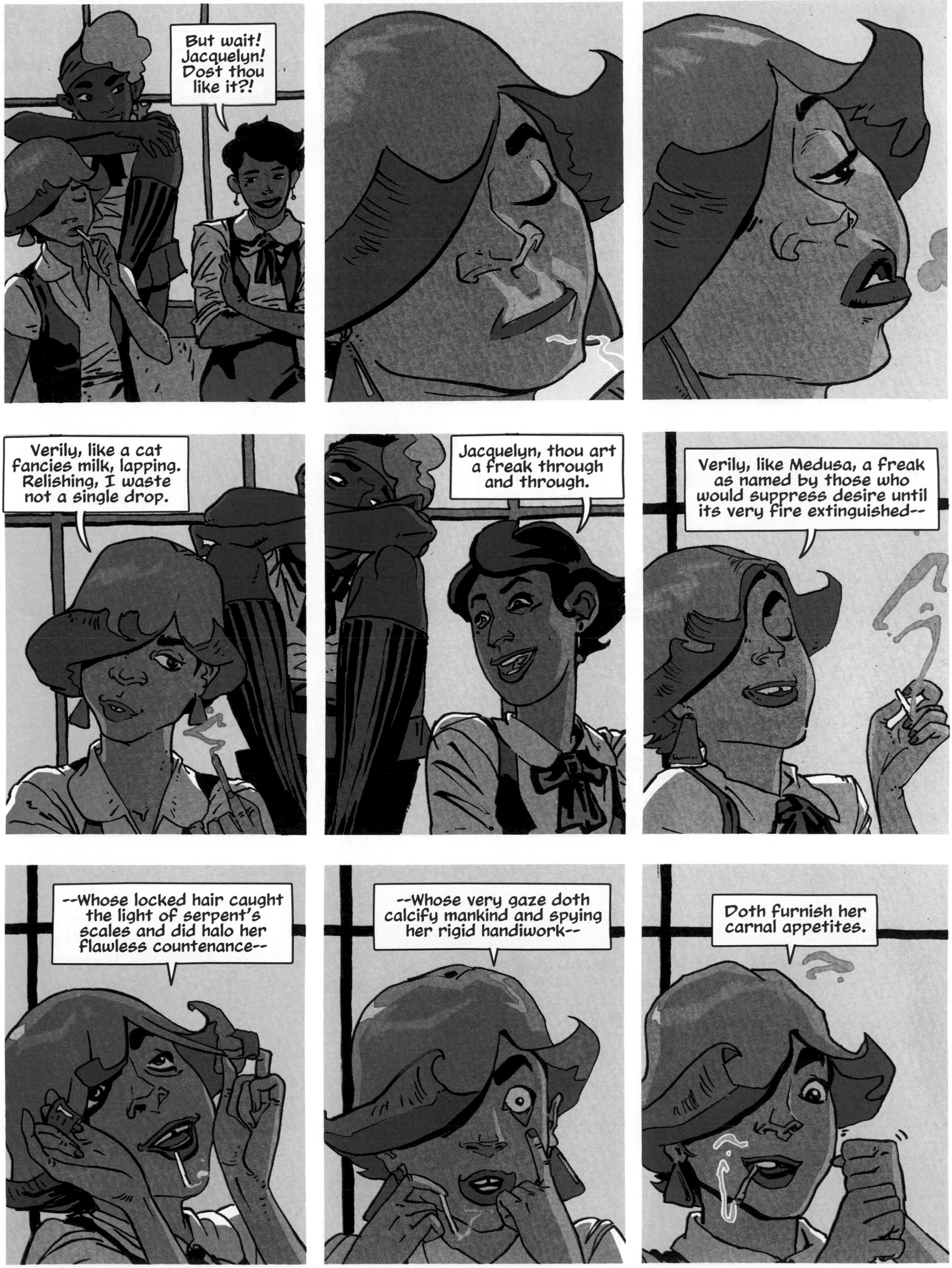
But wait! Jacquelyn! Dost thou like it?!
Verily, like a cat fancies milk, lapping. Relishing, I waste not a single drop.
Jacquelyn, thou art a freak through and through.
Verily, like Medusa, a freak as named by those who would suppress desire until its very fire extinguished--
--Whose locked hair caught the light of serpent's scales and did halo her flawless countenance--
--Whose very gaze doth calcify mankind and spying her rigid handiwork--
Doth furnish her carnal appetites.

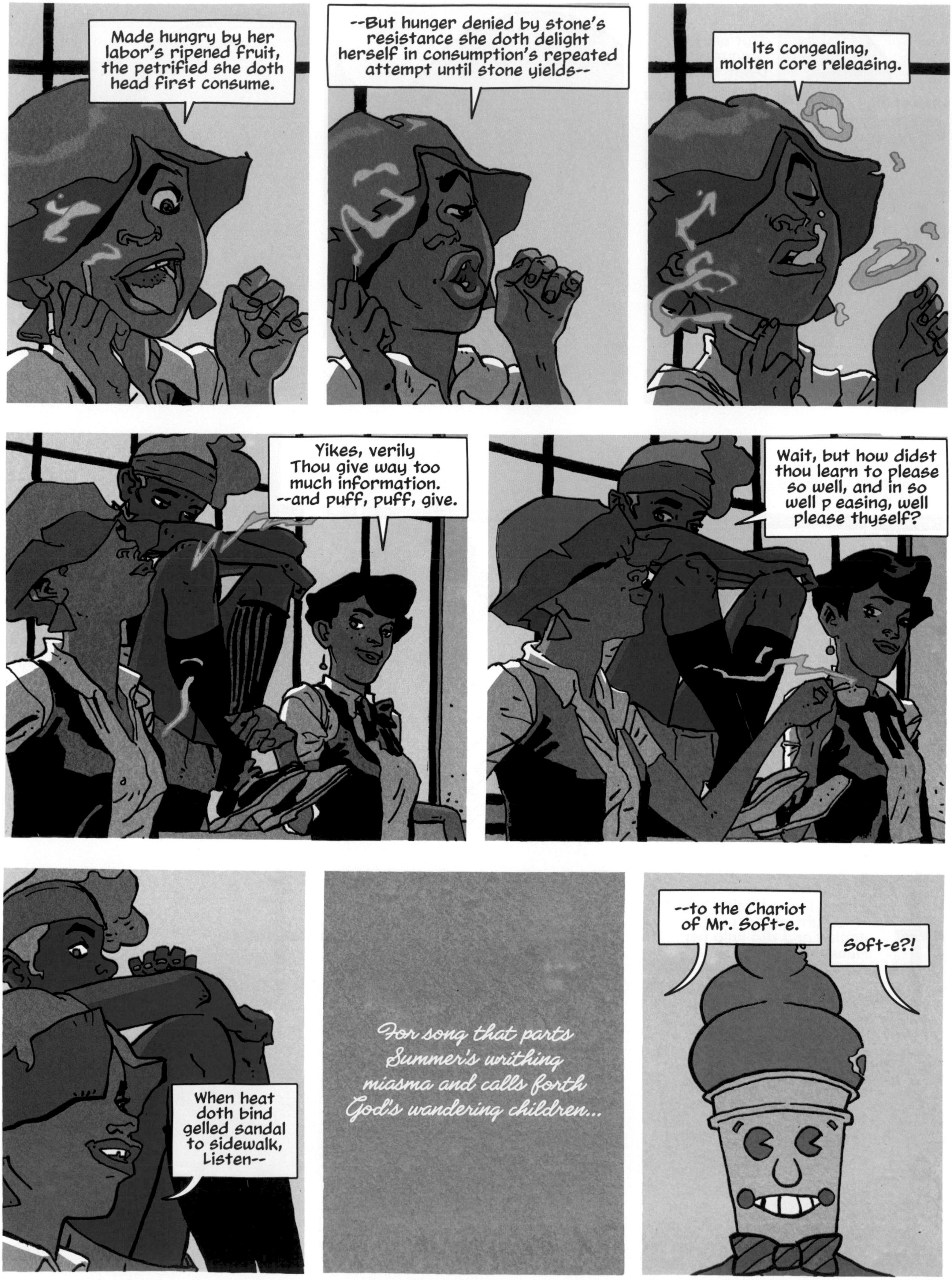
Made hungry by her labor's ripened fruit, the petrified she doth head first consume.
--But hunger denied by stone's resistance she doth delight herself in consumption's repeated attempt until stone yields--
Its congealing, molten core releasing.
Yikes, verily Thou give way too much information. --and puff, puff, give.
Wait, but how didst thou learn to please so well, and in so well p easing, well please thyself?
When heat doth bind gelled sandal to sidewalk, Listen--
For song that parts Summer's writhing miasma and calls forth God's wandering children...
--to the Chariot of Mr. Soft-e.
Soft-e?!

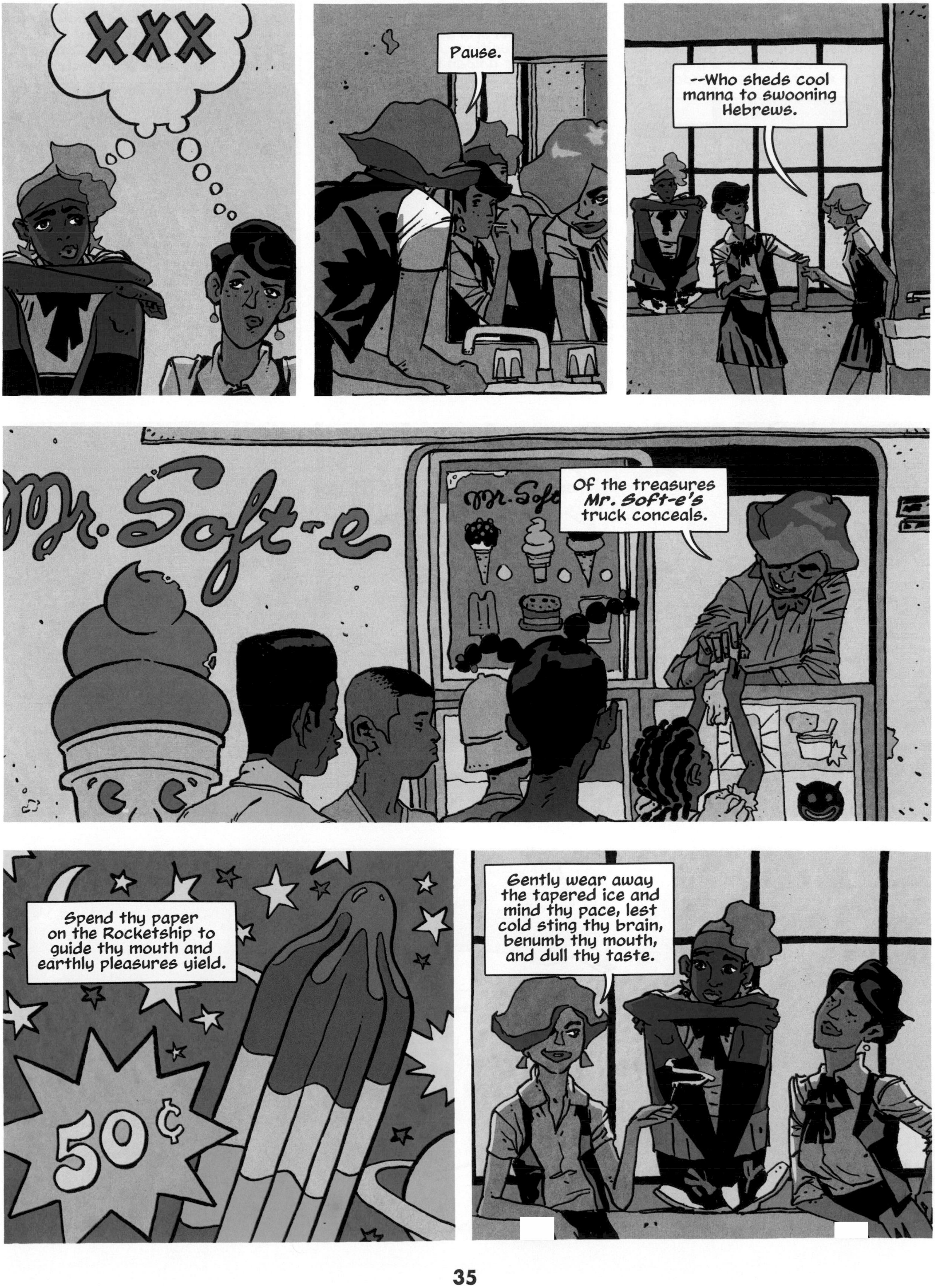
XXX
Pause.
--Who sheds cool manna to swooning Hebrews.
Mr. Soft-e
Of the treasures Mr. Soft-e's truck conceals.
Spend thy paper on the Rocketship to guide thy mouth and earthly pleasures yield.
50¢
Gently wear away the tapered ice and mind thy pace, lest cold sting thy brain, benumb thy mouth, and dull thy taste.

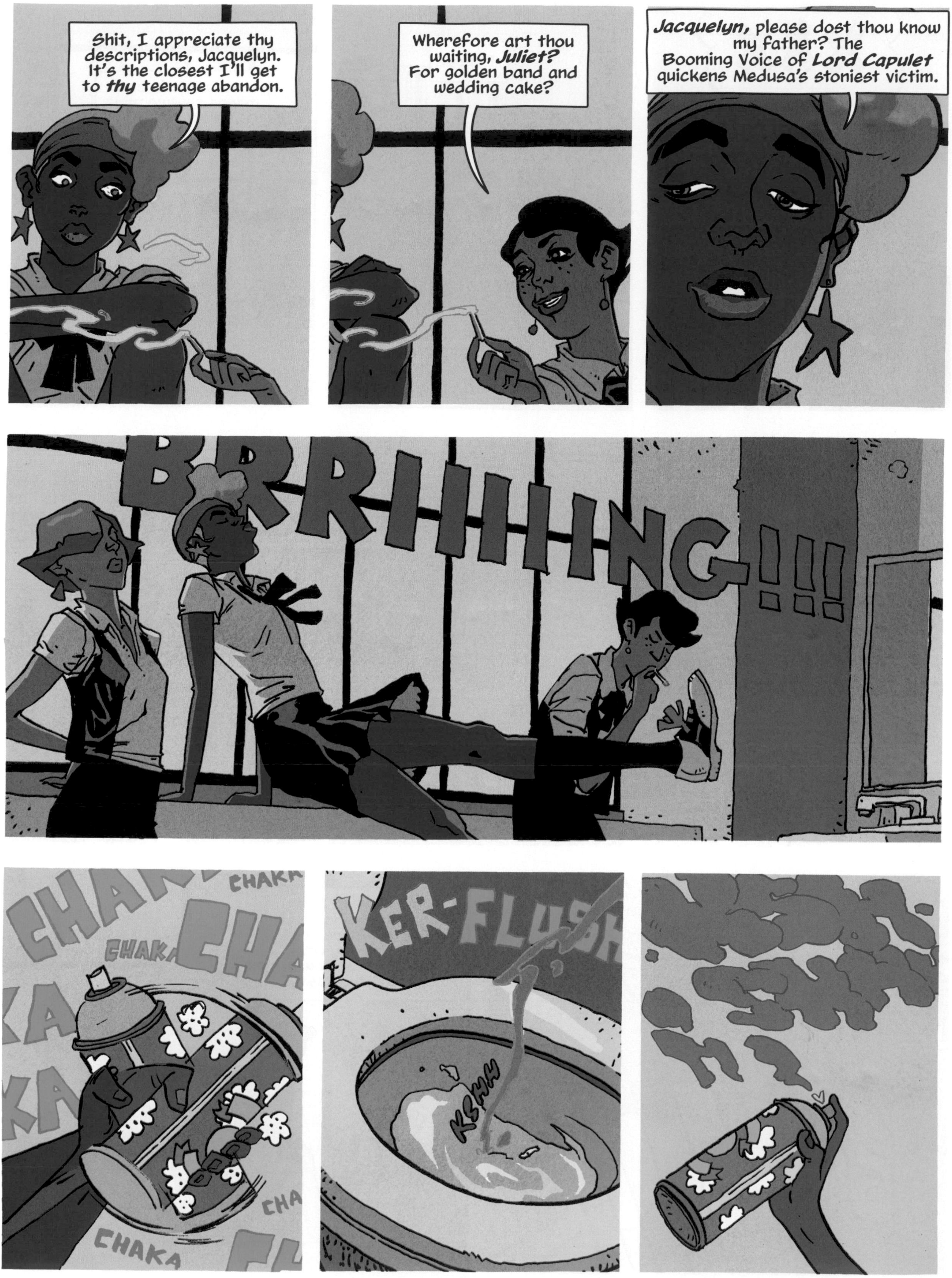
Shit, I appreciate thy descriptions, Jacquelyn. It's the closest I'll get to *thy* teenage abandon.
Wherefore art thou waiting, *Juliet?* For golden band and wedding cake?
*Jacquelyn,* please dost thou know my father? The Booming Voice of *Lord Capulet* quickens Medusa's stoniest victim.
BRRIIIIING!!!
CHAKA
CHAKA
CHAKA
CHAKA
KER-FLUSH
KSHH

Verily, free at last!

My father's enrolled me in summer school.

Juliet, you failed? A shame you'll miss the Mermaid Parade!

Not failed! My dad, he fears my idle hands, binds them with-- Extracurricular Activities.

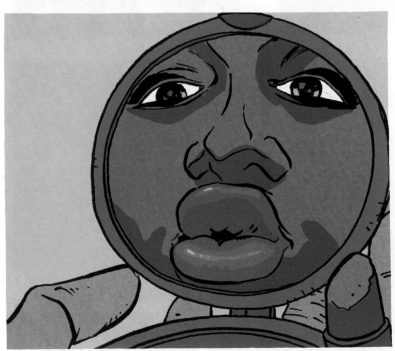

SNAP

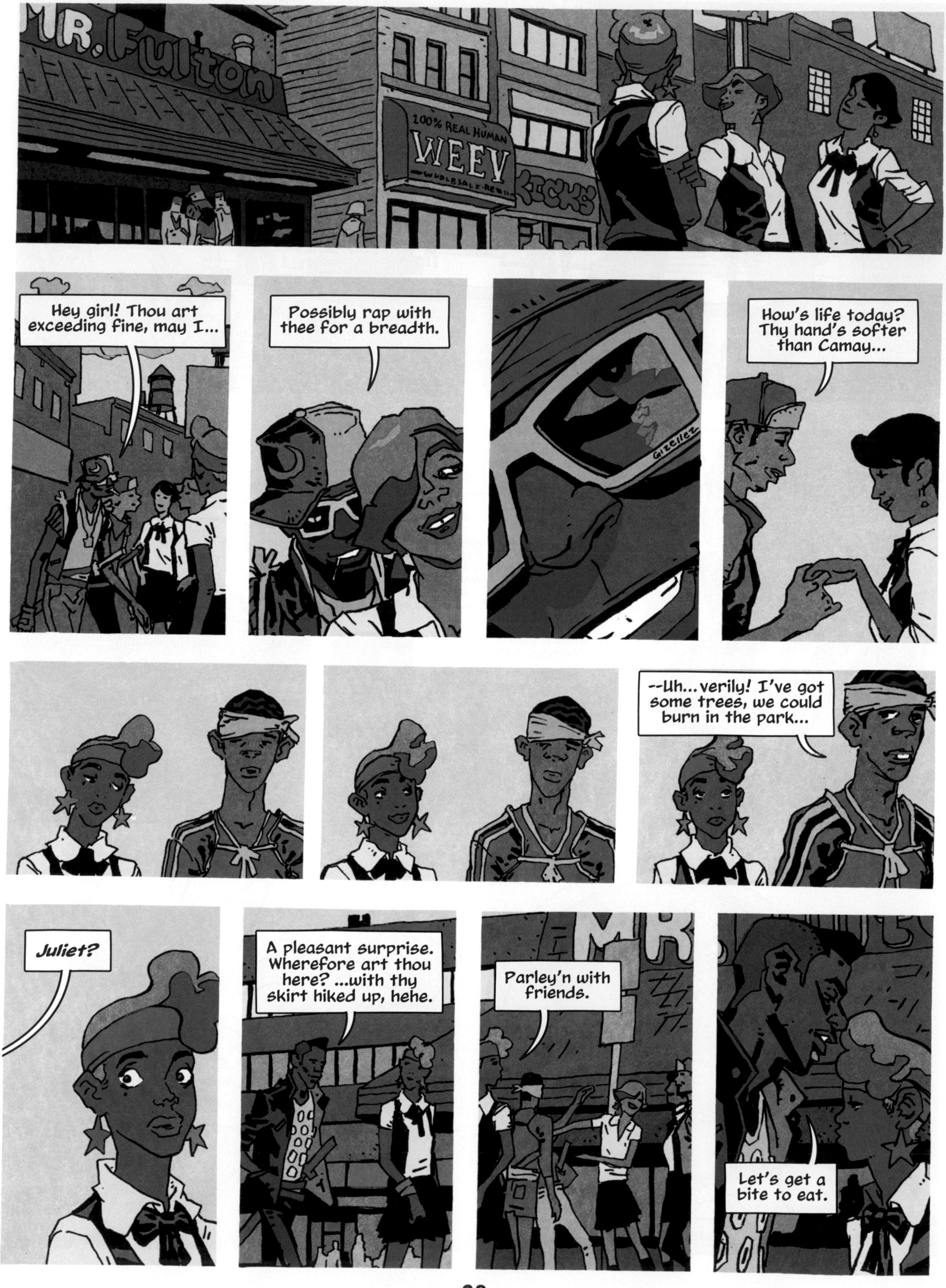
Mr. Fulton
100% REAL HUMAN
WEEV
KICKS
Hey girl! Thou art exceeding fine, may I...
Possibly rap with thee for a breadth.
How's life today? Thy hand's softer than Camay...
--Uh... verily! I've got some trees, we could burn in the park...
Juliet?
A pleasant surprise. Wherefore art thou here? ...with thy skirt hiked up, hehe.
Parley'n with friends.
Let's get a bite to eat.

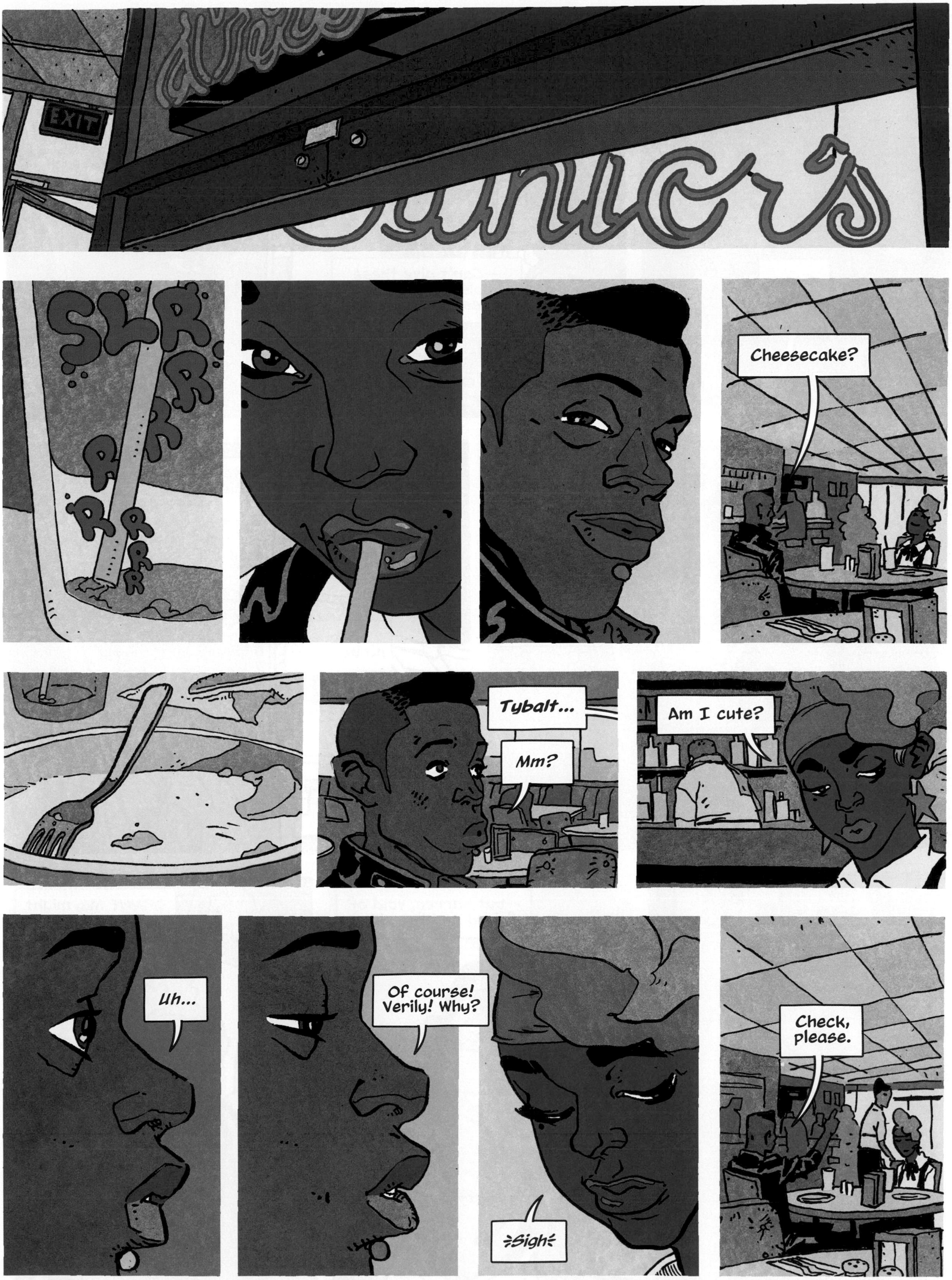
SLRRRRRRRR
Cheesecake?
Tybalt...
Mm?
Am I cute?
Uh...
Of course! Verily! Why?
Sigh
Check, please.

See--

Hahaha, ye look so serious!

--Can't give these fools an inch. Here comes the final boss.

Never dost thou speak of private school, Tybalt. Why?

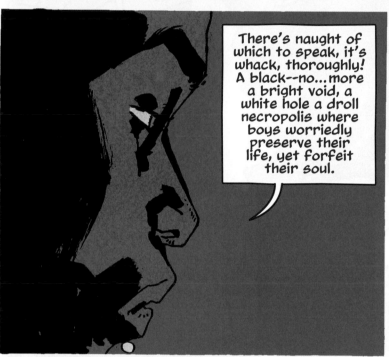

There's naught of which to speak, it's whack, thoroughly! A black--no...more a bright void, a white hole a droll necropolis where boys worriedly preserve their life, yet forfeit their soul.

Surely a better place than this, though.

A place, no better--

--but barren, void of friend and foe alike.

≥Psst≤ Ma, might I have your ear.

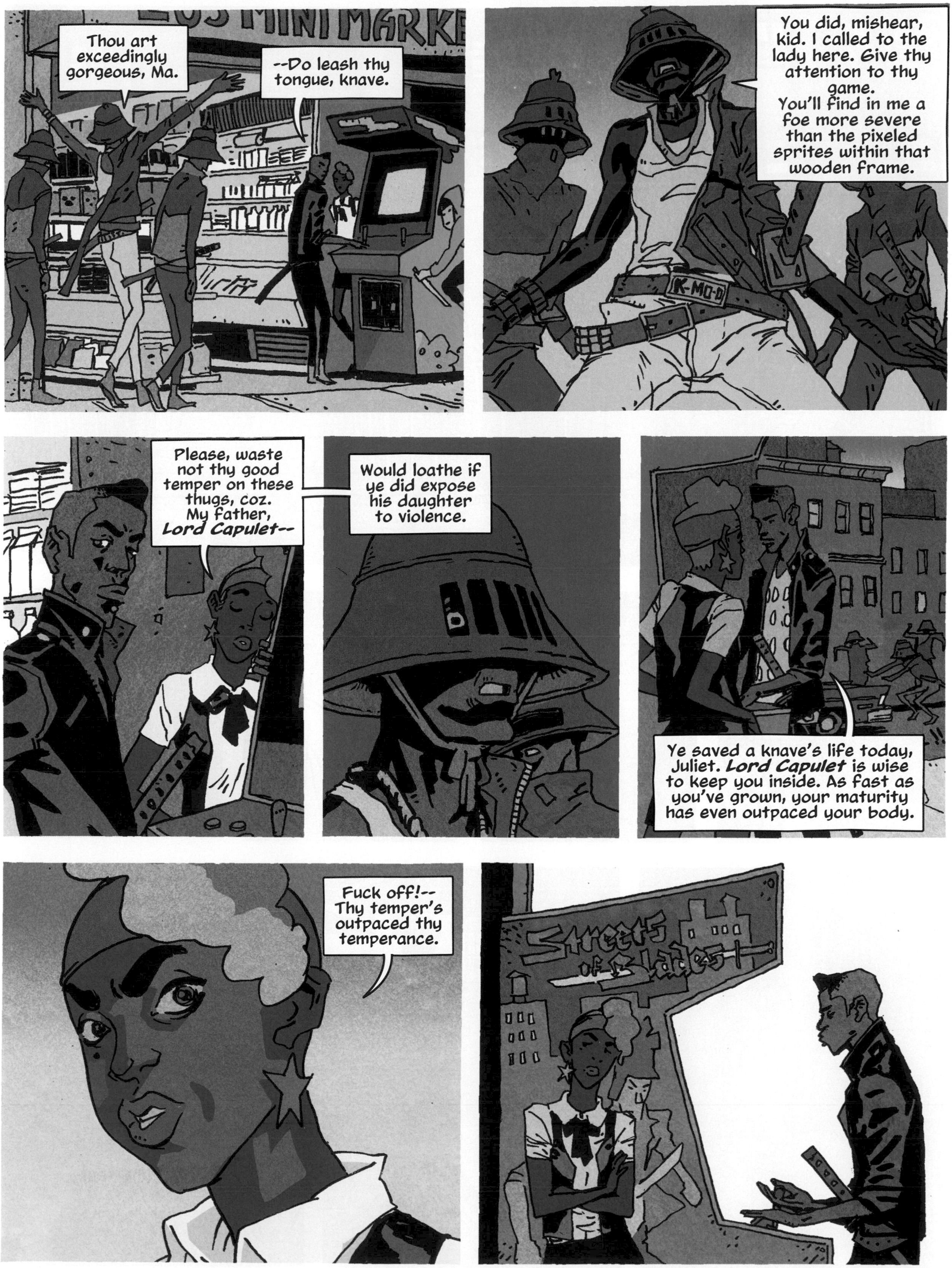
Thou art exceedingly gorgeous, Ma.
--Do leash thy tongue, knave.
You did, mishear, kid. I called to the lady here. Give thy attention to thy game.
You'll find in me a foe more severe than the pixeled sprites within that wooden frame.
K-MO-D
Please, waste not thy good temper on these thugs, coz. My father, ***Lord Capulet***--
Would loathe if ye did expose his daughter to violence.
Ye saved a knave's life today, Juliet. ***Lord Capulet*** is wise to keep you inside. As fast as you've grown, your maturity has even outpaced your body.
Fuck off!-- Thy temper's outpaced thy temperance.
Streets of Blades

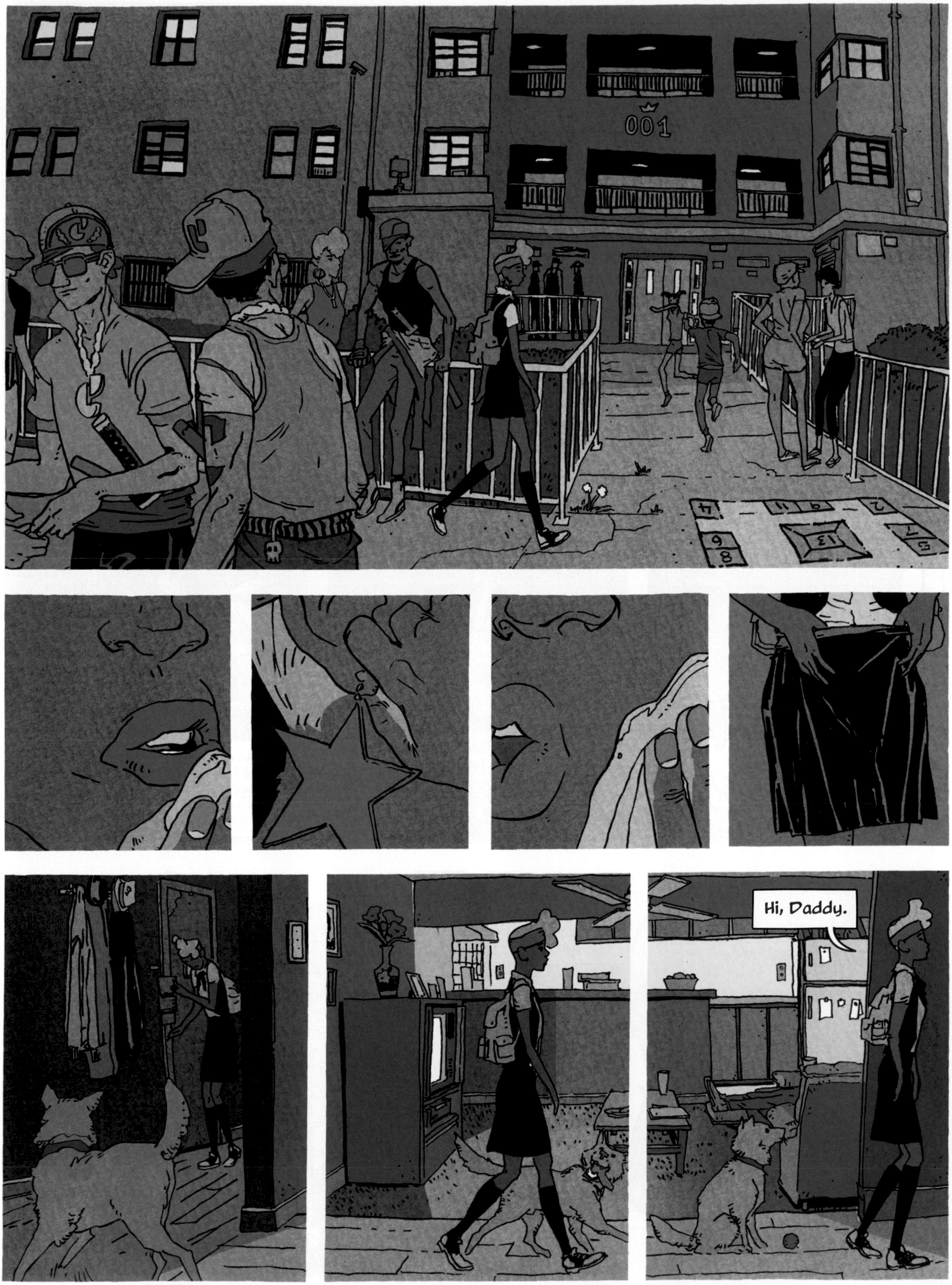
001
Hi, Daddy.

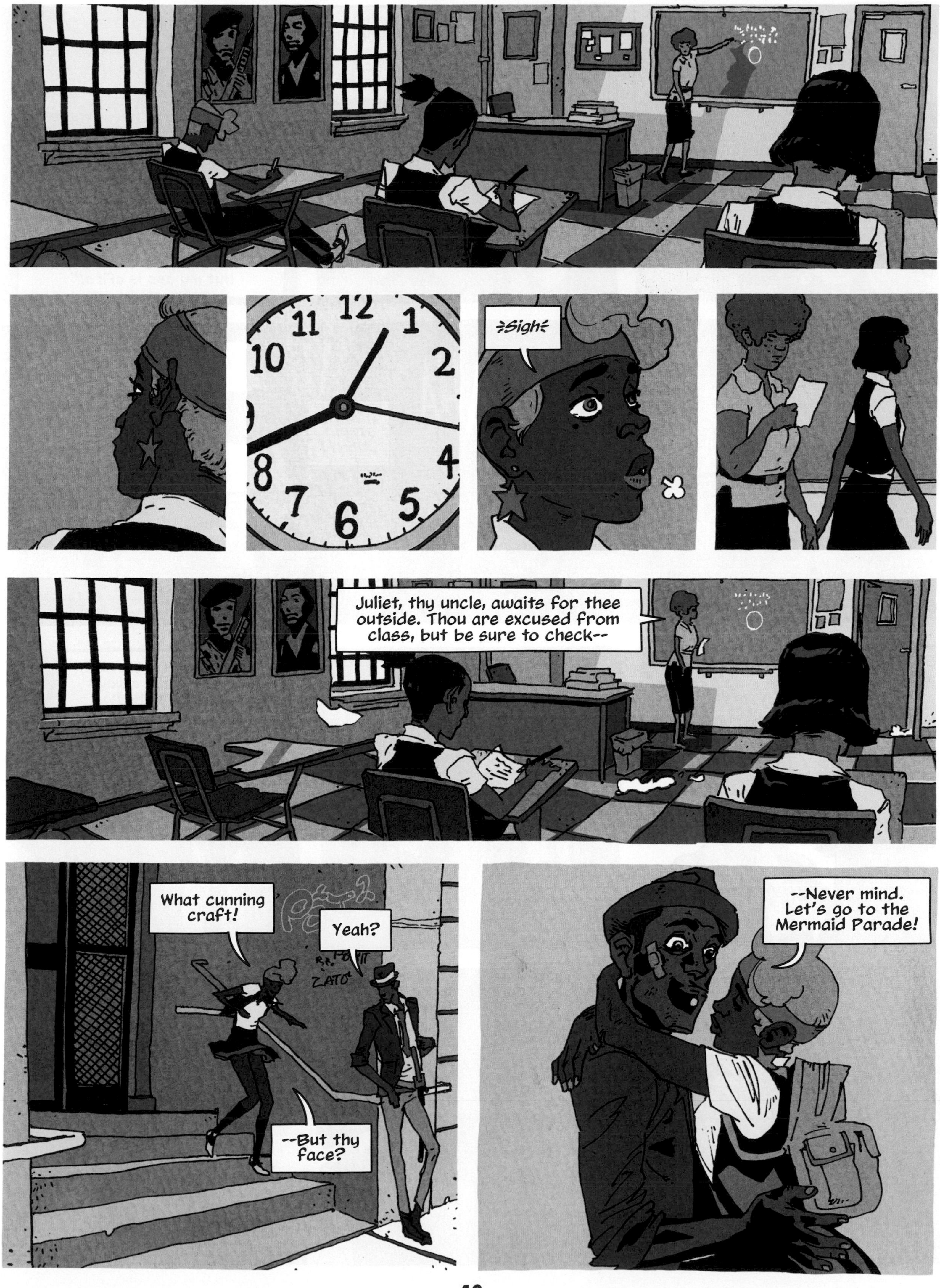

Sigh
Juliet, thy uncle, awaits for thee outside. Thou are excused from class, but be sure to check--
What cunning craft!
Yeah?
--But thy face?
--Never mind. Let's go to the Mermaid Parade!

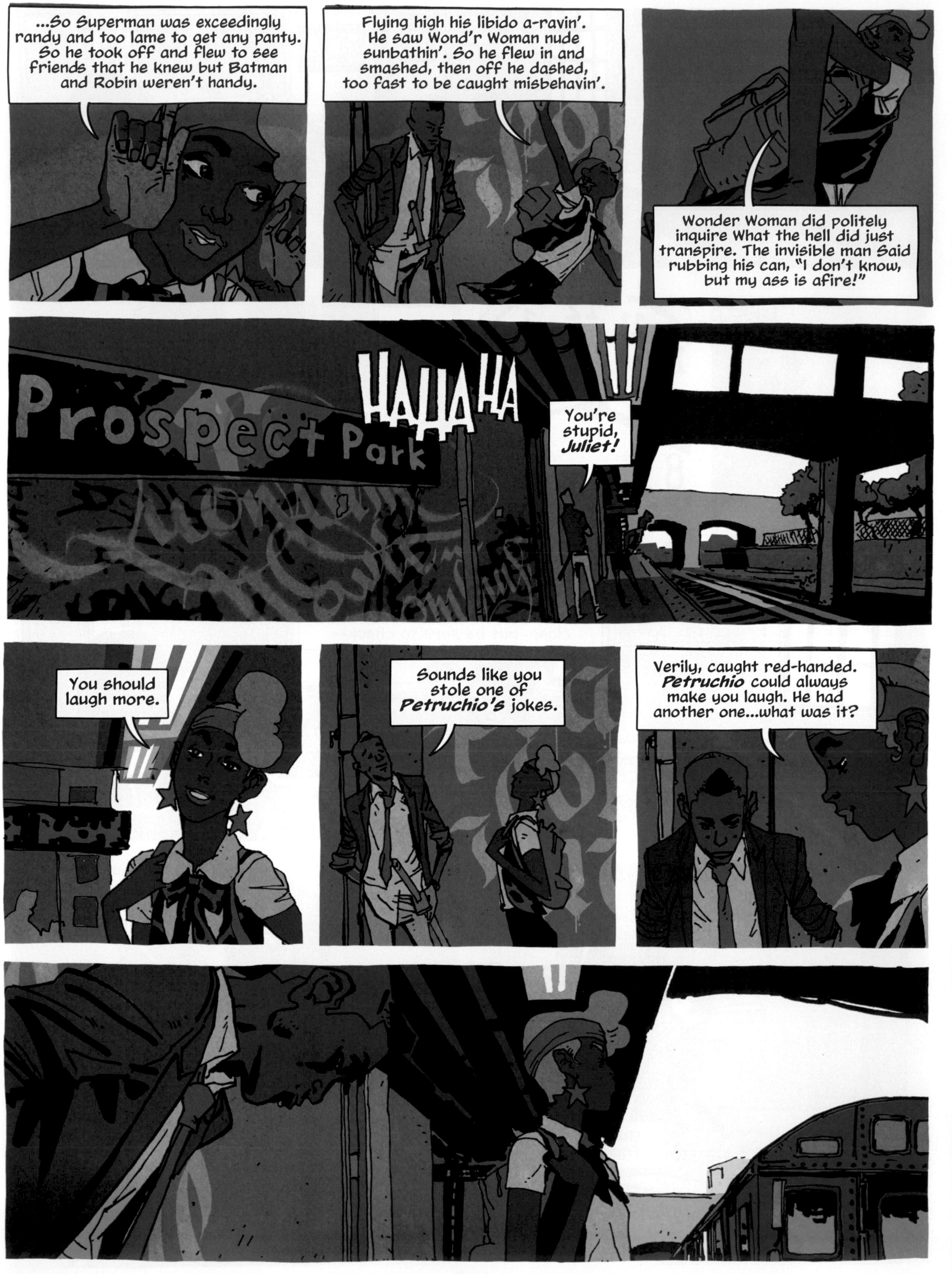
...So Superman was exceedingly randy and too lame to get any panty. So he took off and flew to see friends that he knew but Batman and Robin weren't handy.
Flying high his libido a-ravin'. He saw Wond'r Woman nude sunbathin'. So he flew in and smashed, then off he dashed, too fast to be caught misbehavin'.
Wonder Woman did politely inquire What the hell did just transpire. The invisible man Said rubbing his can, "I don't know, but my ass is afire!"
Prospect Park
HAHAHA
You're stupid, Juliet!
You should laugh more.
Sounds like you stole one of Petruchio's jokes.
Verily, caught red-handed. Petruchio could always make you laugh. He had another one...what was it?

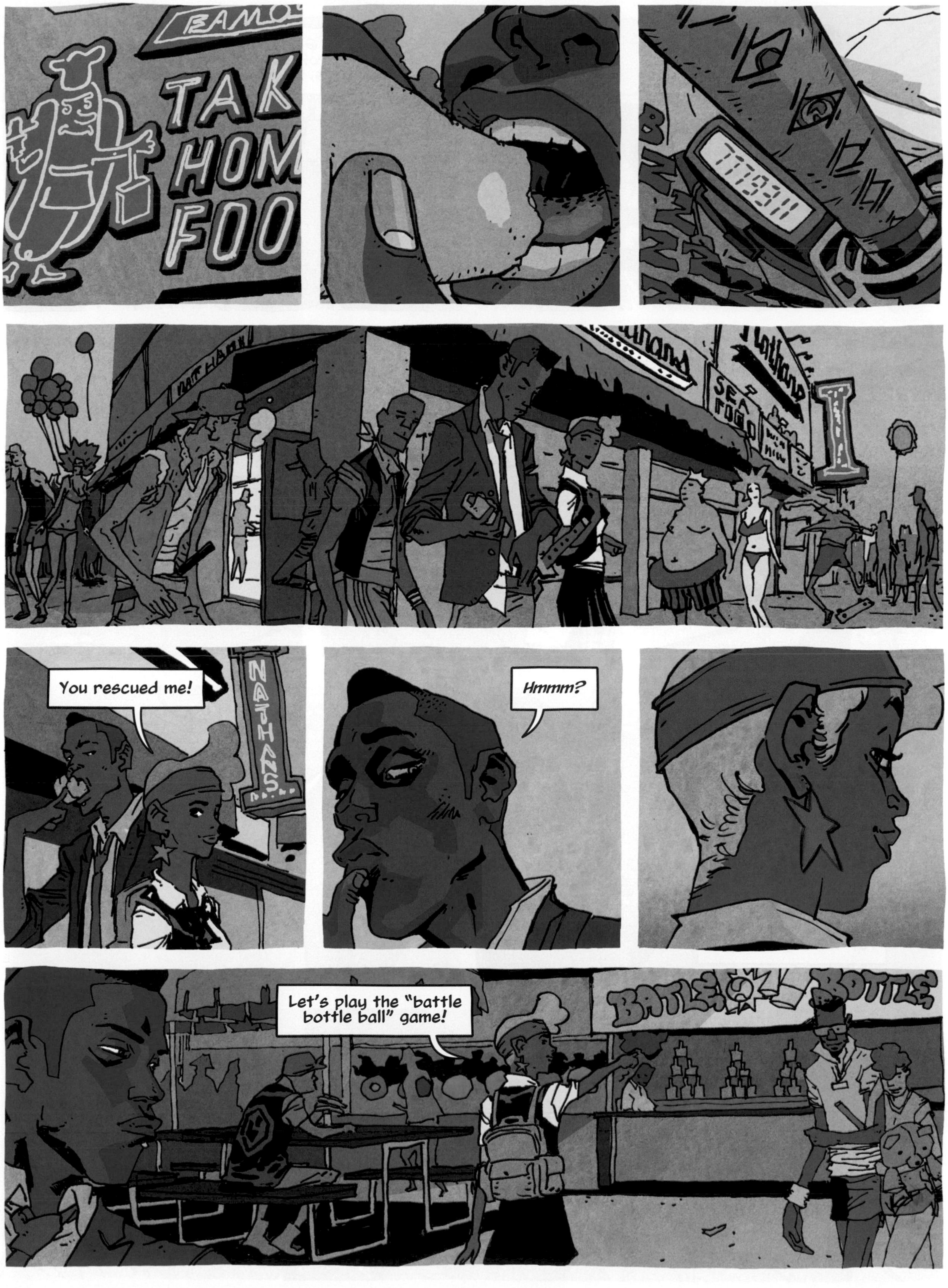
FAMO
TAK
HOM
FOO
7779311
NATHANS
SEA FOOD
NATHANS
You rescued me!
NATHANS
Hmmm?
Let's play the "battle bottle ball" game!
BATTLE BOTTLE

CRASH

Geez, Kiddo, thou art a professional--at busting my balls, take thy prize and scram.

Which will it be, Sweetheart? Take your pick.

What charms are those beneath the plush?

My wife, she makes these, each one by hand each is a one-of-a-kind love charm.

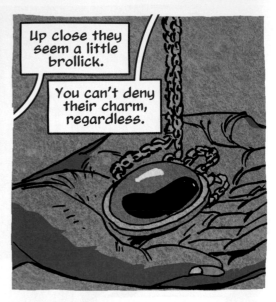

Up close they seem a little brollick.

You can't deny their charm, regardless.

On delicate necks as yours maybe, but on the sturdy neck of your lover, this amulet will rest perfectly, guarding his affections from any other.

Ha, you've no need for trifling trinkets.

I'll take it!

I want the rocketship.

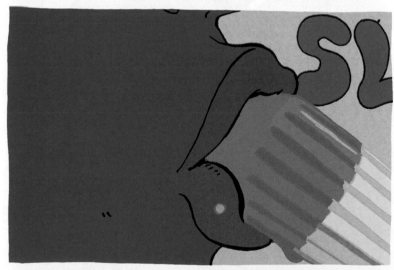

SLURP

Uh...we should catch a ride--

THIRSTY

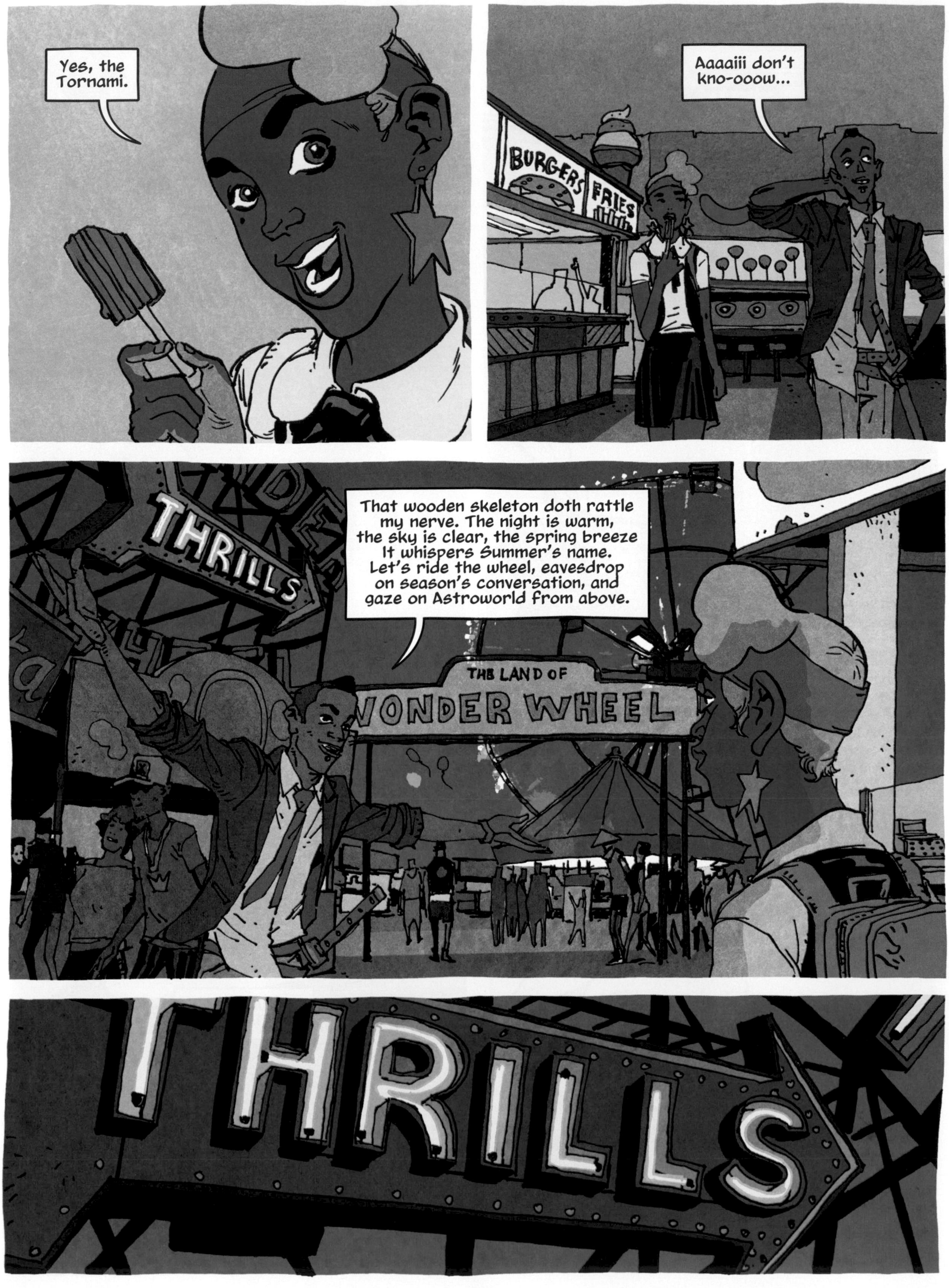
Yes, the Tornami.
Aaaaiii don't kno-ooow...
BURGERS
FRIES
THRILLS
That wooden skeleton doth rattle my nerve. The night is warm, the sky is clear, the spring breeze It whispers Summer's name. Let's ride the wheel, eavesdrop on season's conversation, and gaze on Astroworld from above.
THE LAND OF
WONDER WHEEL
THRILLS

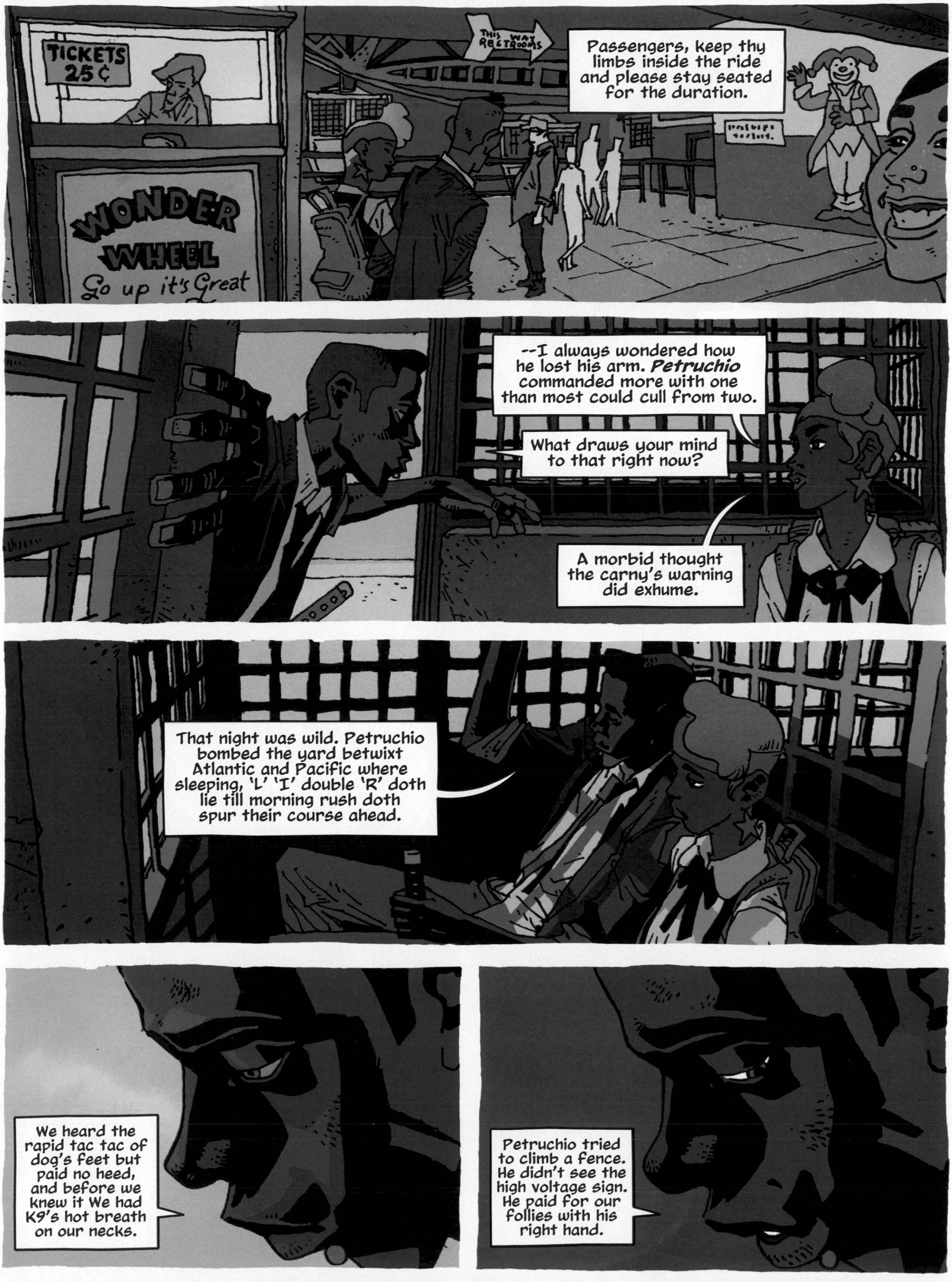
TICKETS 25¢
WONDER WHEEL Go up it's Great
THIS WAY RESTROOMS
Passengers, keep thy limbs inside the ride and please stay seated for the duration.
--I always wondered how he lost his arm. *Petruchio* commanded more with one than most could cull from two.
What draws your mind to that right now?
A morbid thought the carny's warning did exhume.
That night was wild. Petruchio bombed the yard betwixt Atlantic and Pacific where sleeping, 'L' 'I' double 'R' doth lie till morning rush doth spur their course ahead.
We heard the rapid tac tac of dog's feet but paid no heed, and before we knew it We had K9's hot breath on our necks.
Petruchio tried to climb a fence. He didn't see the high voltage sign. He paid for our follies with his right hand.

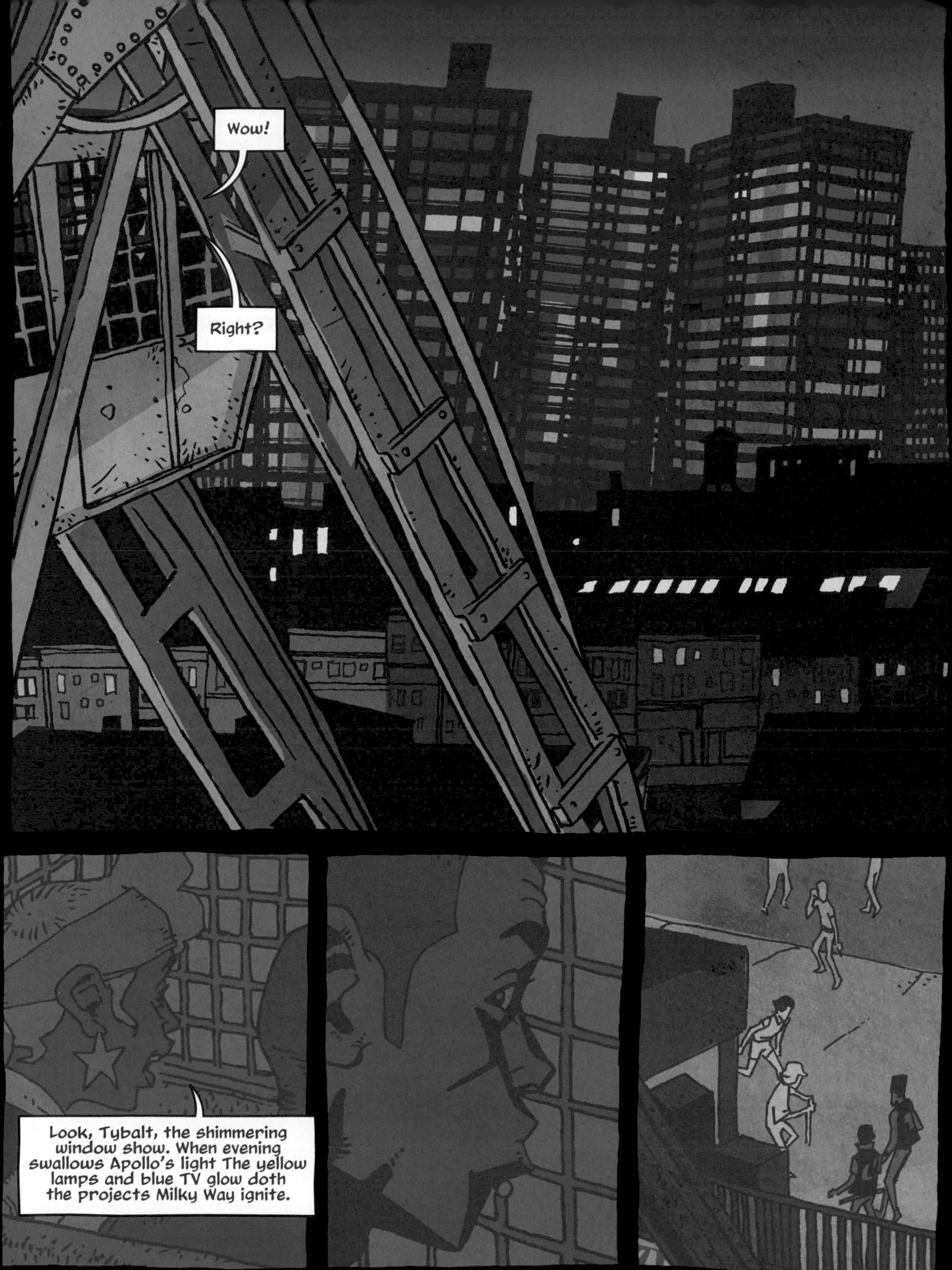
Wow!
Right?
Look, Tybalt, the shimmering window show. When evening swallows Apollo's light The yellow lamps and blue TV glow doth the projects Milky Way ignite.

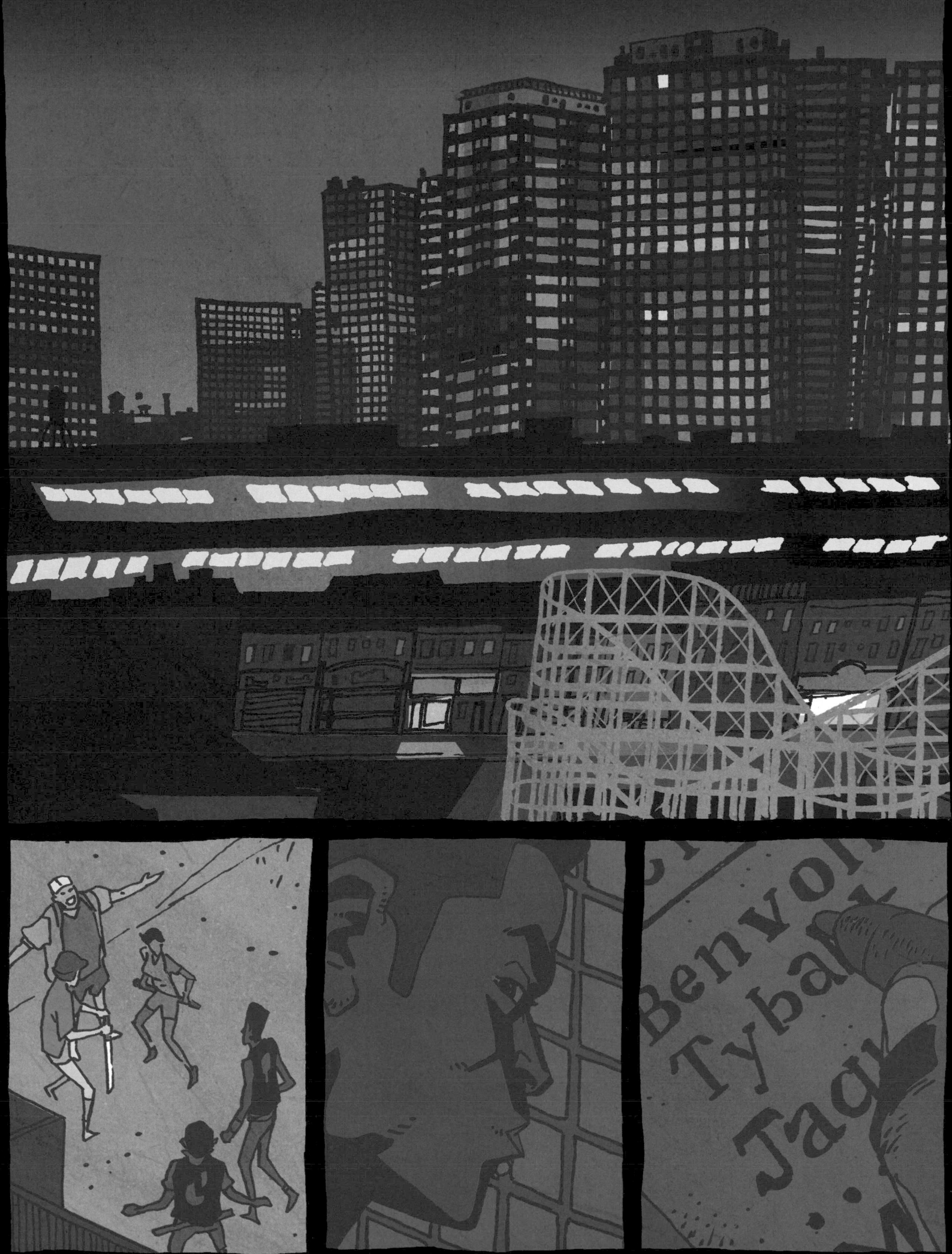
Benvo
Tyba
Jaq

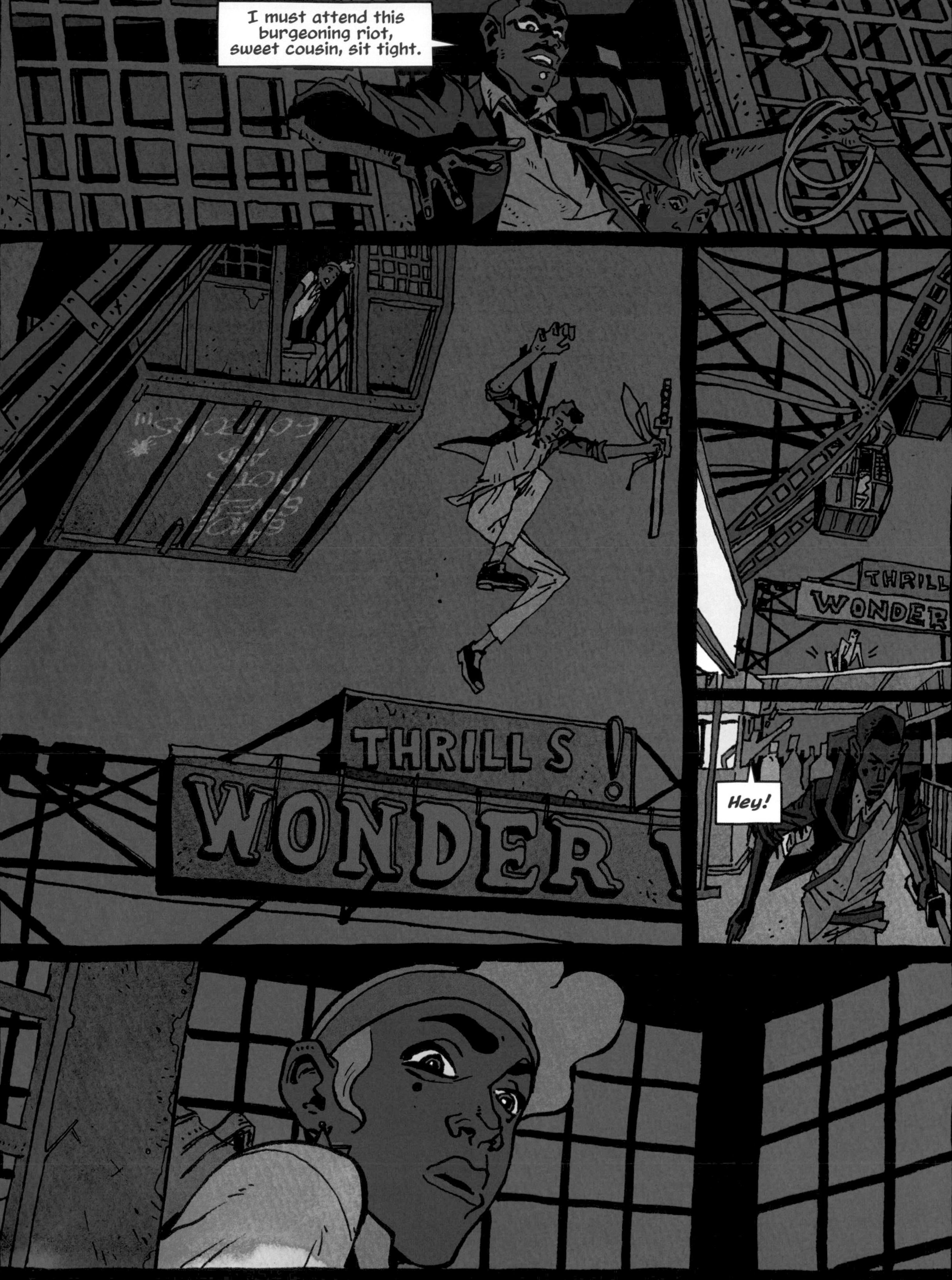
I must attend this burgeoning riot, sweet cousin, sit tight.
THRILLS!
WONDER
THRILL
WONDER
Hey!

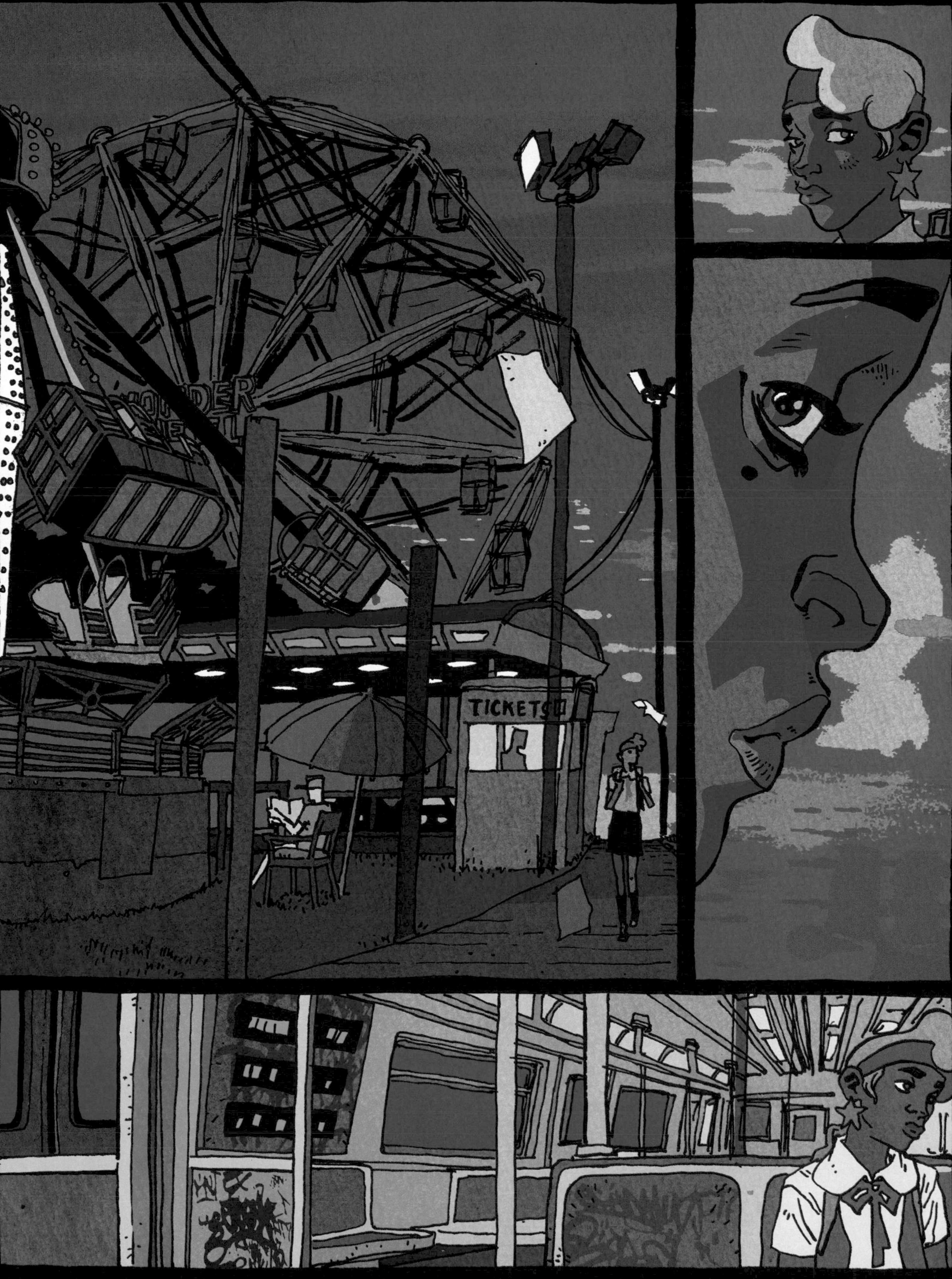
TICKETS

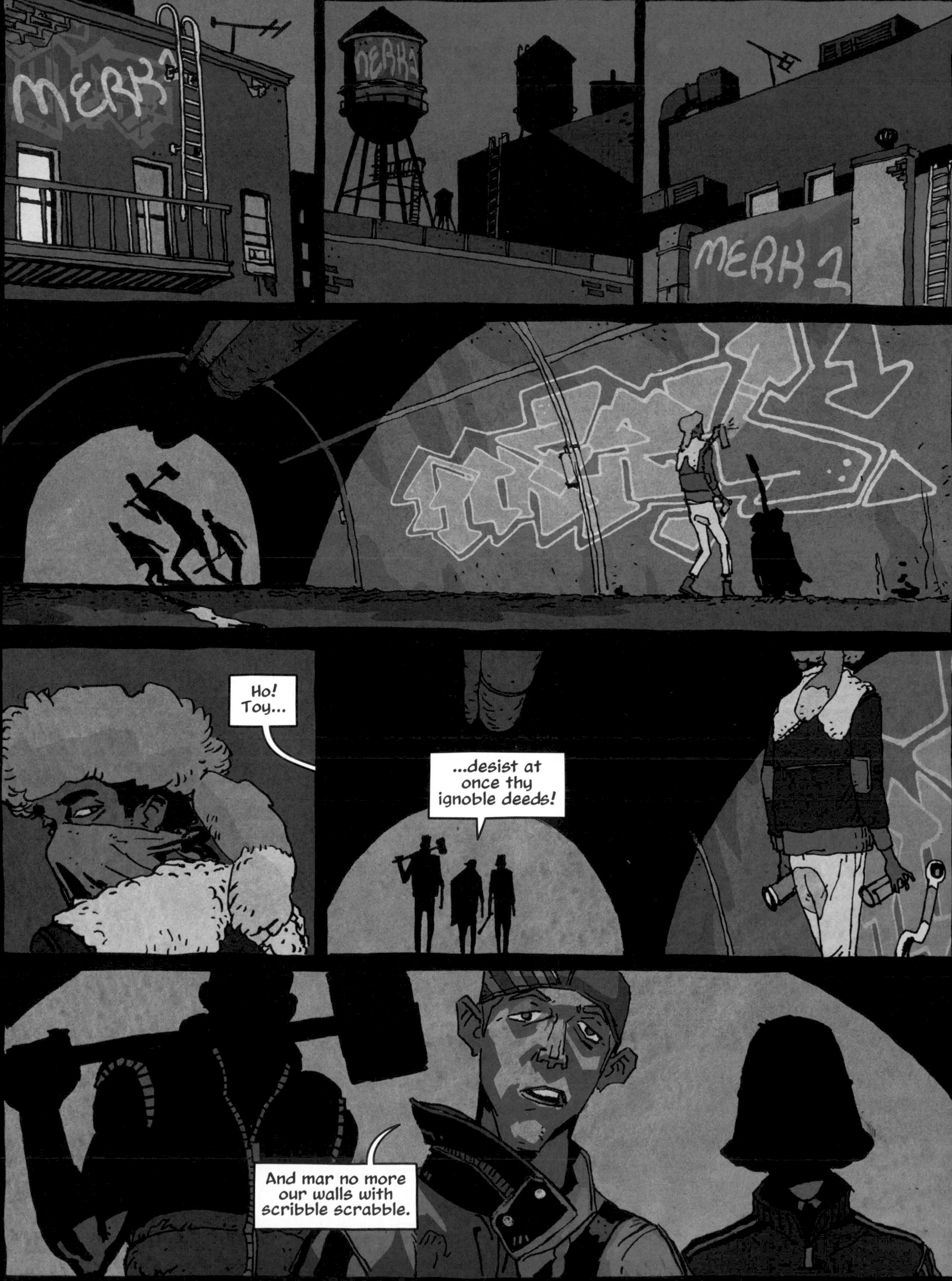
MERK 1
Ho! Toy...
...desist at once thy ignoble deeds!
And mar no more our walls with scribble scrabble.

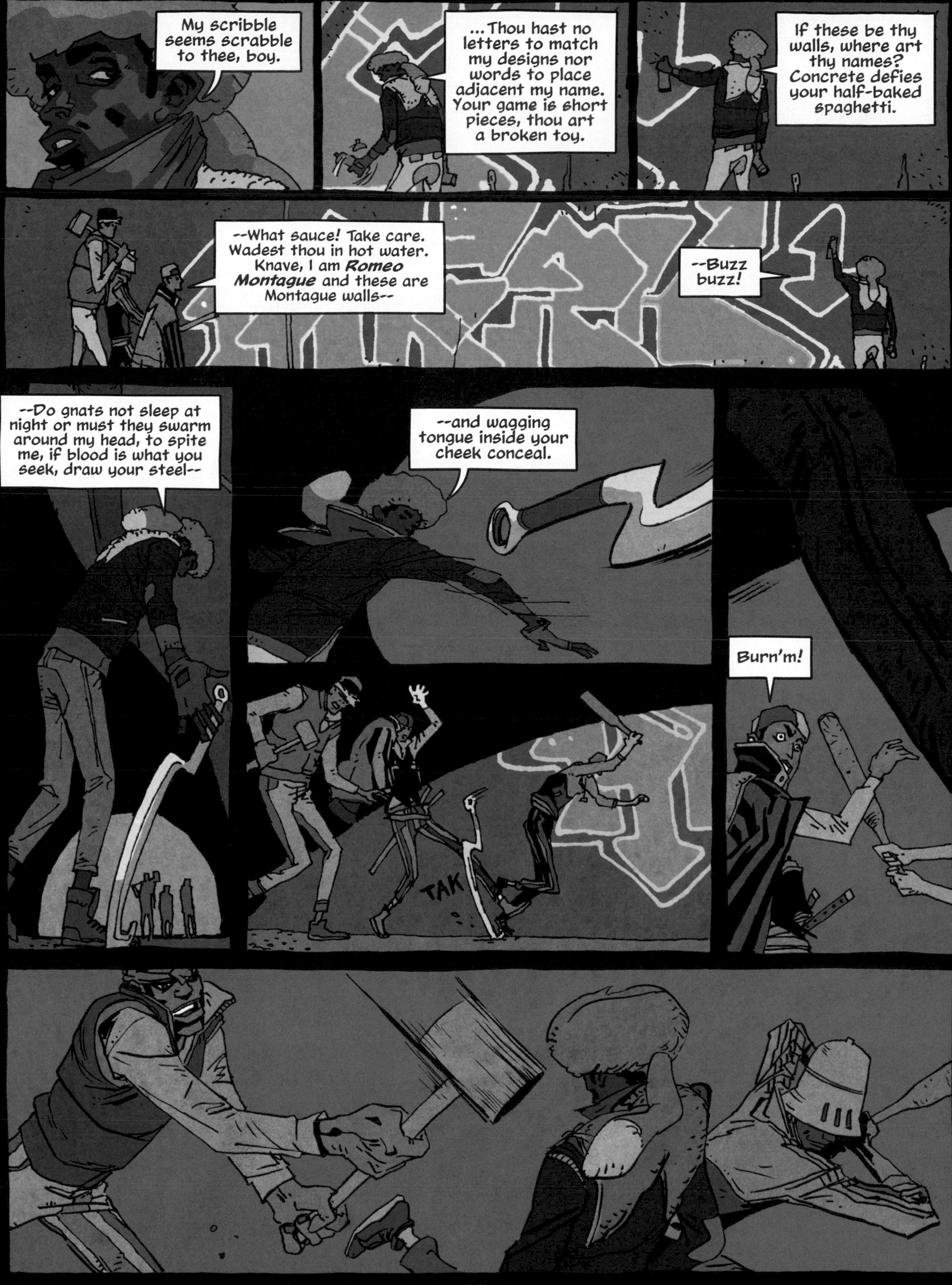
My scribble seems scrabble to thee, boy.
...Thou hast no letters to match my designs nor words to place adjacent my name. Your game is short pieces, thou art a broken toy.
If these be thy walls, where art thy names? Concrete defies your half-baked spaghetti.
--What sauce! Take care. Wadest thou in hot water. Knave, I am *Romeo Montague* and these are Montague walls--
--Buzz buzz!
--Do gnats not sleep at night or must they swarm around my head, to spite me, if blood is what you seek, draw your steel--
--and wagging tongue inside your cheek conceal.
TAK
Burn'm!

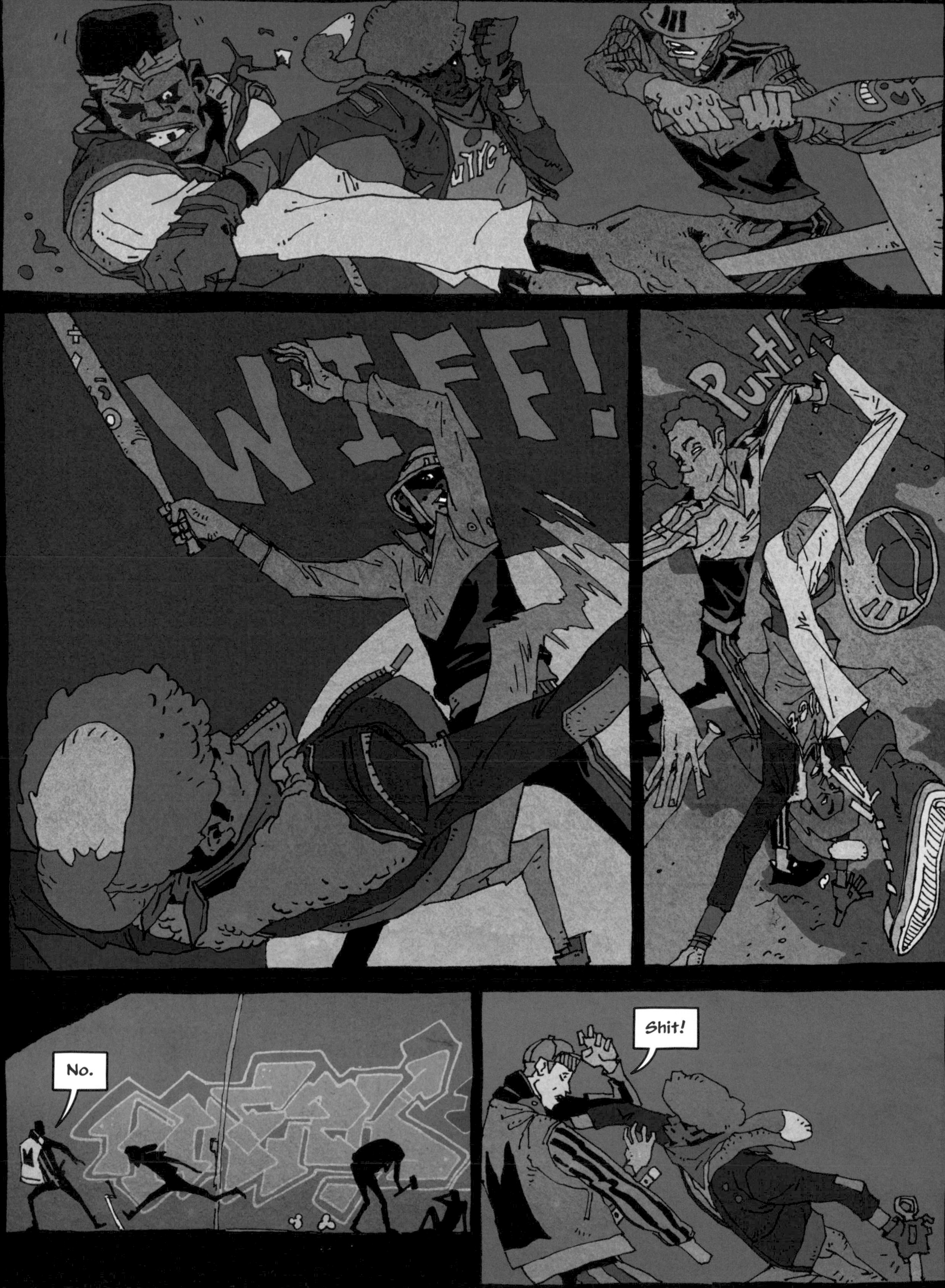
WIFF!
Punt!
No.
Shit!

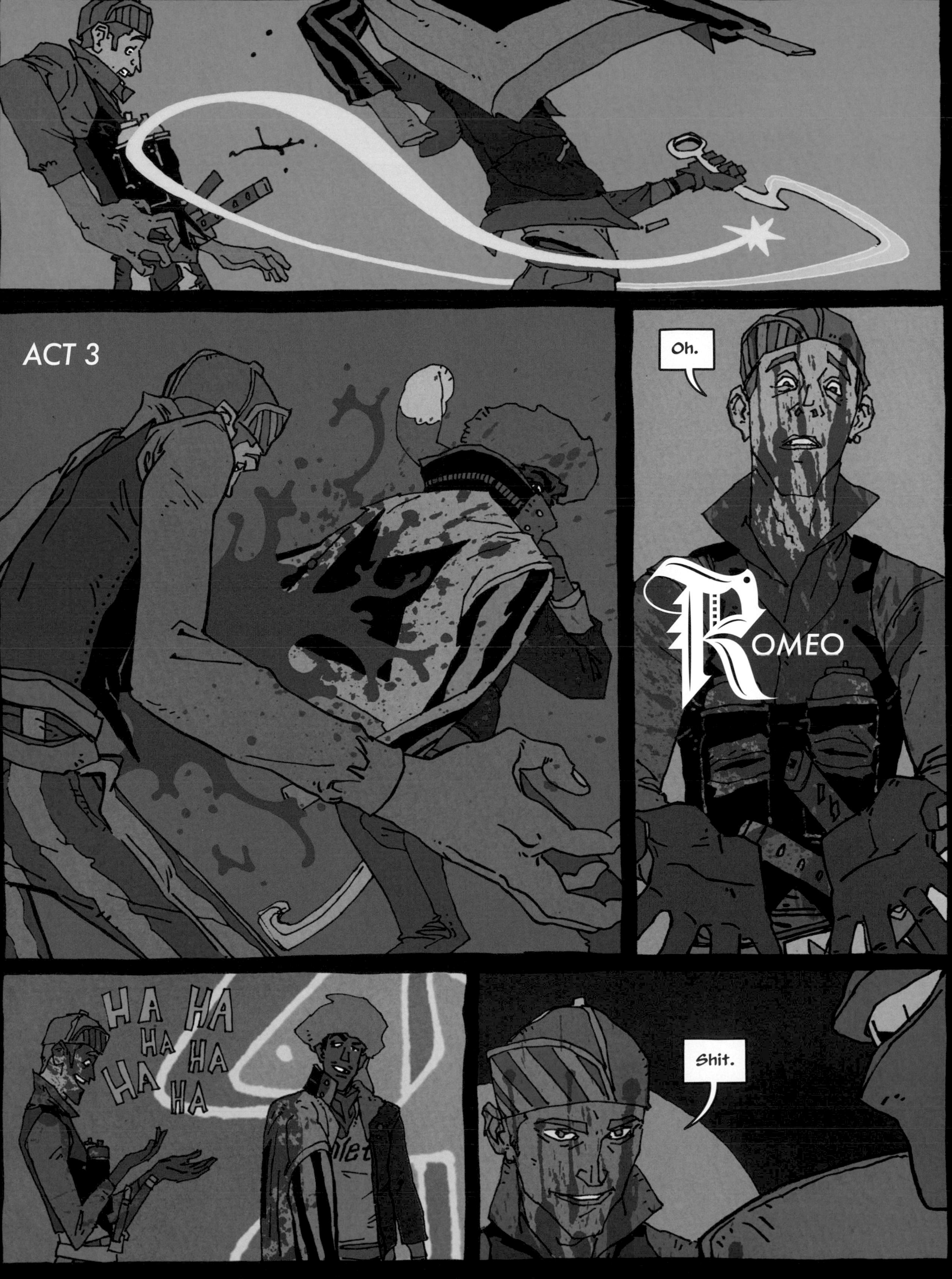
ACT 3
Oh.
ROMEO
HA HA HA HA HA HA HA
Shit.

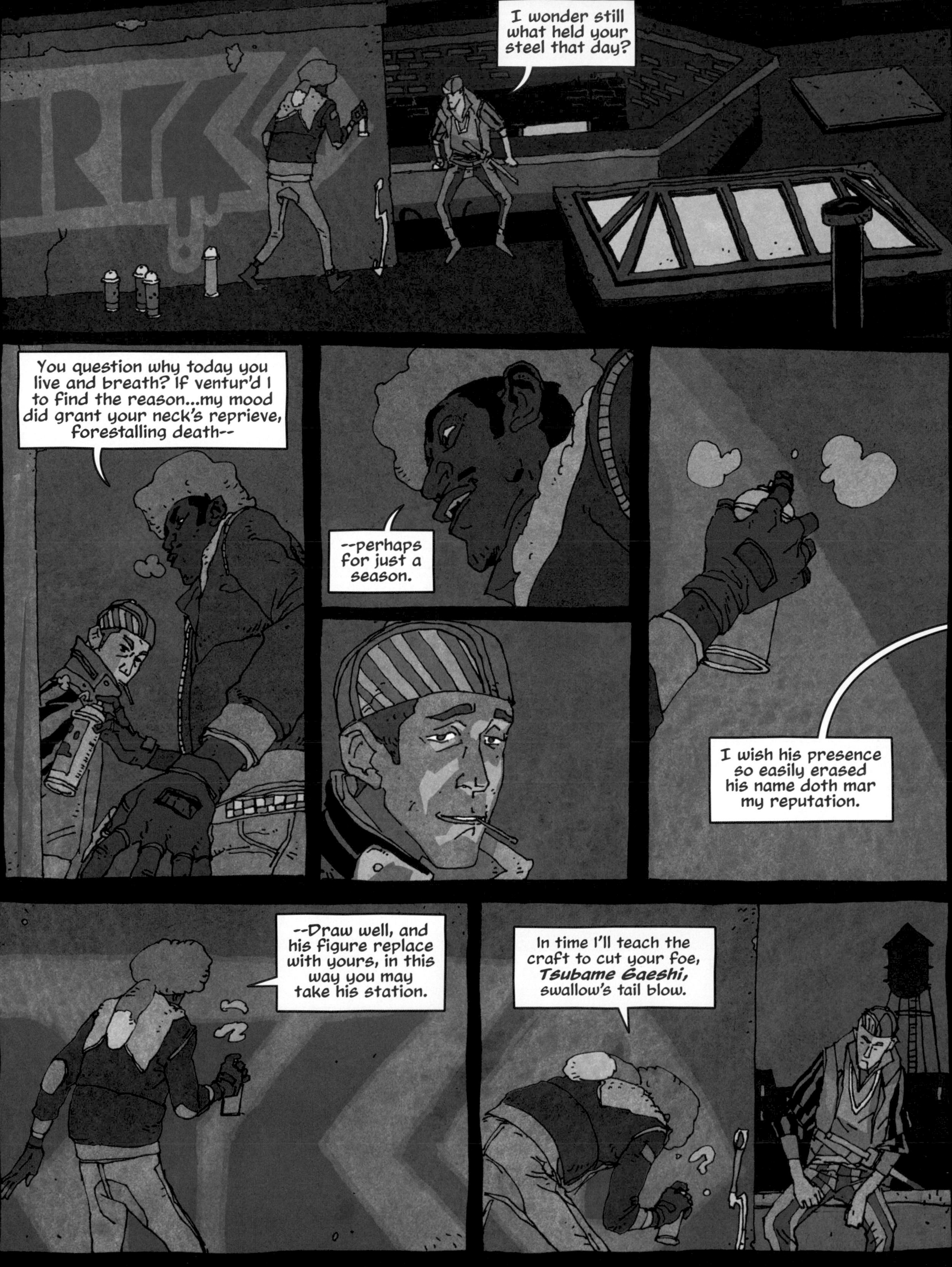
I wonder still what held your steel that day?
You question why today you live and breath? If ventur'd I to find the reason...my mood did grant your neck's reprieve, forestalling death--
--perhaps for just a season.
I wish his presence so easily erased his name doth mar my reputation.
--Draw well, and his figure replace with yours, in this way you may take his station.
In time I'll teach the craft to cut your foe, *Tsubame Gaeshi,* swallow's tail blow.

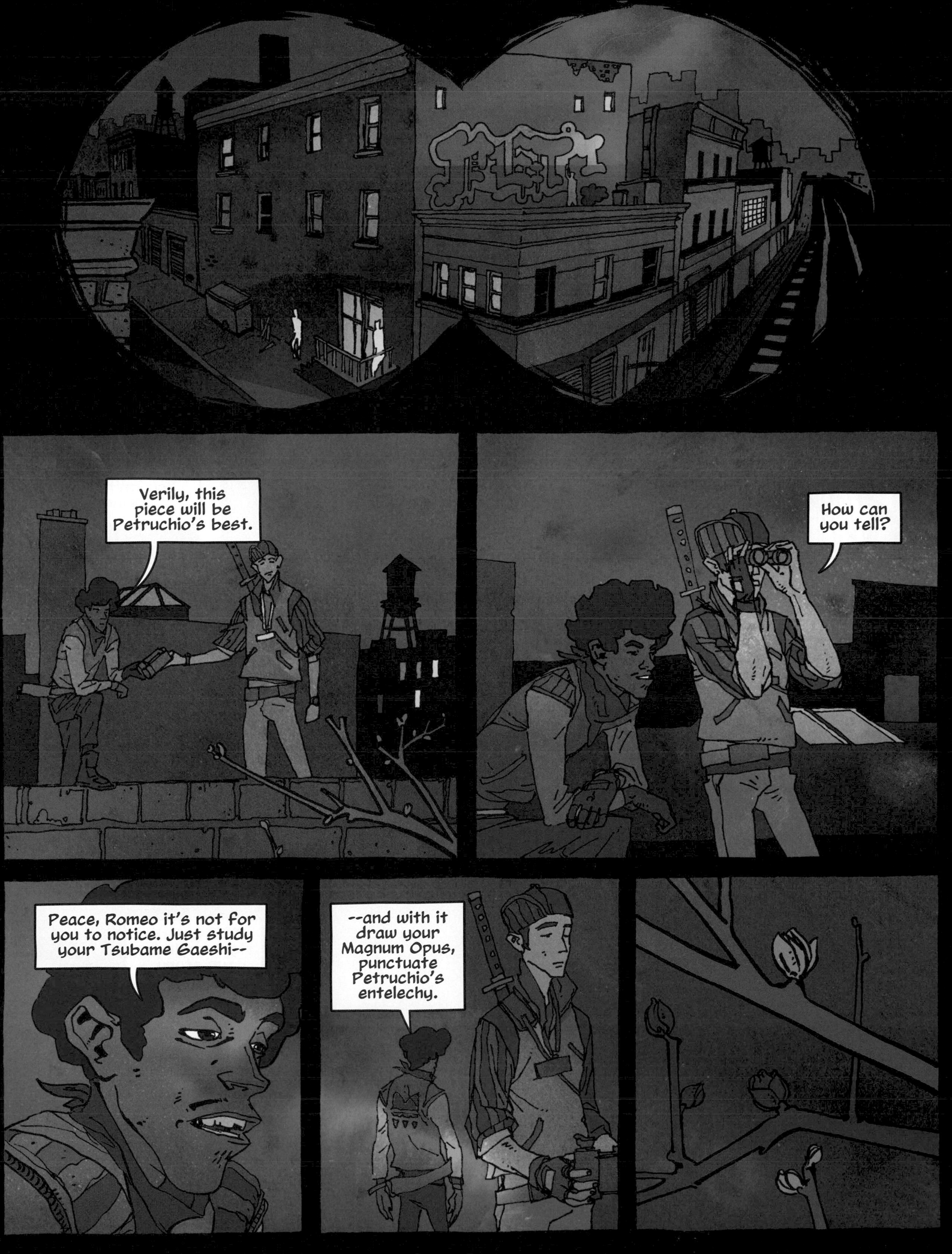
Verily, this piece will be Petruchio's best.
How can you tell?
Peace, Romeo it's not for you to notice. Just study your Tsubame Gaeshi--
--and with it draw your Magnum Opus, punctuate Petruchio's entelechy.

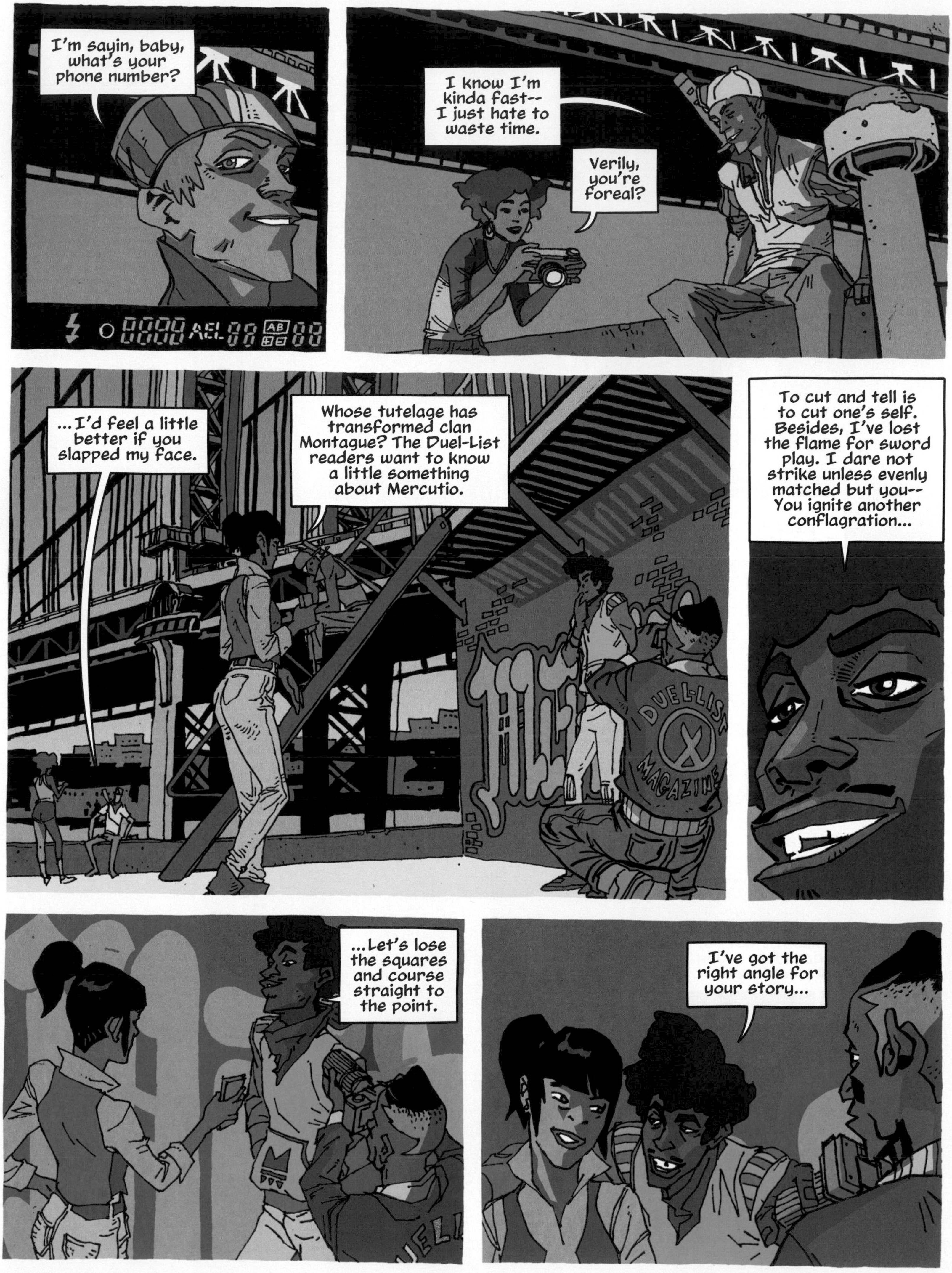

I'm sayin, baby, what's your phone number?
I know I'm kinda fast-- I just hate to waste time.
Verily, you're foreal?
...I'd feel a little better if you slapped my face.
Whose tutelage has transformed clan Montague? The Duel-List readers want to know a little something about Mercutio.
DUEL-LIST MAGAZINE
To cut and tell is to cut one's self. Besides, I've lost the flame for sword play. I dare not strike unless evenly matched but you-- You ignite another conflagration...
...Let's lose the squares and course straight to the point.
I've got the right angle for your story...

RIIIIIIING

RIIIIIIING

RIIIIIIING

CLICK

ACT 4

...Please leave your name, number, and a message after the chime.

Rosalyn, sweetheart. I've put thy name on the list--Oh, shit!

STETSASONIC

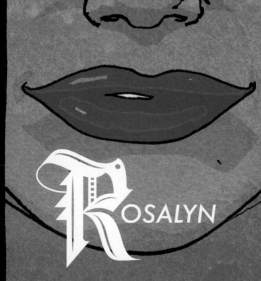

ROSALYN

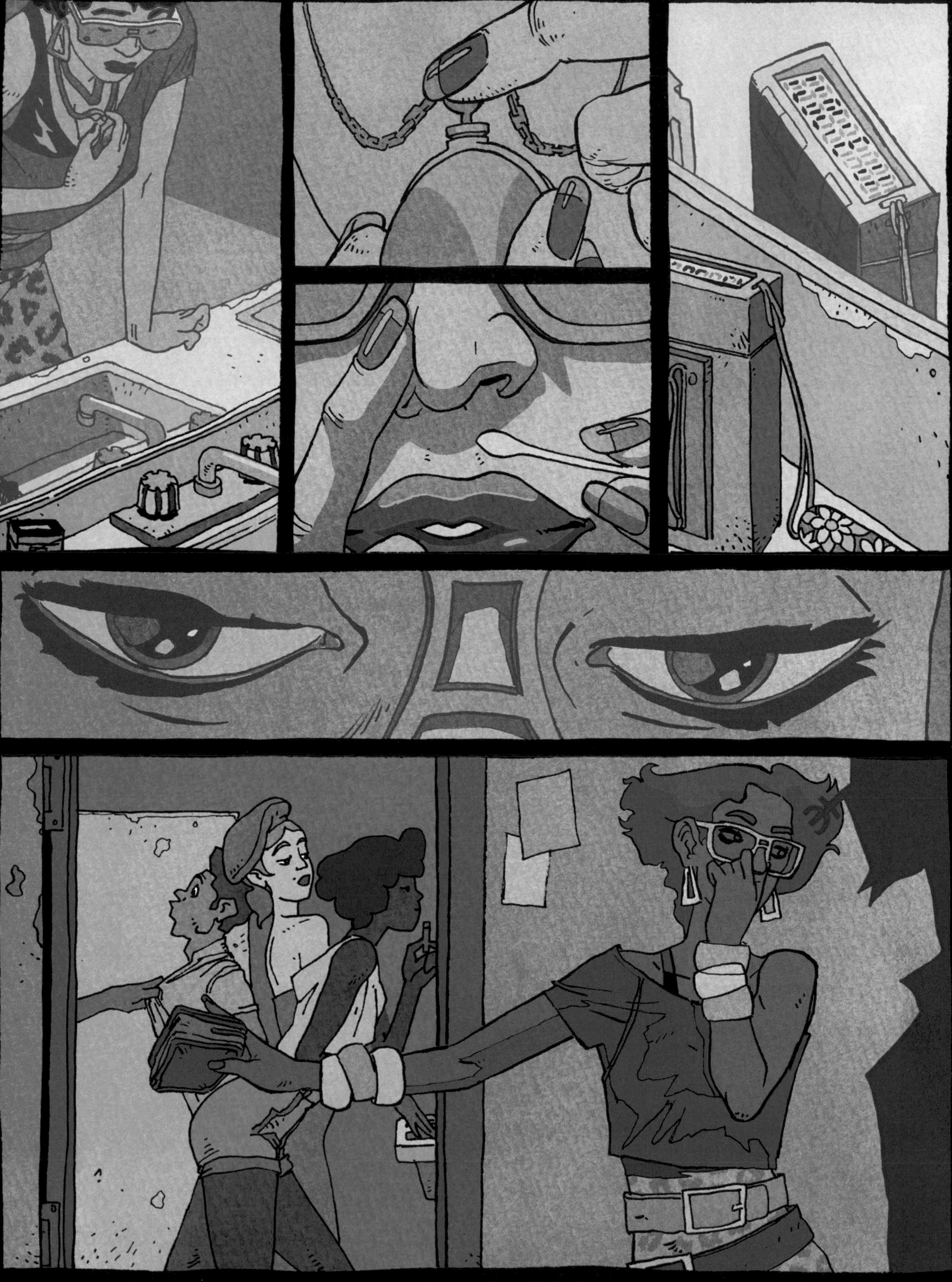

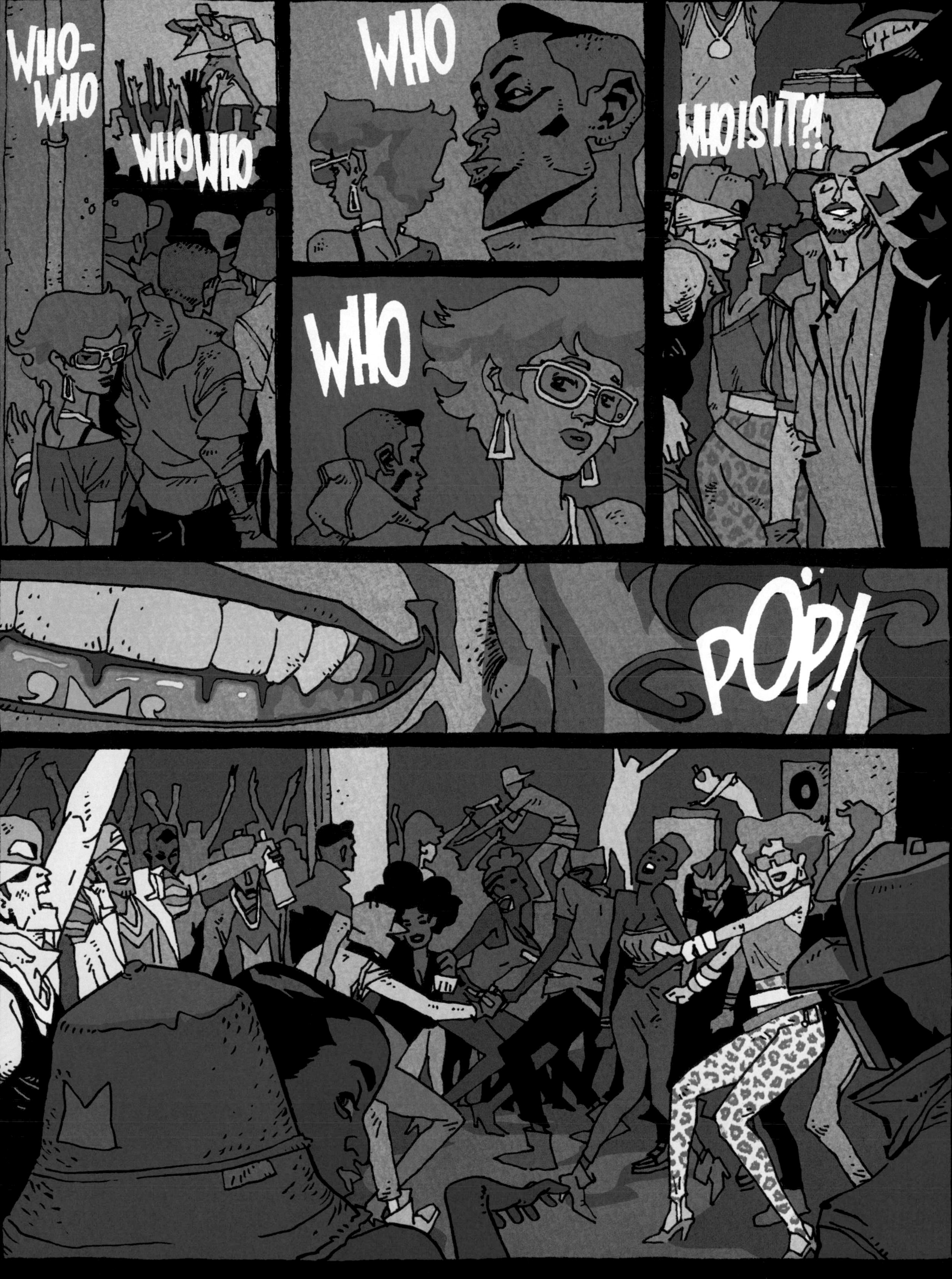
WHO-
WHO
WHOWHO
WHO
WHO
WHOISIT?!
POP!

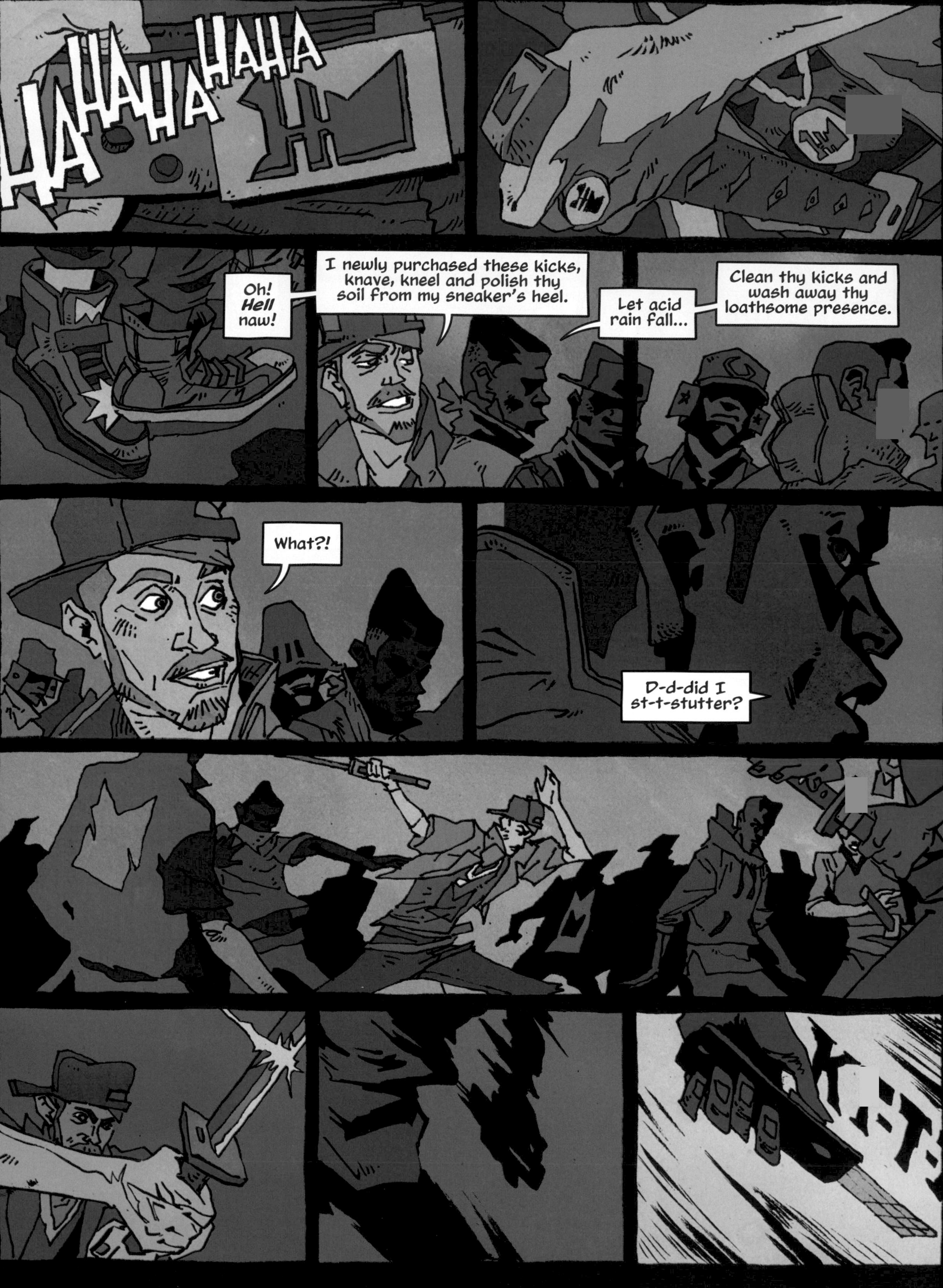
HAHAHAHAHAHA
Oh! *Hell* naw!
I newly purchased these kicks, knave, kneel and polish thy soil from my sneaker's heel.
Let acid rain fall...
Clean thy kicks and wash away thy loathsome presence.
What?!
D-d-did I st-t-stutter?

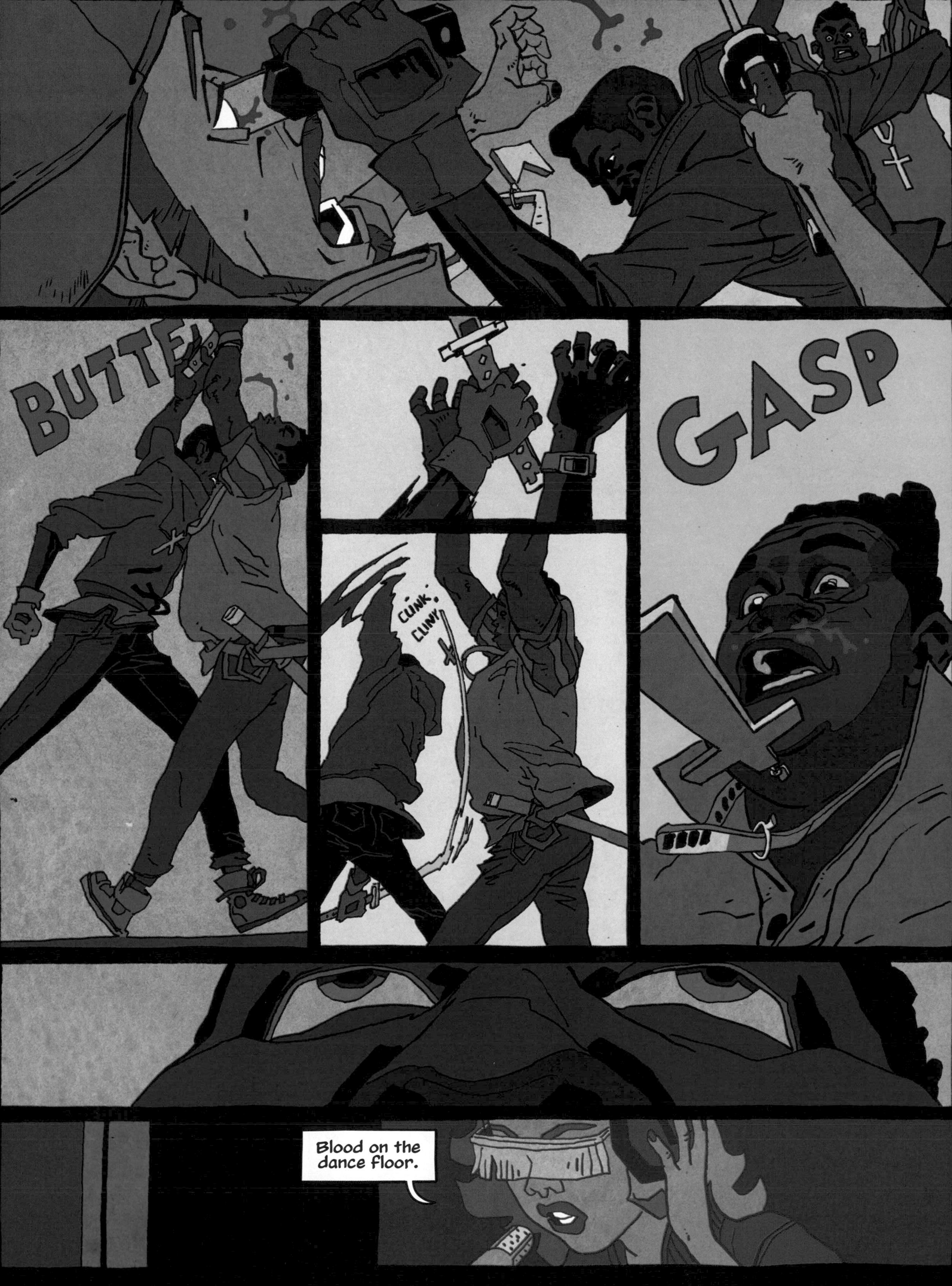
BUTTE
CLINK
CLINK
GASP
Blood on the dance floor.

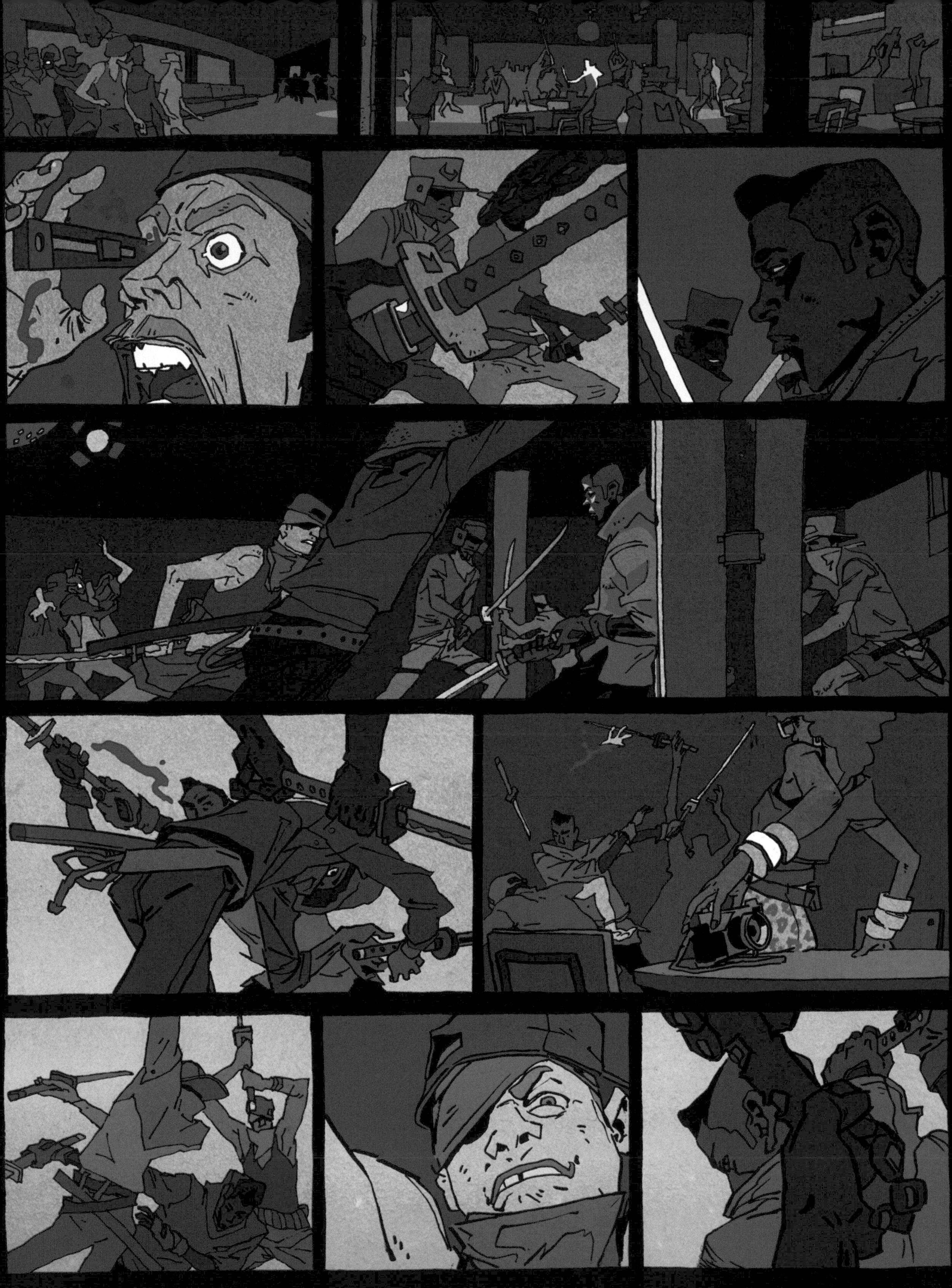

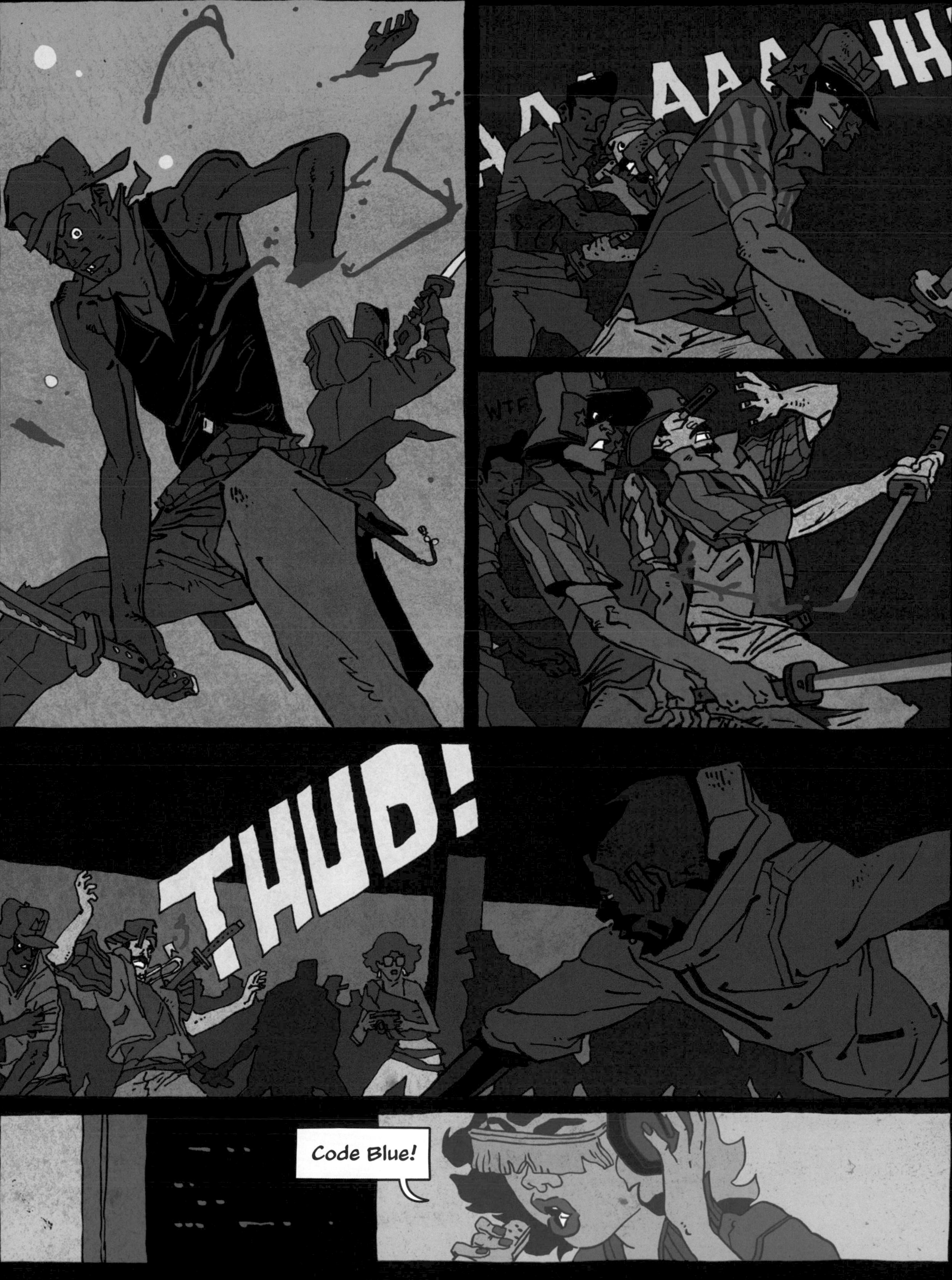
AAAAAHH
WTF
THUD!
Code Blue!

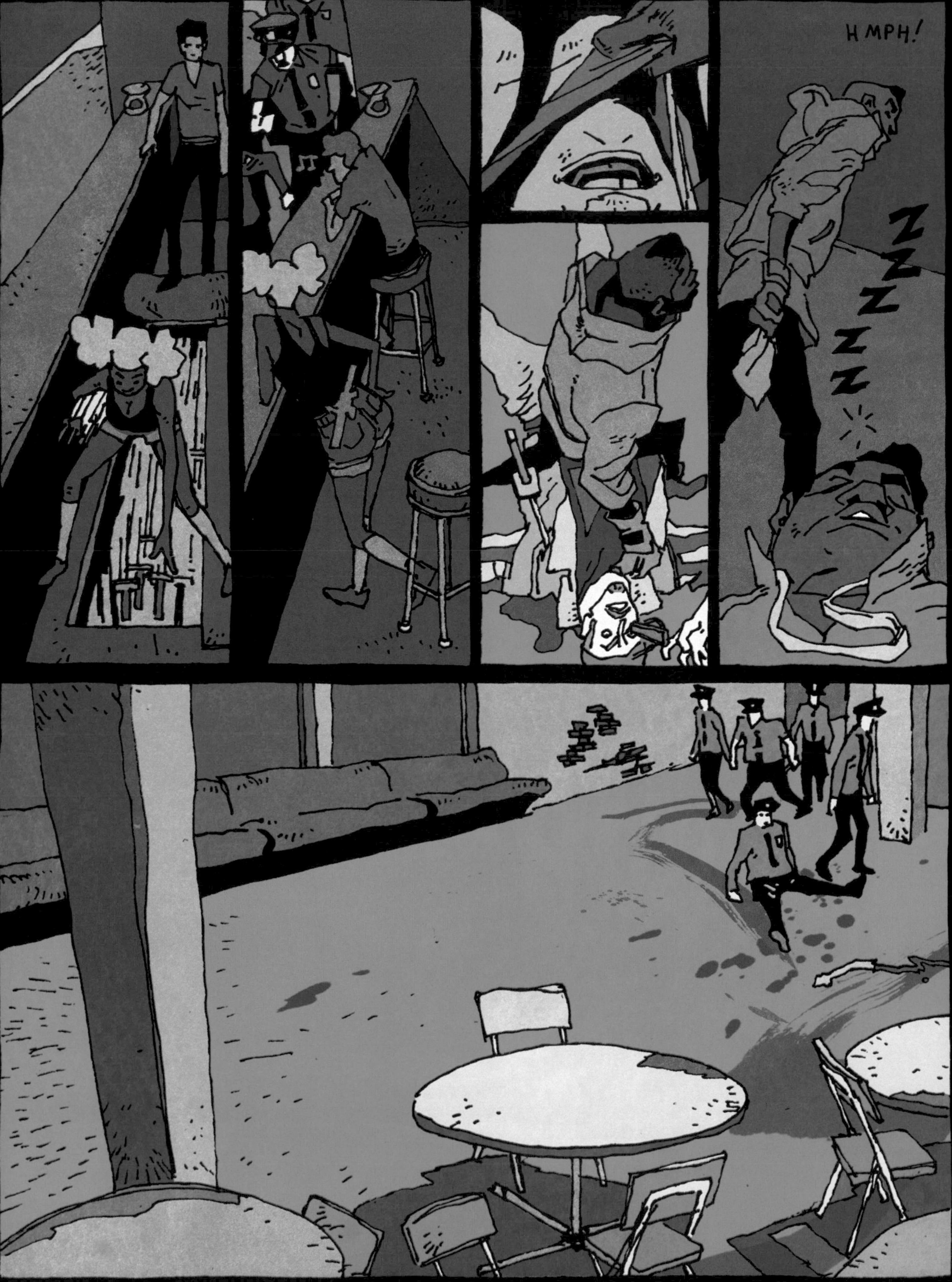
HMPH!
ZZZZZ

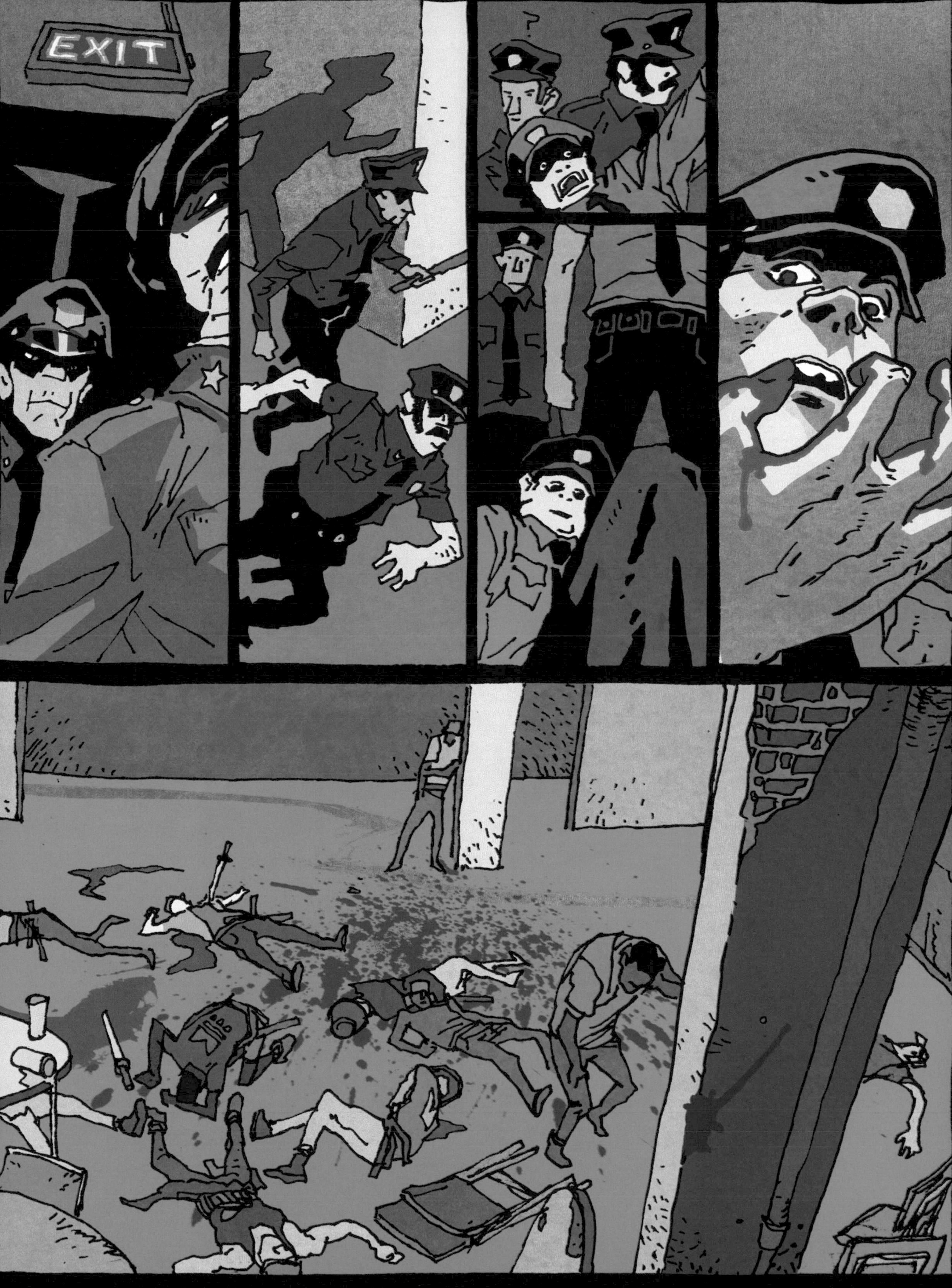
EXIT
?

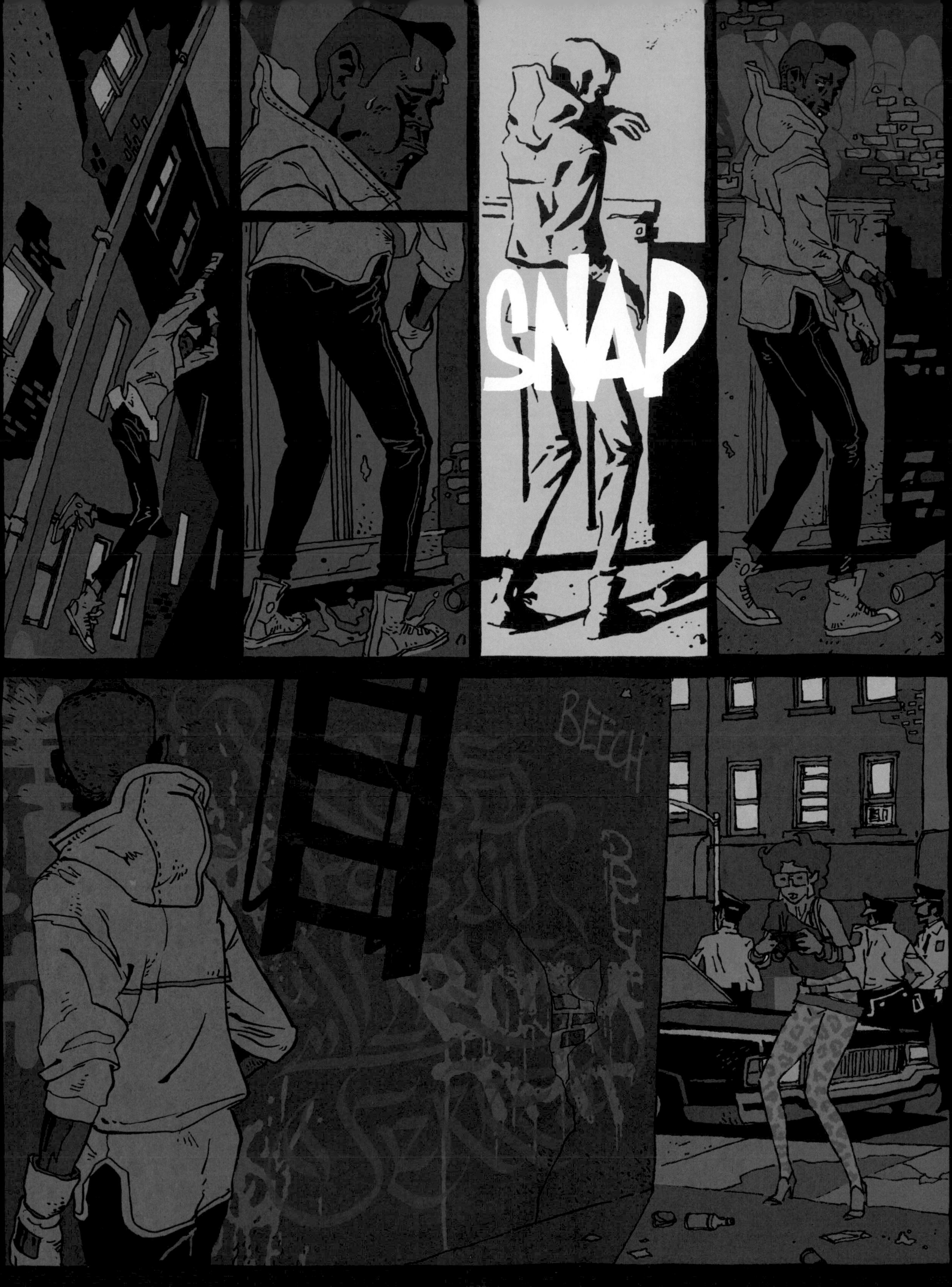
SNAP
BEECH

SNAP
SNAP

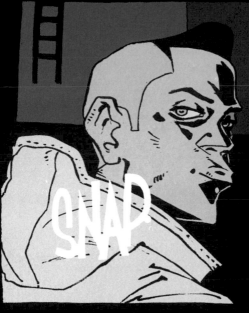

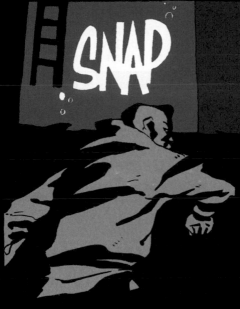

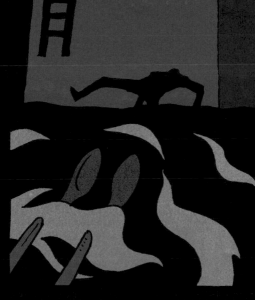

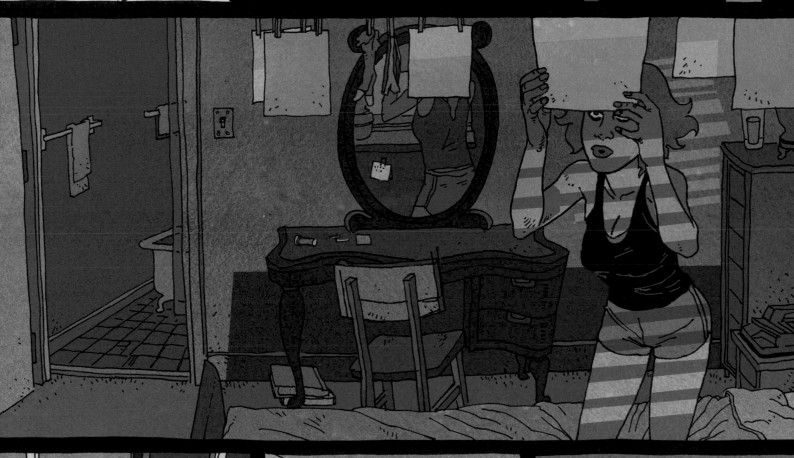

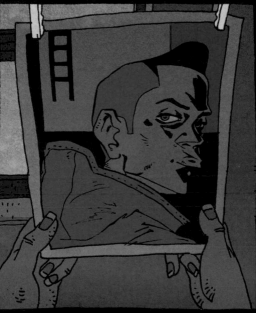

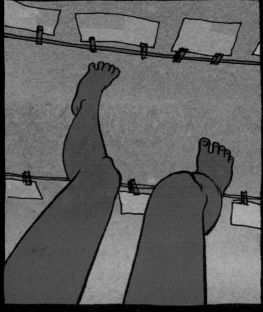

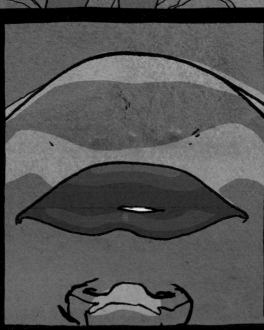

Dear Rosalyn, our time is up. I've got business to which I must attend.

Yes, certainly. I've got plenty here.

--A challenge!? On my life.

Romeo will answer it.

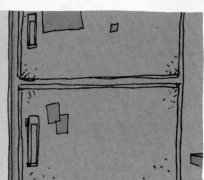

Any man that can write may answer a letter.

Nay, he will answer the letter's master, how he dares, being dared.

Alas poor Romeo! He is already dead; stabbed with a white wench's black eye; shot through the ear with a love-song; the very pin of his heart cleft with the blind bow-boy's butt-shaft: and is he a man to encounter Tybalt?

Why, what is Tybalt?

CRACK

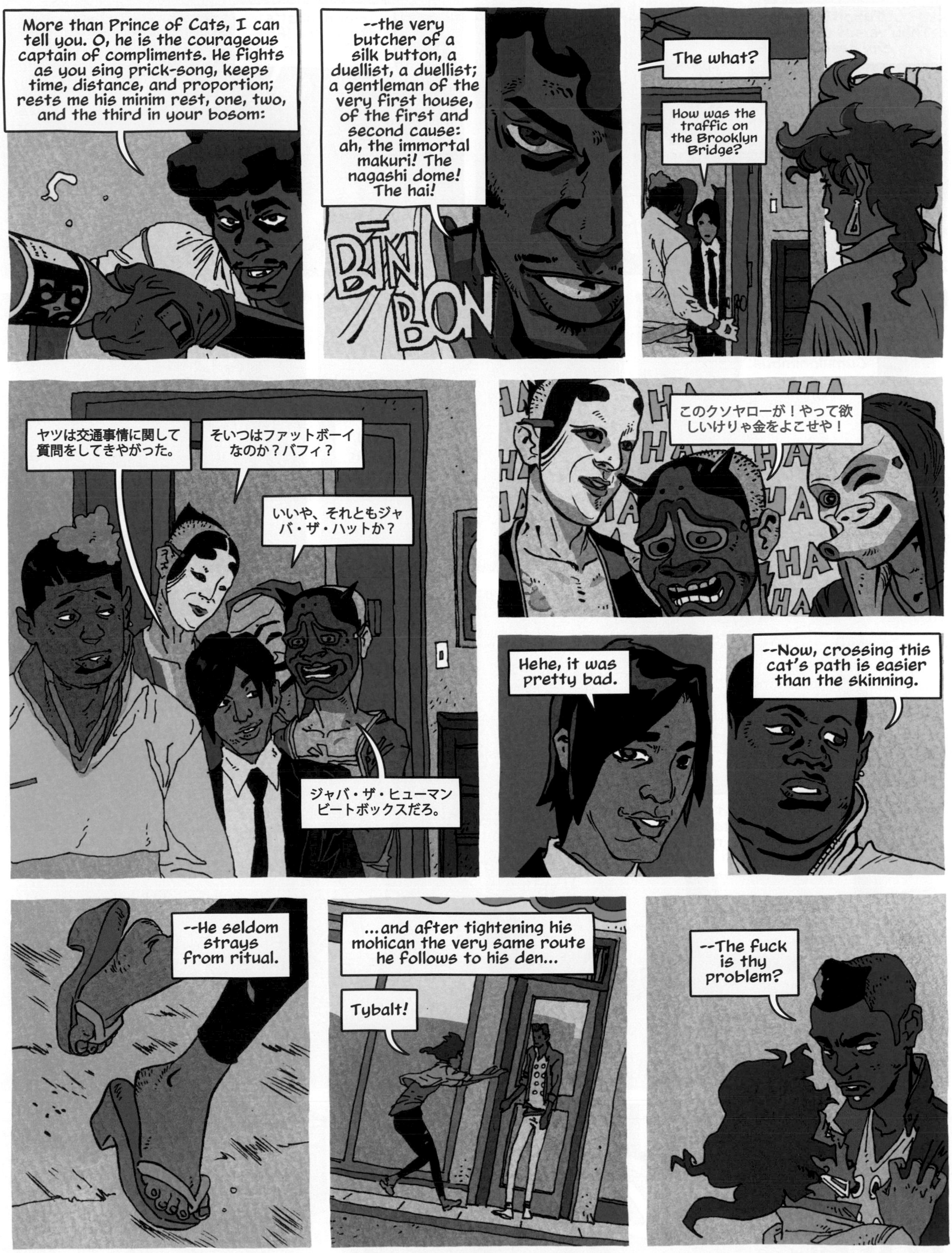

More than Prince of Cats, I can tell you. O, he is the courageous captain of compliments. He fights as you sing prick-song, keeps time, distance, and proportion; rests me his minim rest, one, two, and the third in your bosom:
--the very butcher of a silk button, a duellist, a duellist; a gentleman of the very first house, of the first and second cause: ah, the immortal makuri! The nagashi dome! The hai!
BIN
BON
The what?
How was the traffic on the Brooklyn Bridge?
ヤツは交通事情に関して質問をしてきやがった。
そいつはファットボーイなのか？バフィ？
いいや、それともジャバ・ザ・ハットか？
ジャバ・ザ・ヒューマンビートボックスだろ。
このクソヤローが！やって欲しいけりゃ金をよこせや！
HA HA HA HA HA HA HA HA
Hehe, it was pretty bad.
--Now, crossing this cat's path is easier than the skinning.
--He seldom strays from ritual.
...and after tightening his mohican the very same route he follows to his den...
Tybalt!
--The fuck is thy problem?

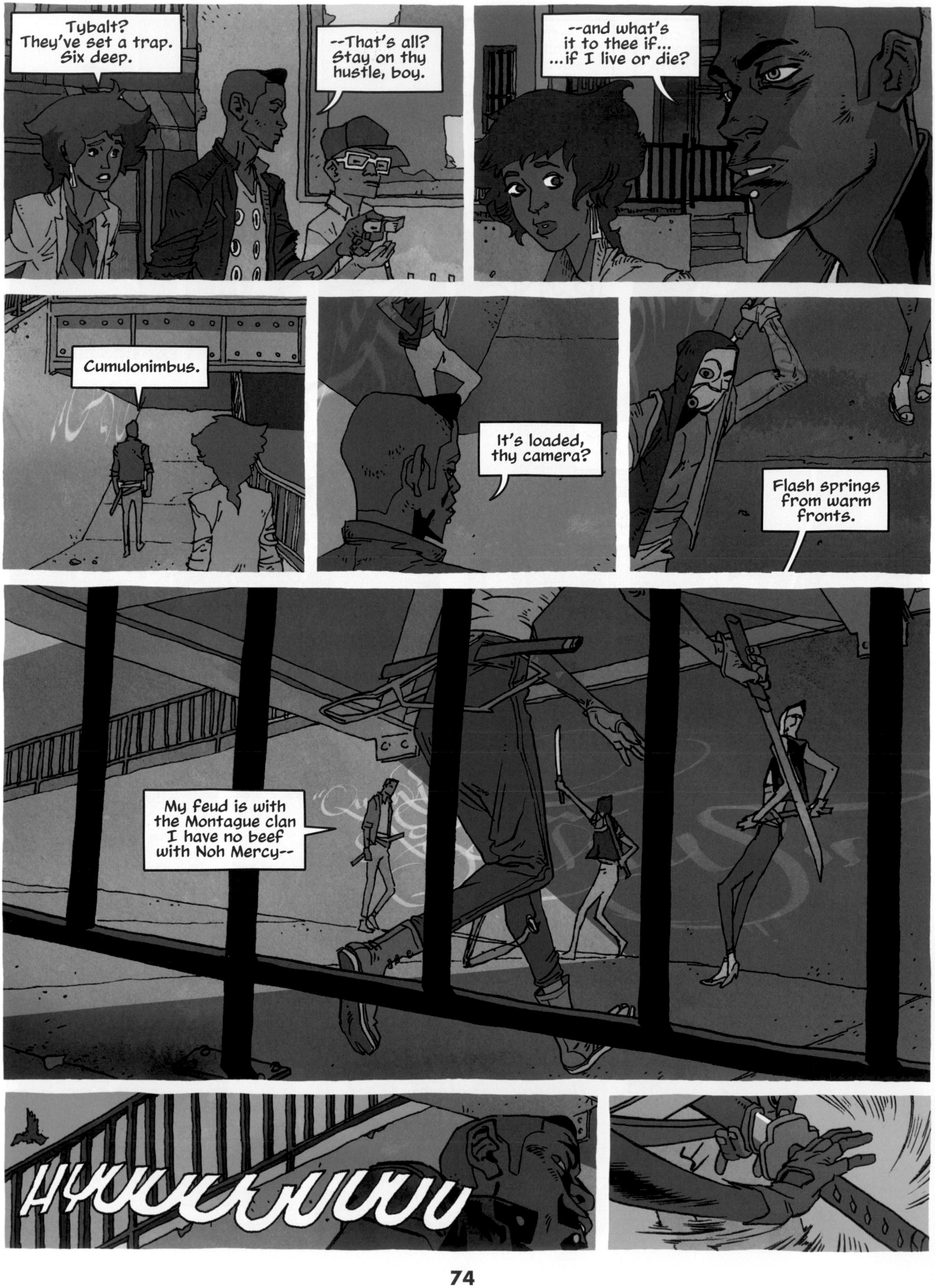

Tybalt? They've set a trap. Six deep.
--That's all? Stay on thy hustle, boy.
--and what's it to thee if... ...if I live or die?
Cumulonimbus.
It's loaded, thy camera?
Flash springs from warm fronts.
My feud is with the Montague clan I have no beef with Noh Mercy--
HYUUUUUUUUU

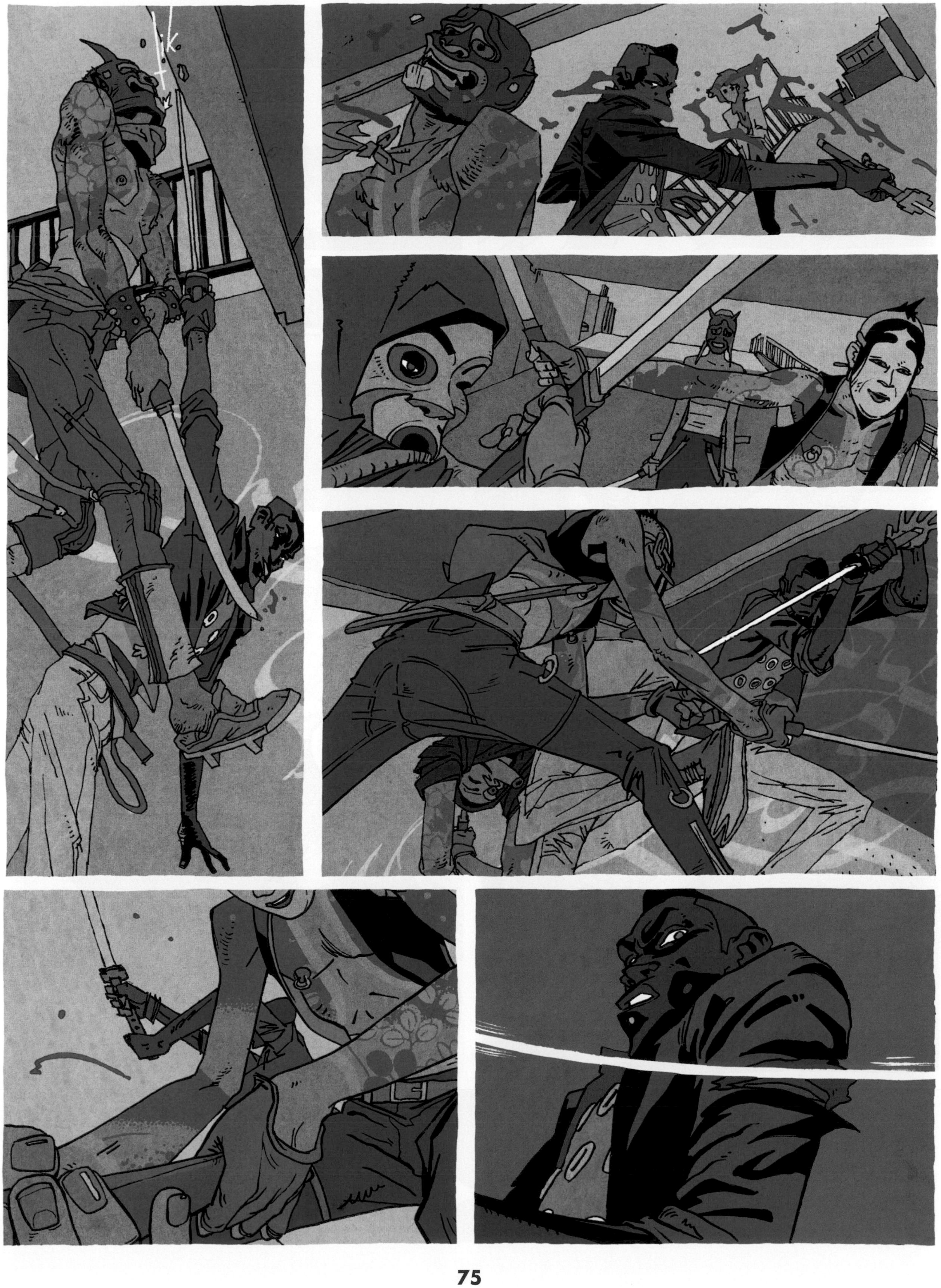

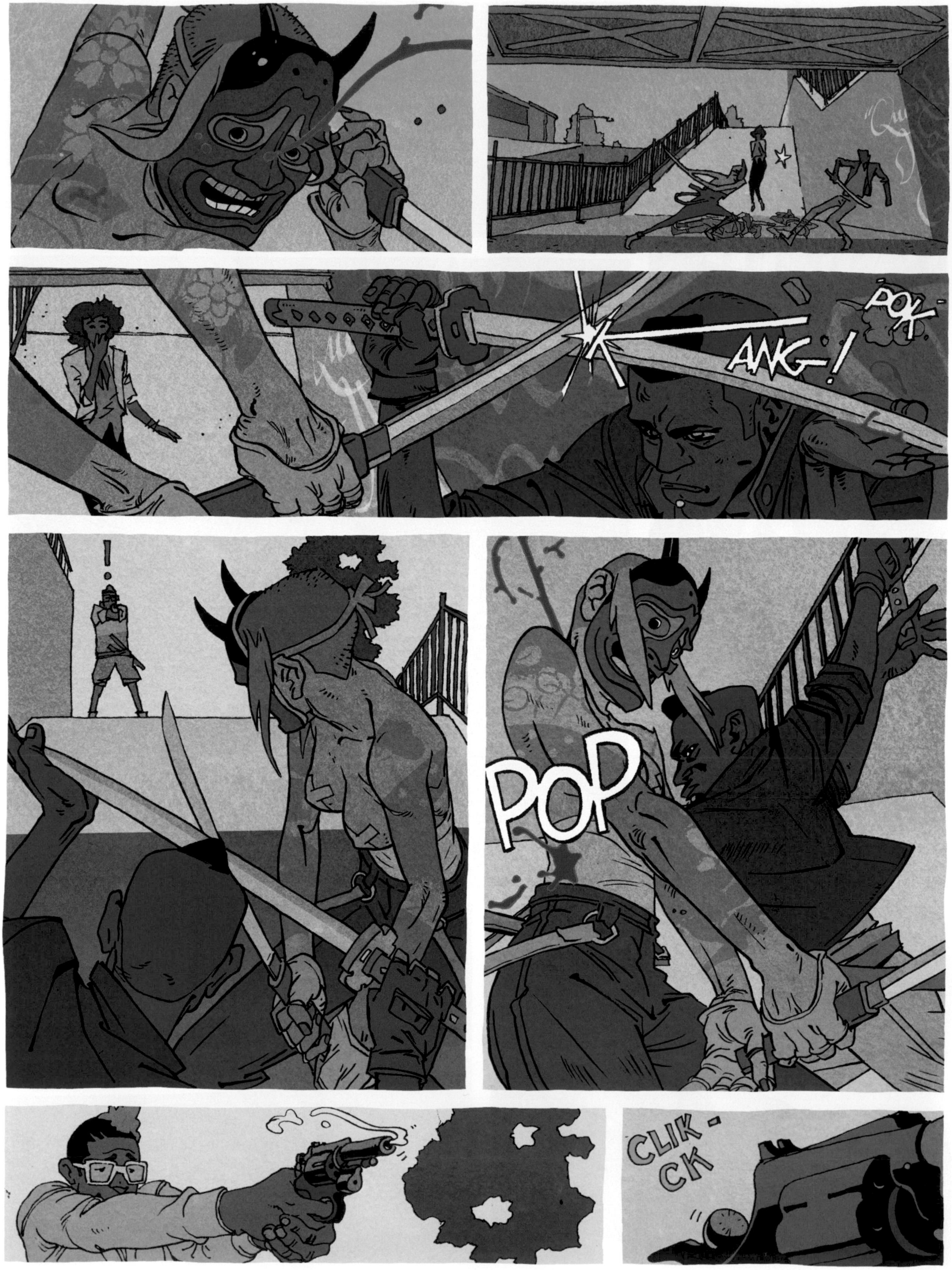
POK
ANG-!
POP
CLIK-CK

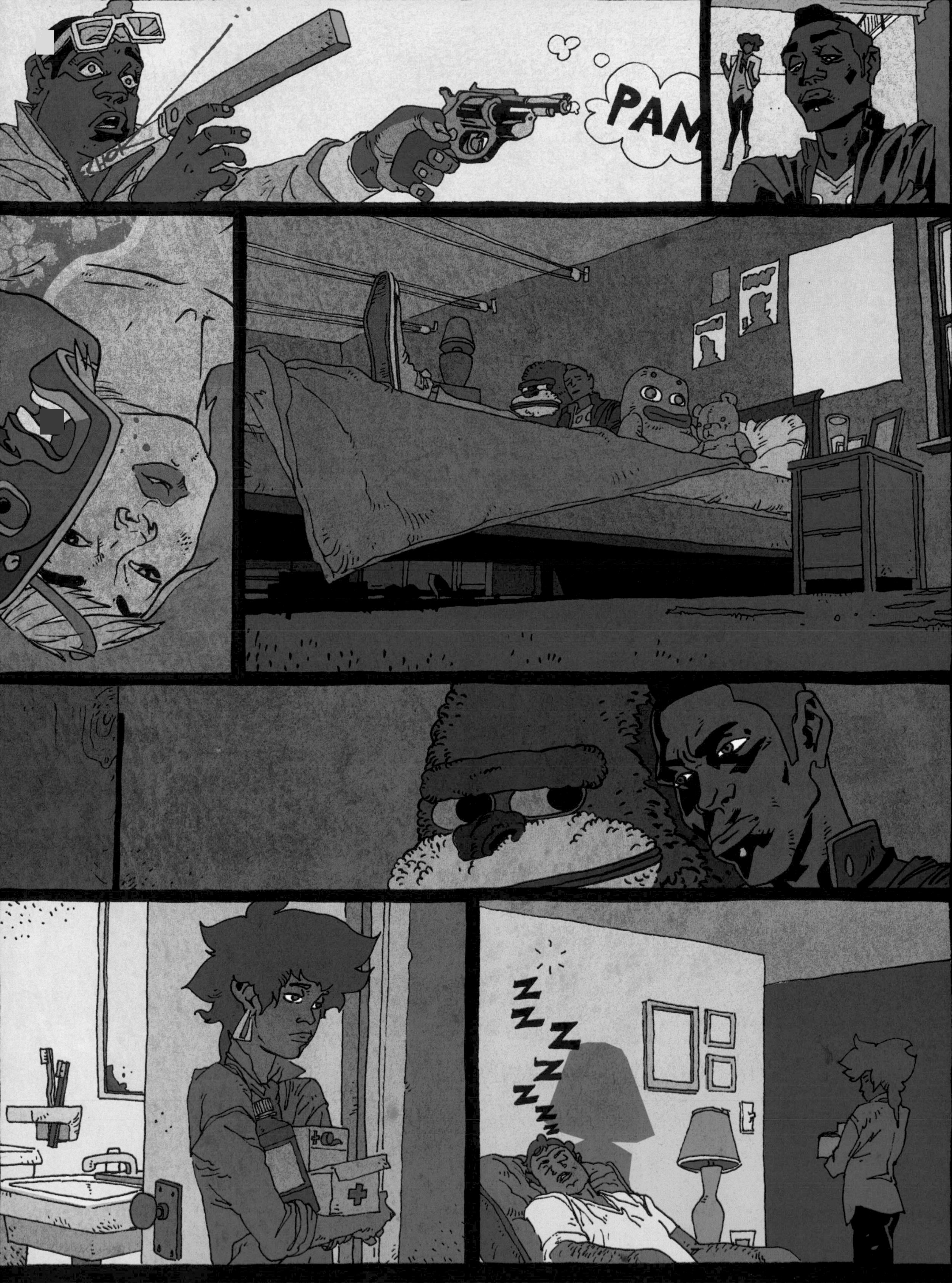
PAM

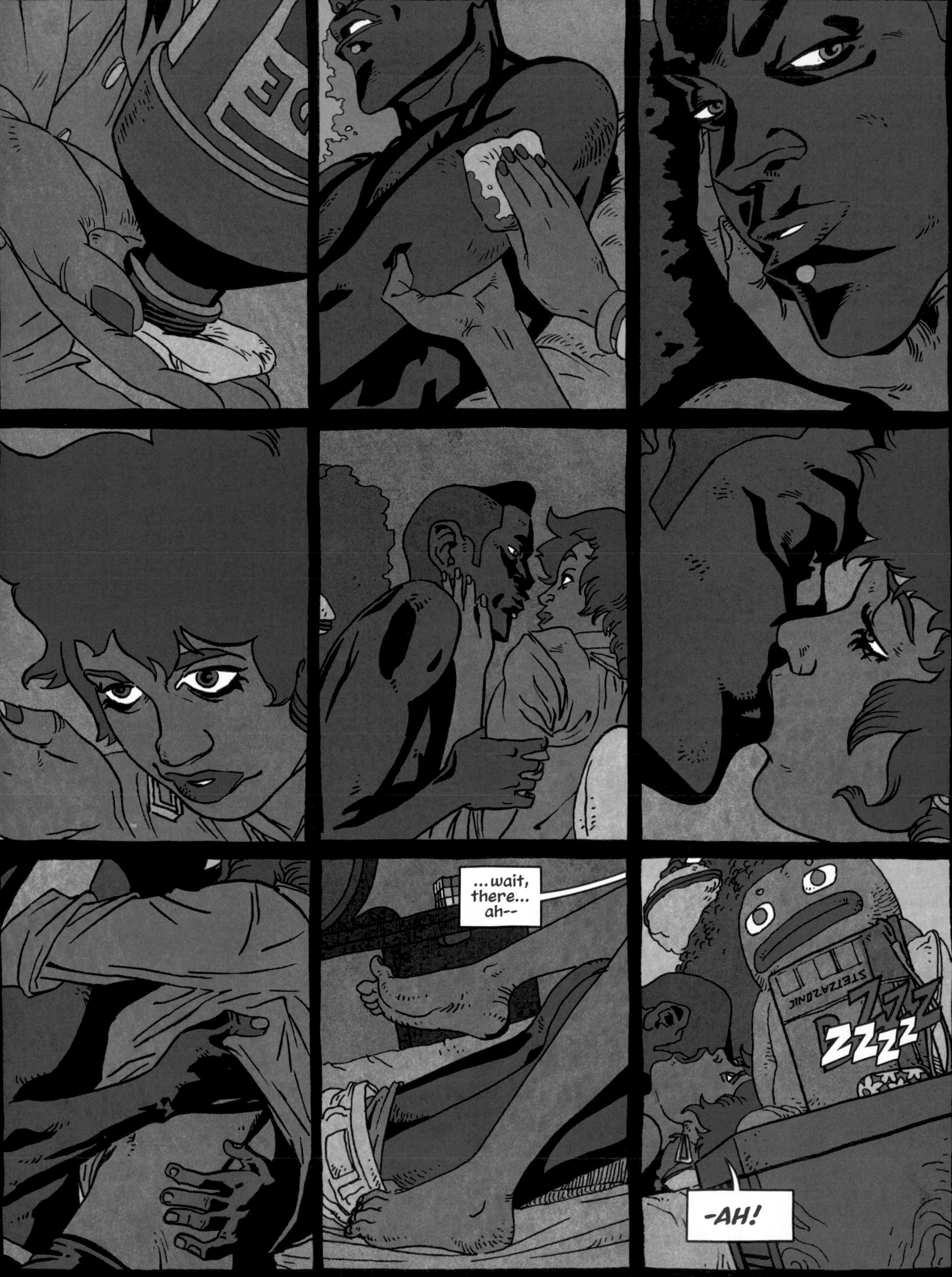
...wait, there... ah--
STETZAZONIC
ZZZ
ZZZZ
-AH!

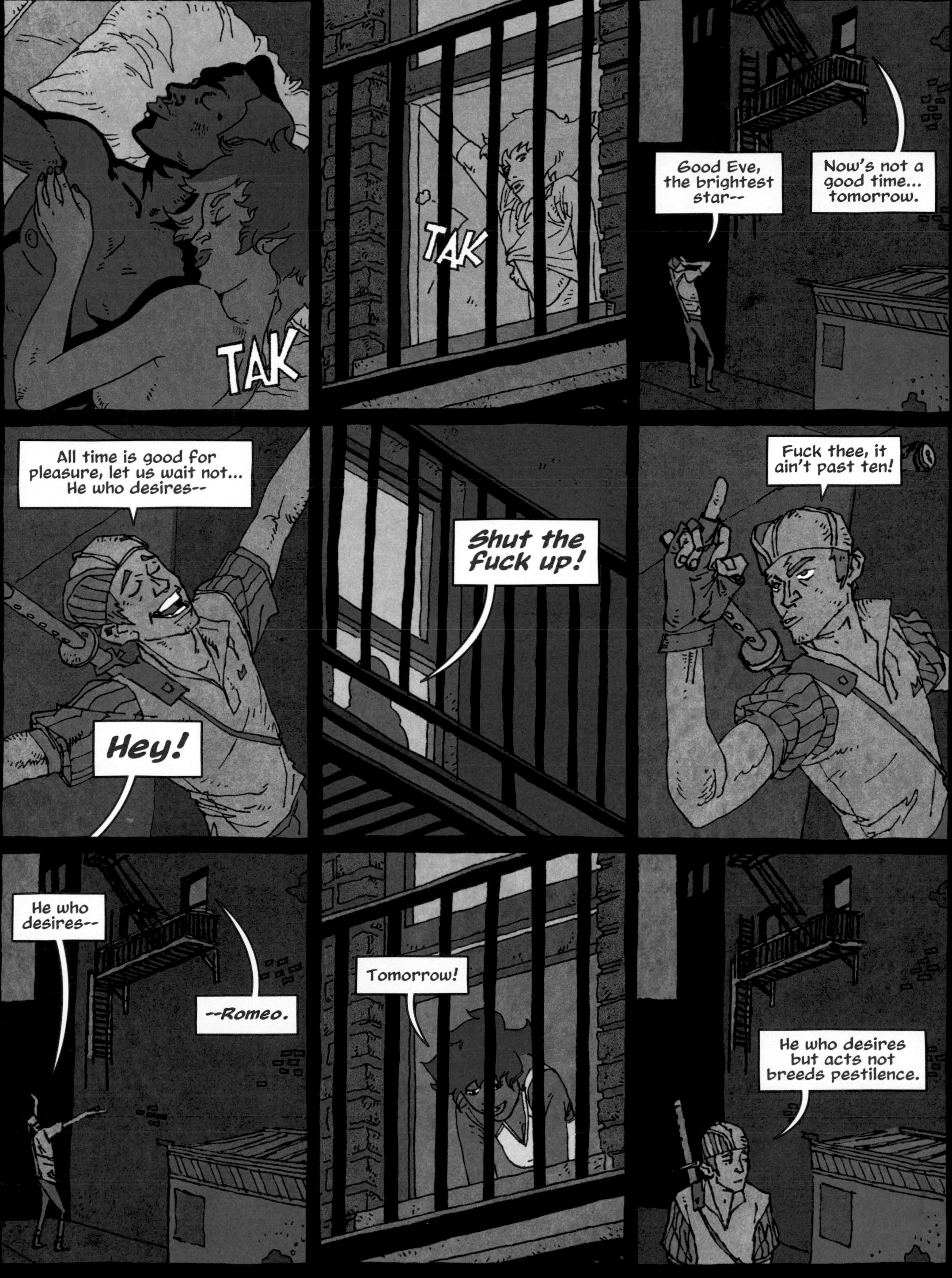
TAK
TAK
Good Eve, the brightest star--
Now's not a good time... tomorrow.
All time is good for pleasure, let us wait not... He who desires--
Hey!
Shut the fuck up!
Fuck thee, it ain't past ten!
He who desires--
--Romeo.
Tomorrow!
He who desires but acts not breeds pestilence.

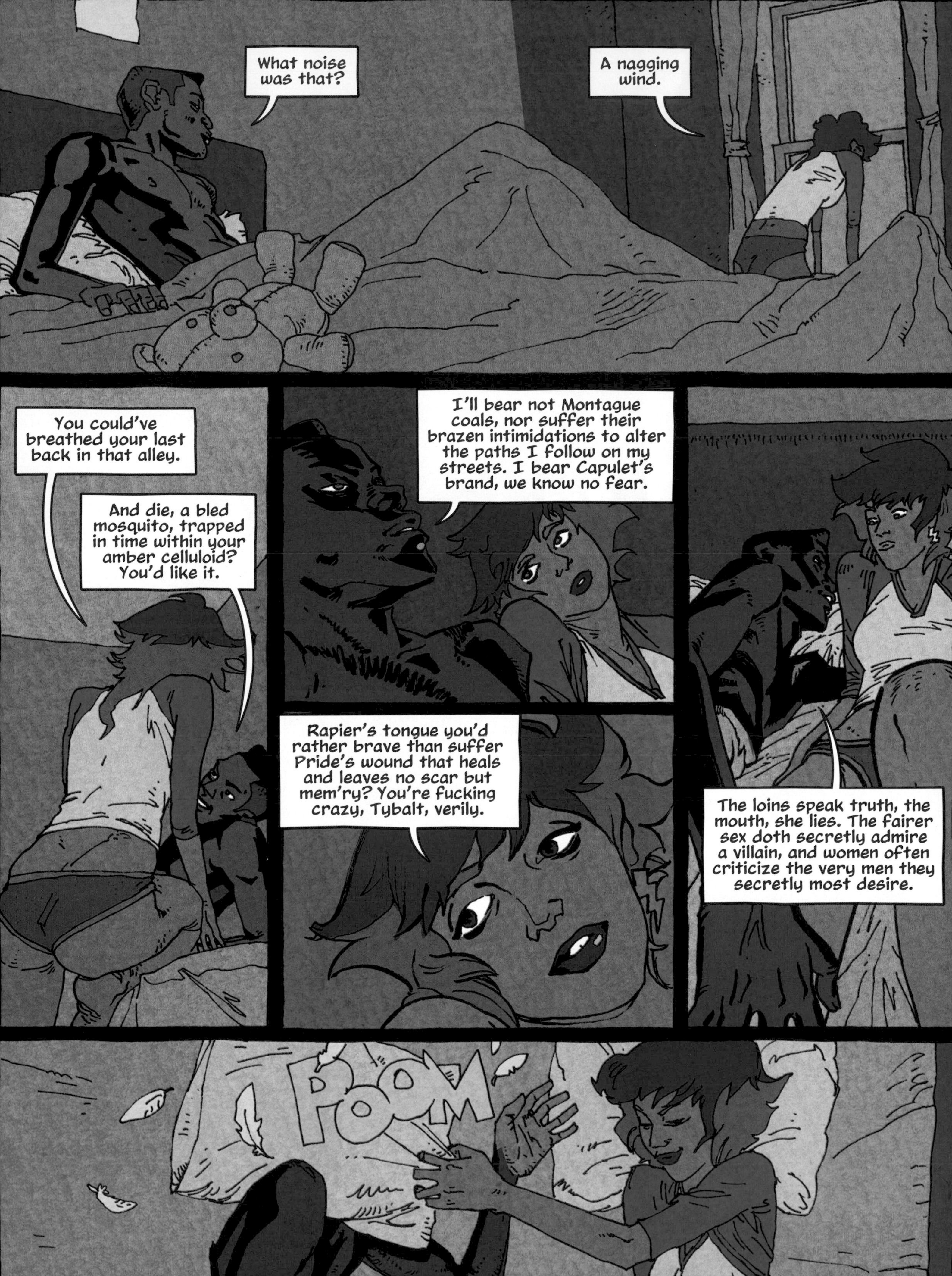
What noise was that?
A nagging wind.
You could've breathed your last back in that alley.
And die, a bled mosquito, trapped in time within your amber celluloid? You'd like it.
I'll bear not Montague coals, nor suffer their brazen intimidations to alter the paths I follow on my streets. I bear Capulet's brand, we know no fear.
Rapier's tongue you'd rather brave than suffer Pride's wound that heals and leaves no scar but mem'ry? You're fucking crazy, Tybalt, verily.
The loins speak truth, the mouth, she lies. The fairer sex doth secretly admire a villain, and women often criticize the very men they secretly most desire.
POOM

Chaste?...As caterpillar doth choose fairest leaves on which to lay her eggs, so the priest doth lay his curse on the fairest of joys.

No more. Your words, though sweet, will not repeal my final verdict on our concupiscence.

But Rosalyn--

--Art naught worse than rejection I'd feel a might better if you'd slap my face.

How many times art thou to page this boy, damn!?

Don't play thyself. He's no different from the others.

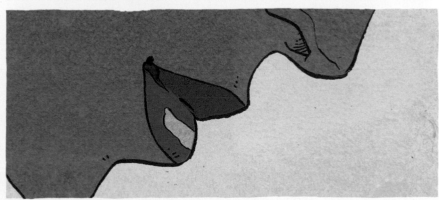

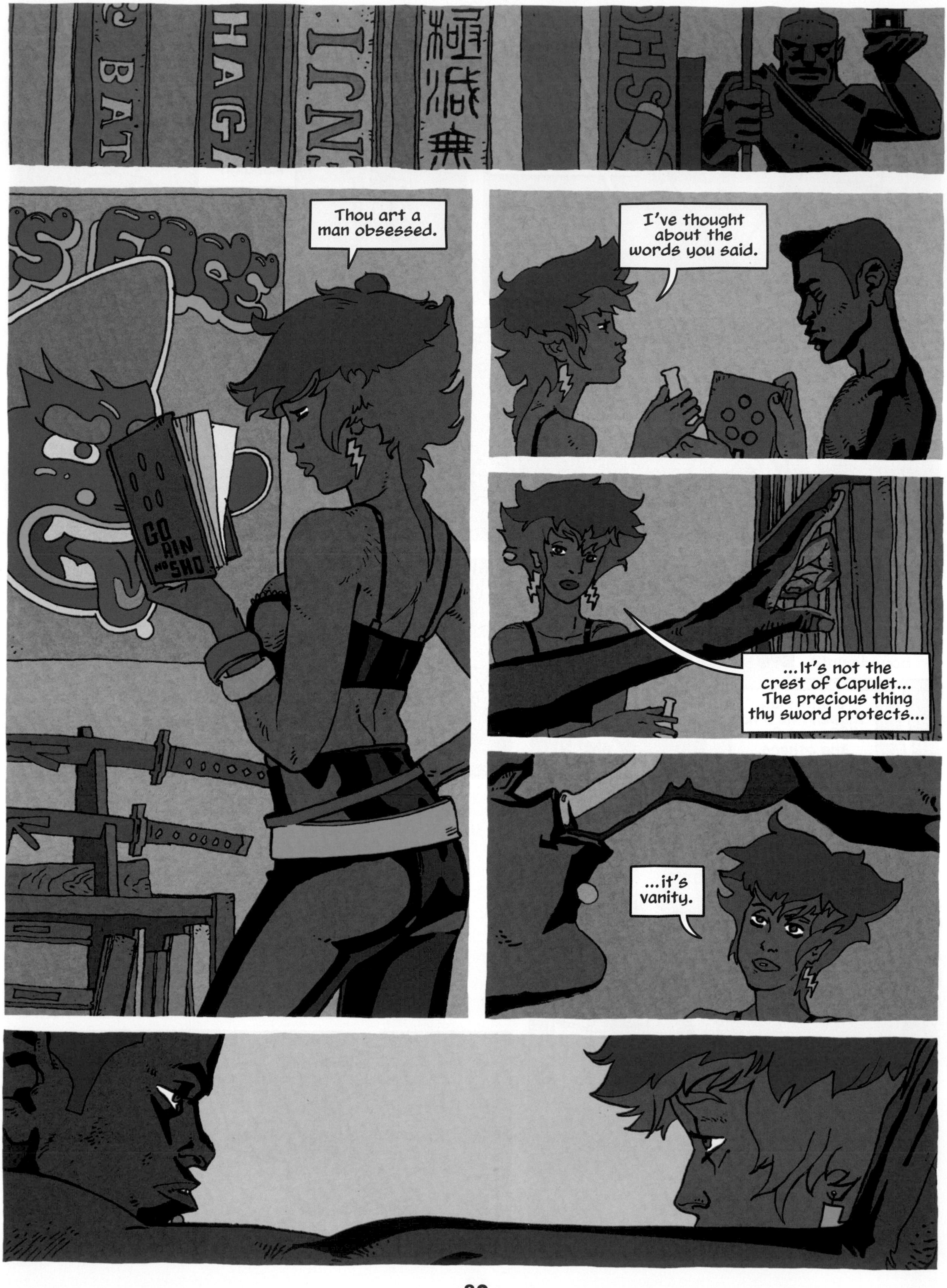
Thou art a man obsessed.
GO RIN NO SHO
I've thought about the words you said.
...It's not the crest of Capulet... The precious thing thy sword protects...
...it's vanity.

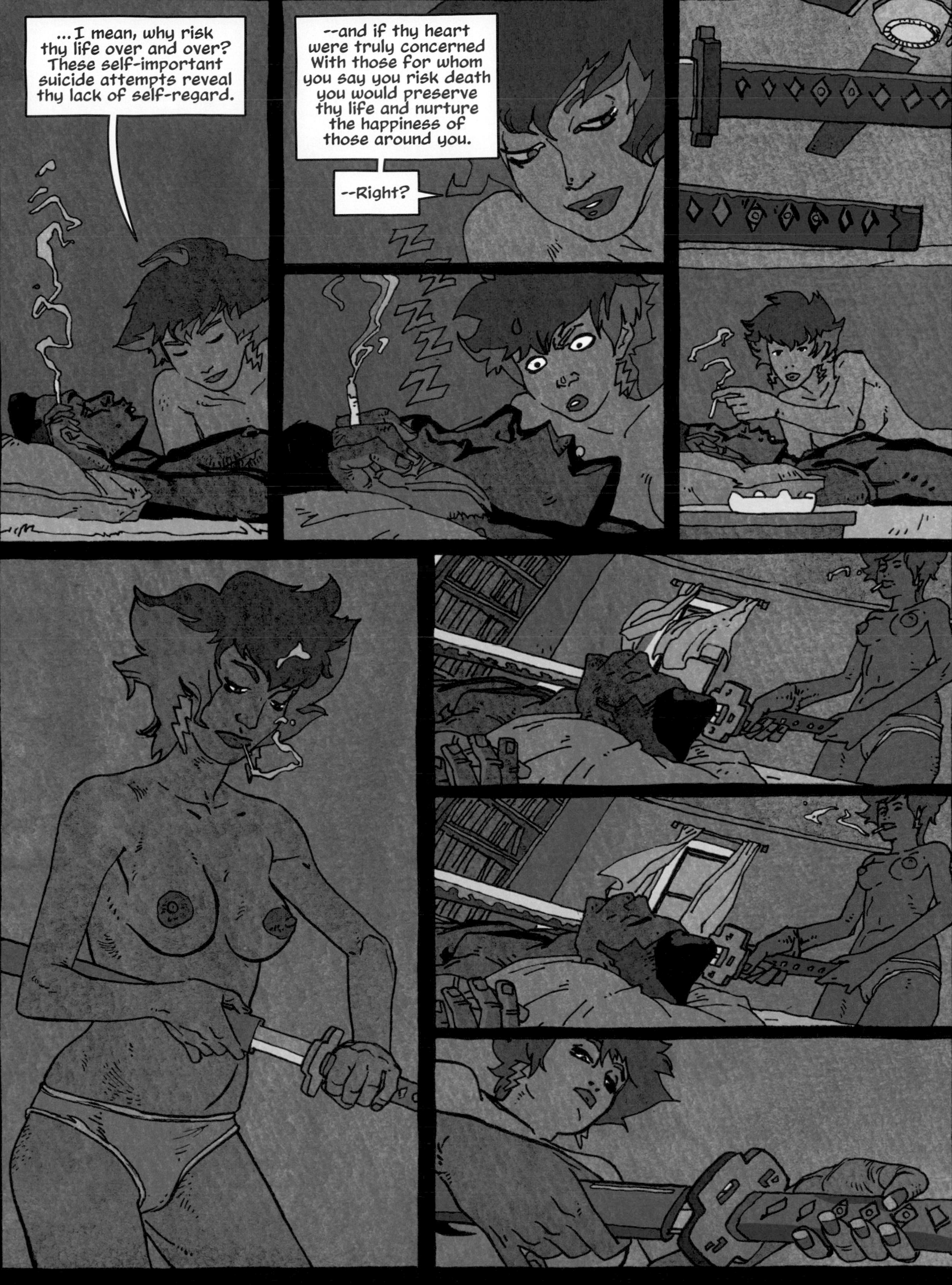

...I mean, why risk thy life over and over? These self-important suicide attempts reveal thy lack of self-regard.
--and if thy heart were truly concerned With those for whom you say you risk death you would preserve thy life and nurture the happiness of those around you.
--Right?

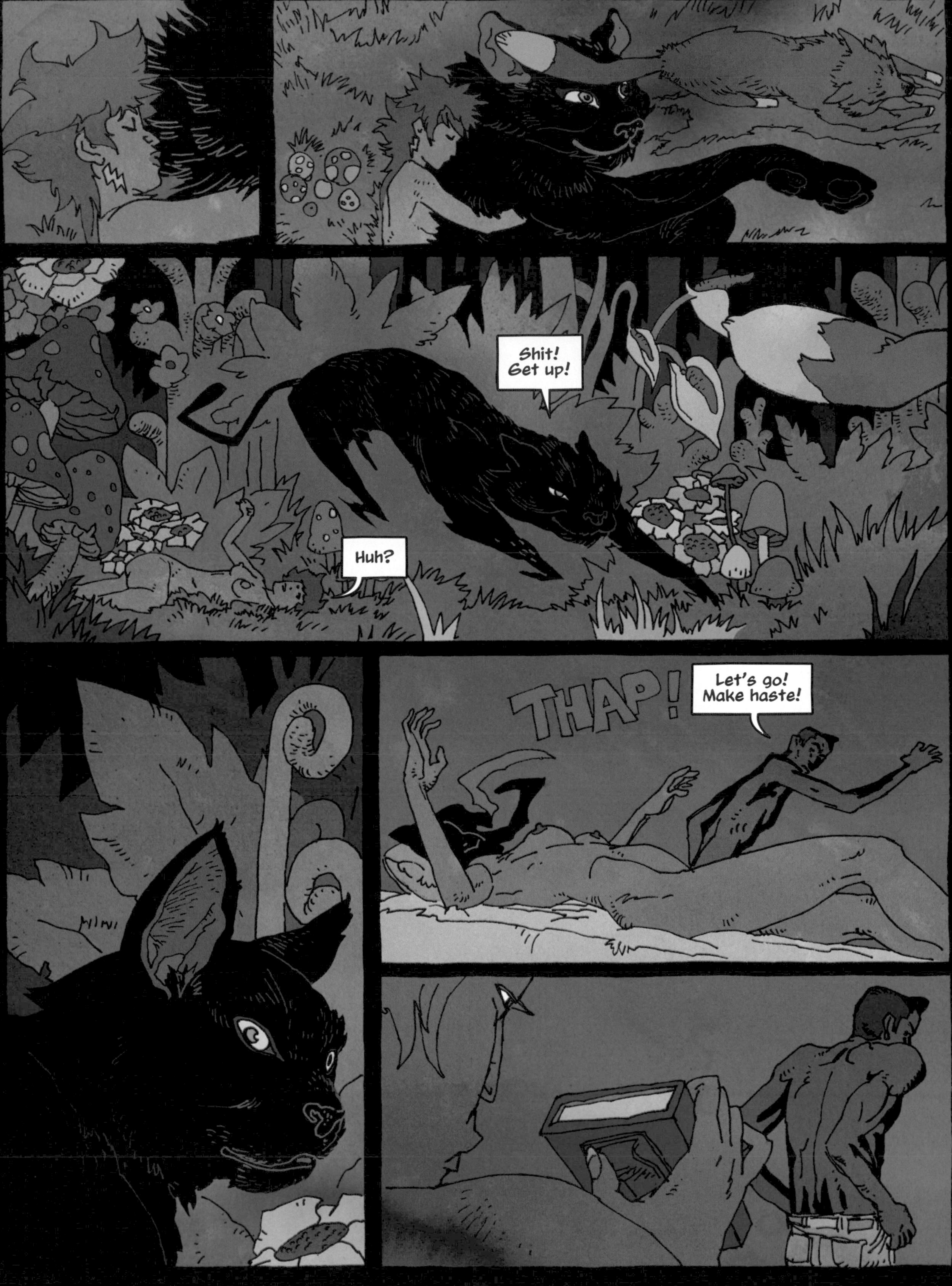
Shit!
Get up!
Huh?
THAP!
Let's go!
Make haste!

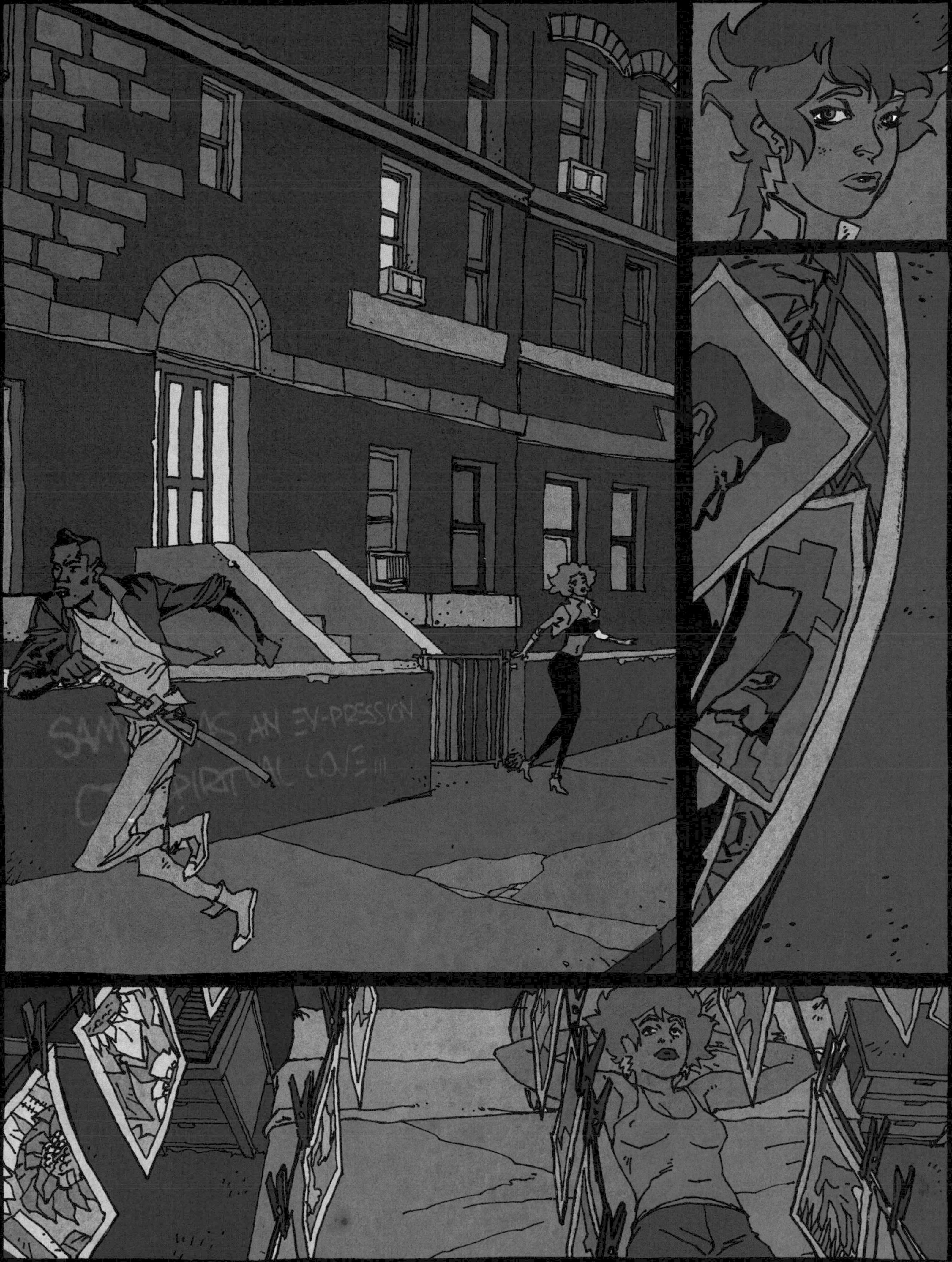
AN EV-PRESSION
LOVE!!!

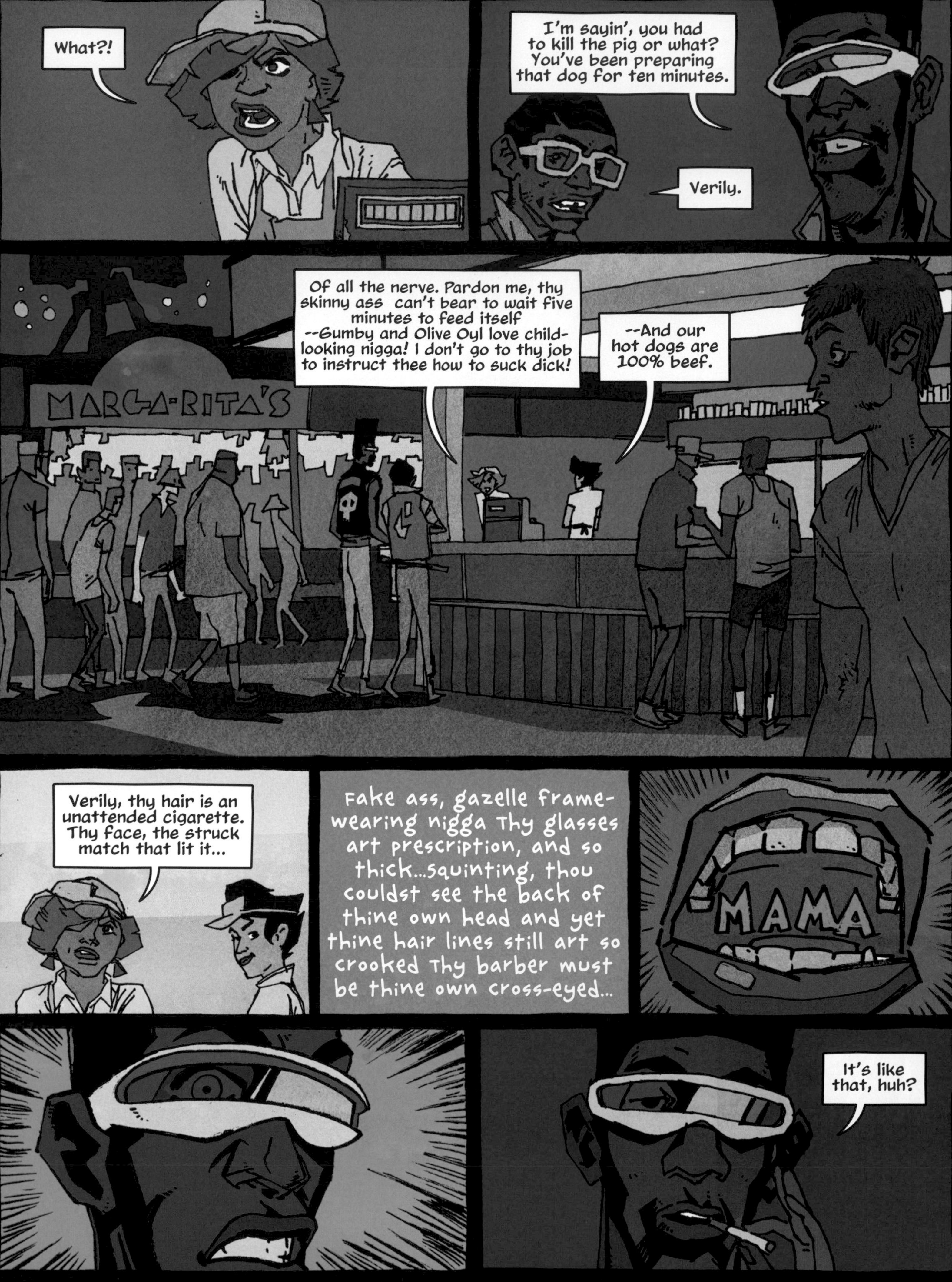
What?!
I'm sayin', you had to kill the pig or what? You've been preparing that dog for ten minutes.
Verily.
Of all the nerve. Pardon me, thy skinny ass can't bear to wait five minutes to feed itself --Gumby and Olive Oyl love child-looking nigga! I don't go to thy job to instruct thee how to suck dick!
--And our hot dogs are 100% beef.
MARGA-RITA'S
Verily, thy hair is an unattended cigarette. Thy face, the struck match that lit it...
Fake ass, gazelle frame-wearing nigga Thy glasses art prescription, and so thick...squinting, thou couldst see the back of thine own head and yet thine hair lines still art so crooked Thy barber must be thine own cross-eyed...
MAMA
It's like that, huh?

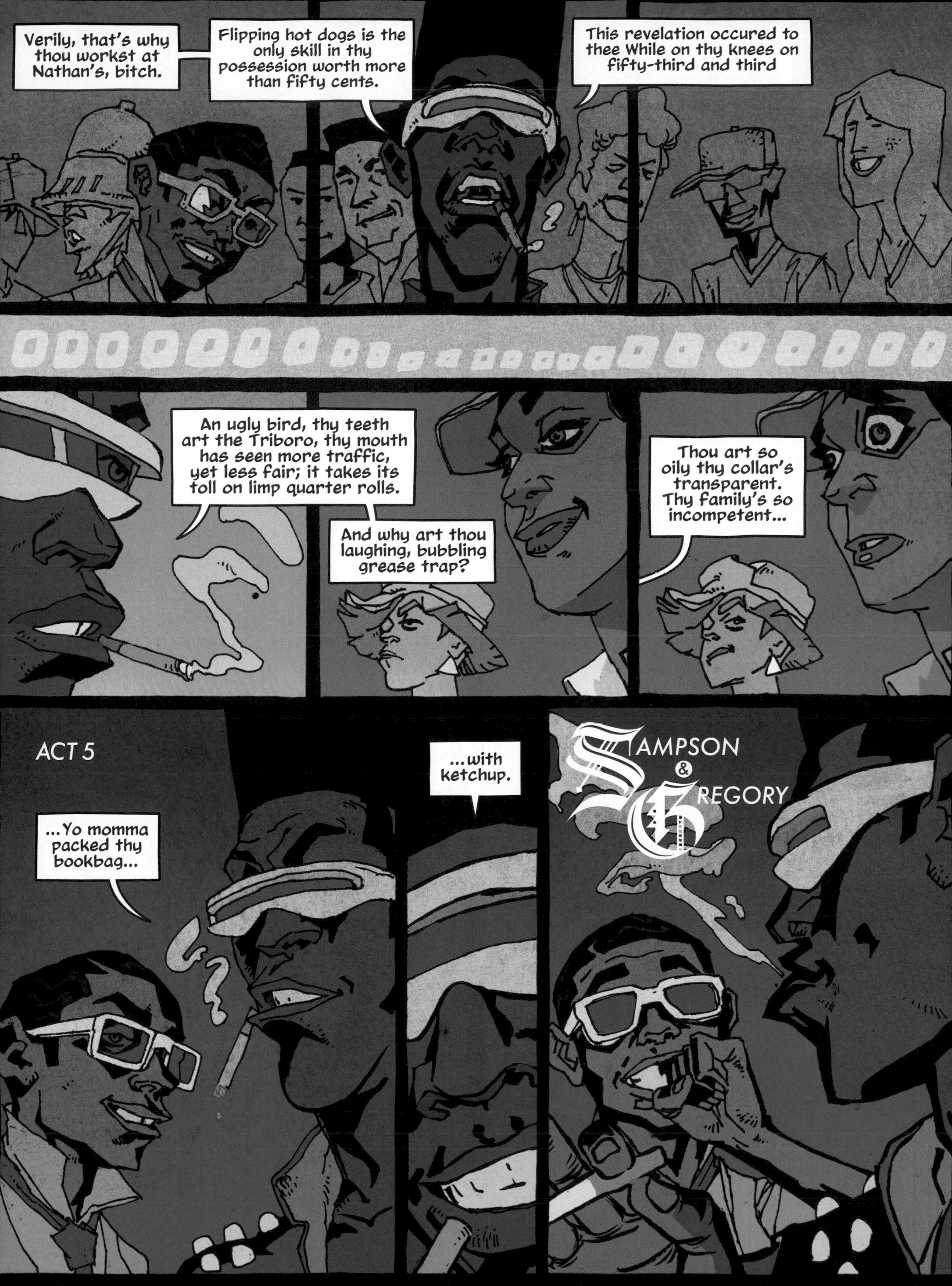
Verily, that's why thou workst at Nathan's, bitch.
Flipping hot dogs is the only skill in thy possession worth more than fifty cents.
This revelation occured to thee While on thy knees on fifty-third and third
An ugly bird, thy teeth art the Triboro, thy mouth has seen more traffic, yet less fair; it takes its toll on limp quarter rolls.
And why art thou laughing, bubbling grease trap?
Thou art so oily thy collar's transparent. Thy family's so incompetent...
ACT 5
...Yo momma packed thy bookbag...
...with ketchup.
SAMPSON & GREGORY

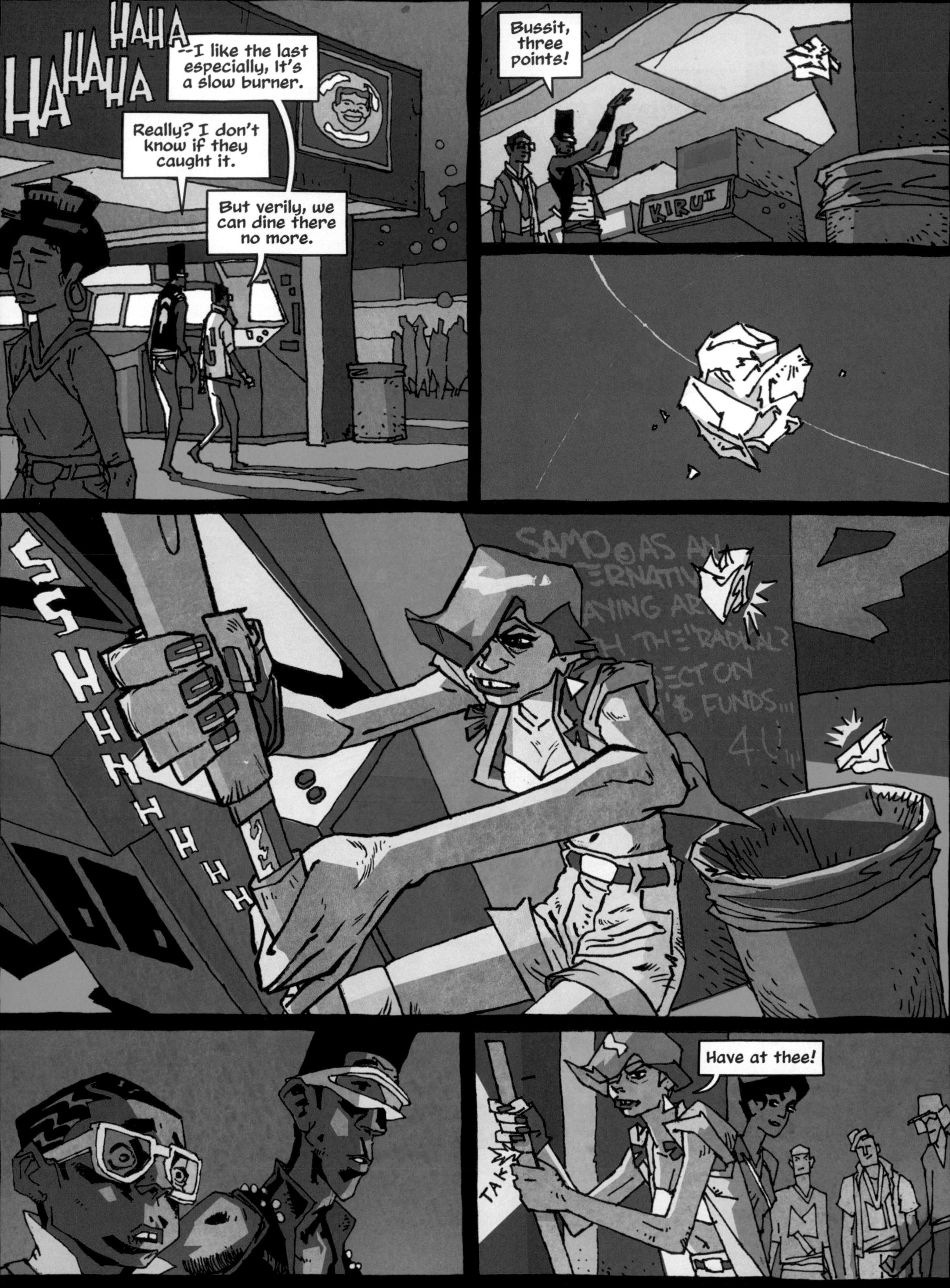

HAHA HAHAHA
--I like the last especially, It's a slow burner.
Really? I don't know if they caught it.
But verily, we can dine there no more.
Bussit, three points!
SSHHHHHHHH
Have at thee!
TAK

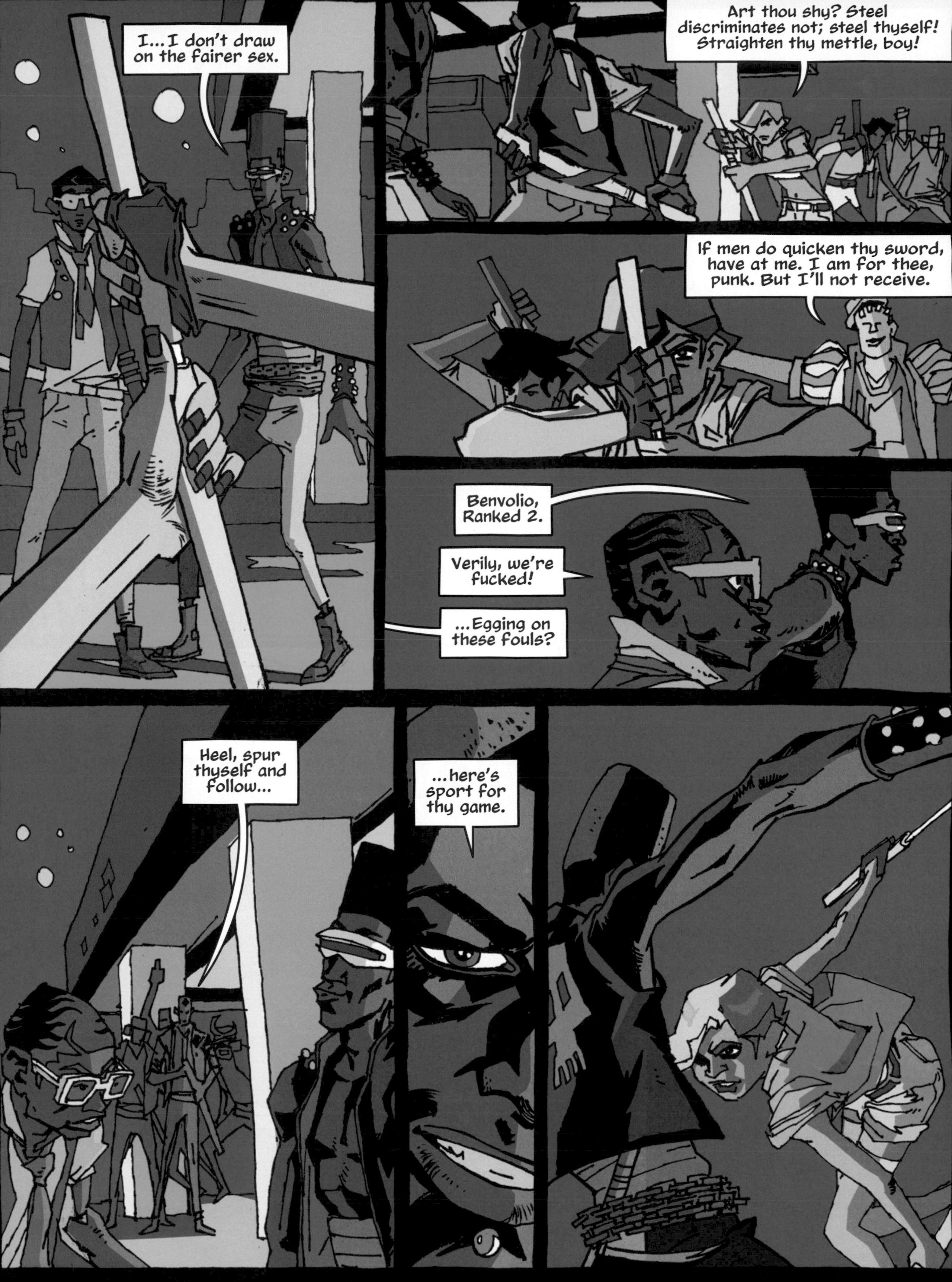
I... I don't draw on the fairer sex.
Art thou shy? Steel discriminates not; steel thyself! Straighten thy mettle, boy!
If men do quicken thy sword, have at me. I am for thee, punk. But I'll not receive.
Benvolio, Ranked 2.
Verily, we're fucked!
...Egging on these fouls?
Heel, spur thyself and follow...
...here's sport for thy game.

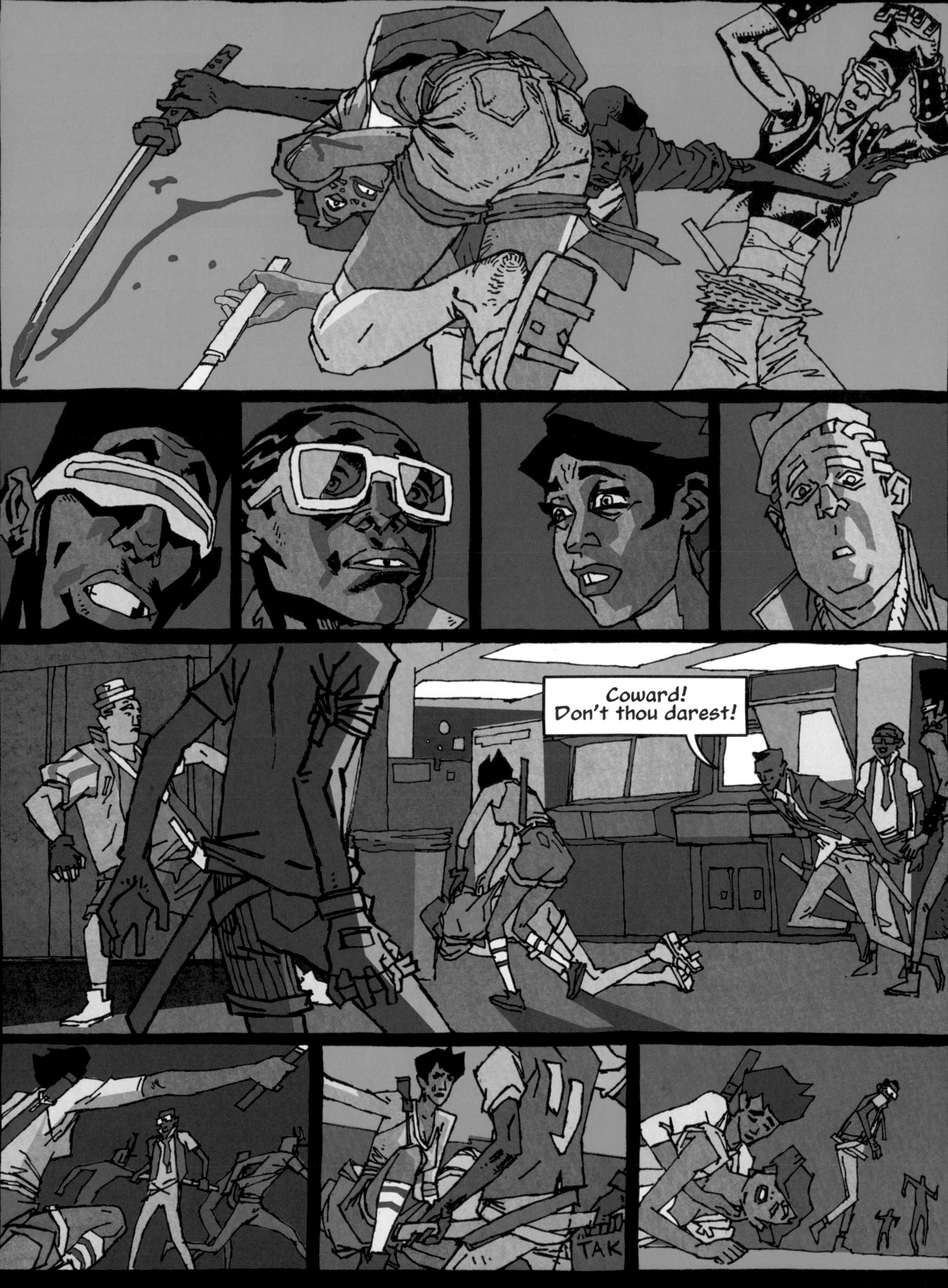
Coward!
Don't thou darest!
TAK

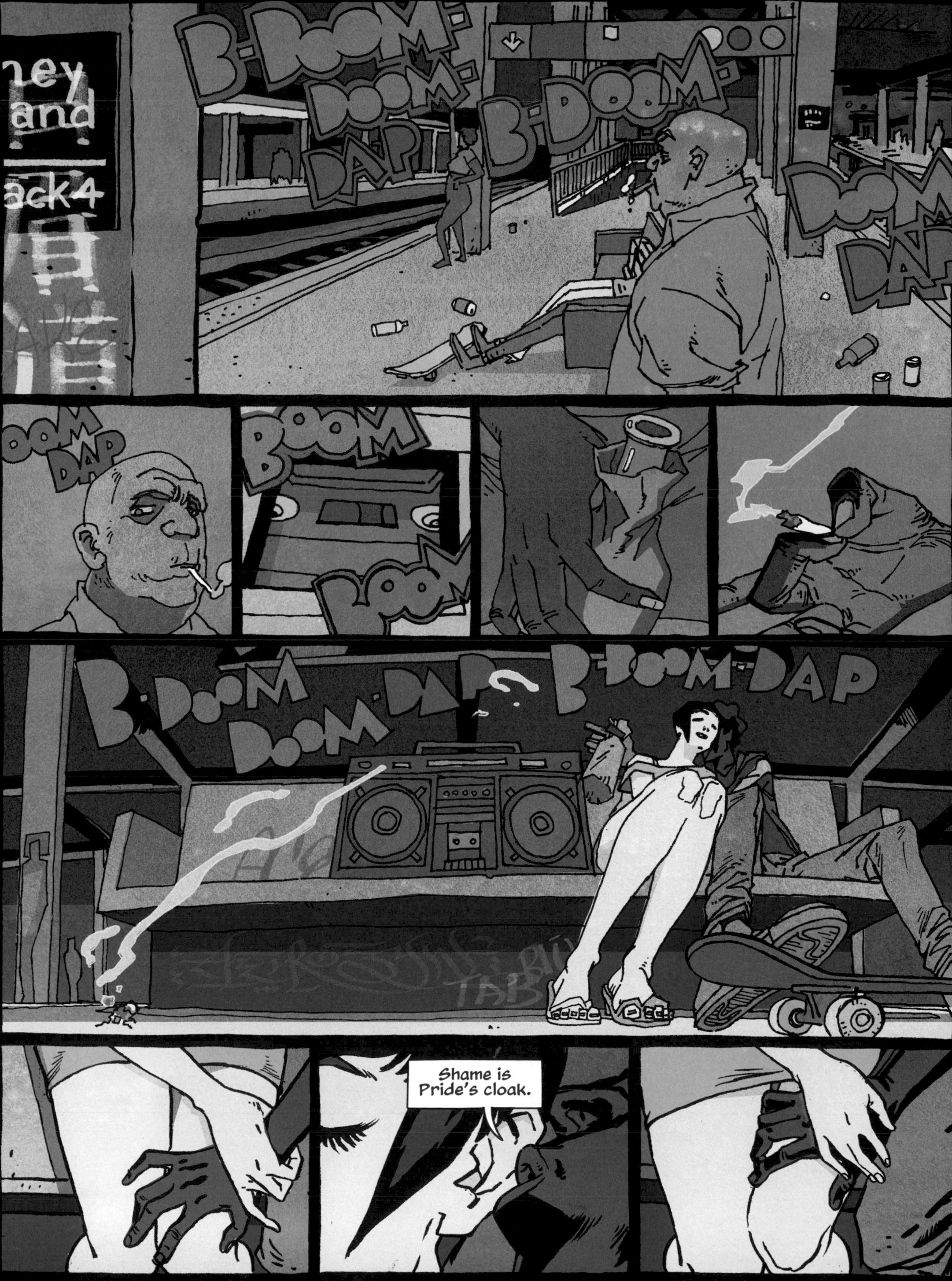
ney
and
ack4
B-DOOM-DOOM-DAP
B-DOOM
DOOM DAP
DOOM DAP
BOOM
BOOM
B-DOOM-DOOM-DAP
B-DOOM-DAP
Shame is Pride's cloak.

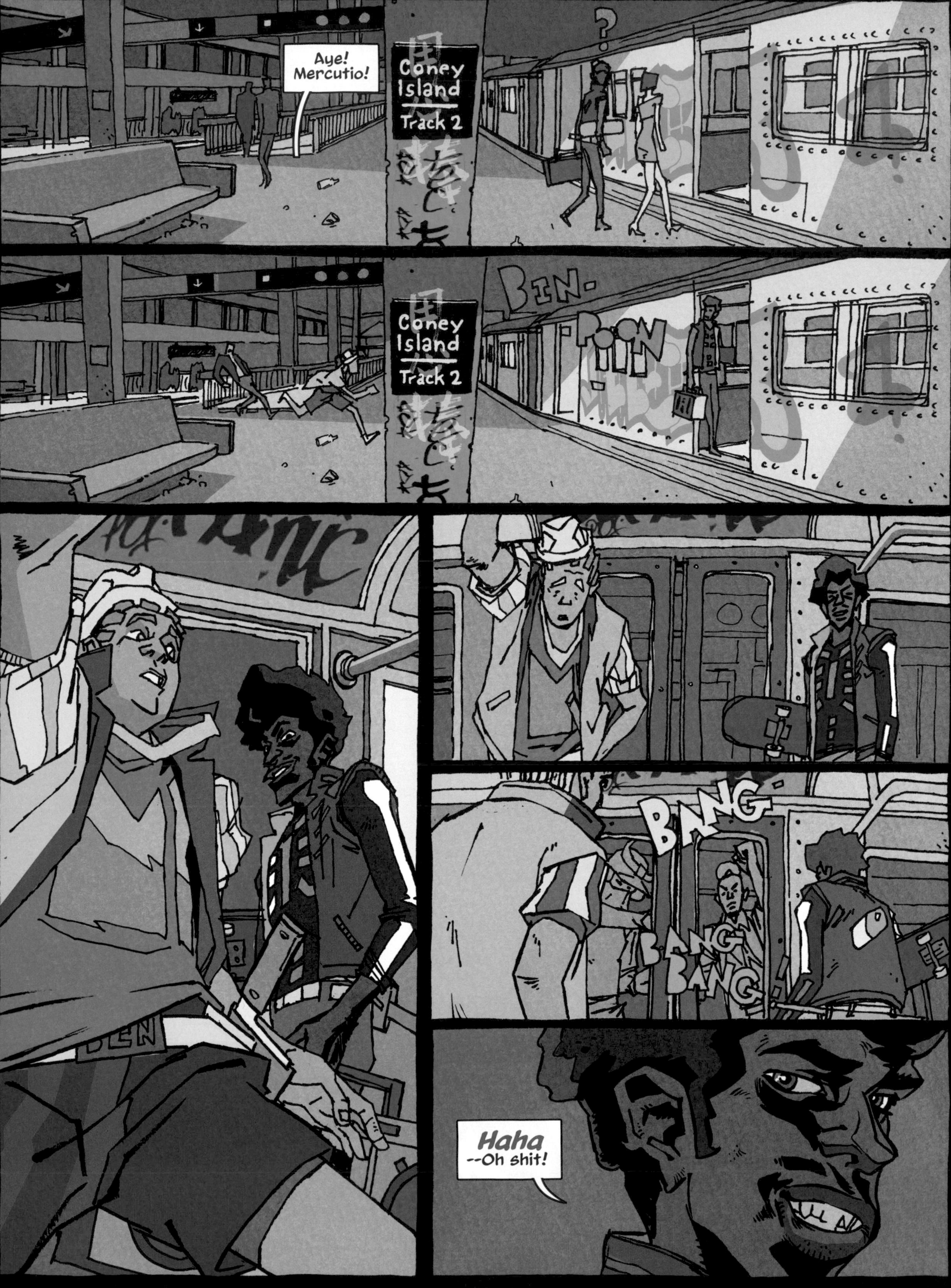
Aye! Mercutio!
Coney Island
Track 2
Coney Island
Track 2
BIN-
BANG
BANG
BANG
Haha --Oh shit!

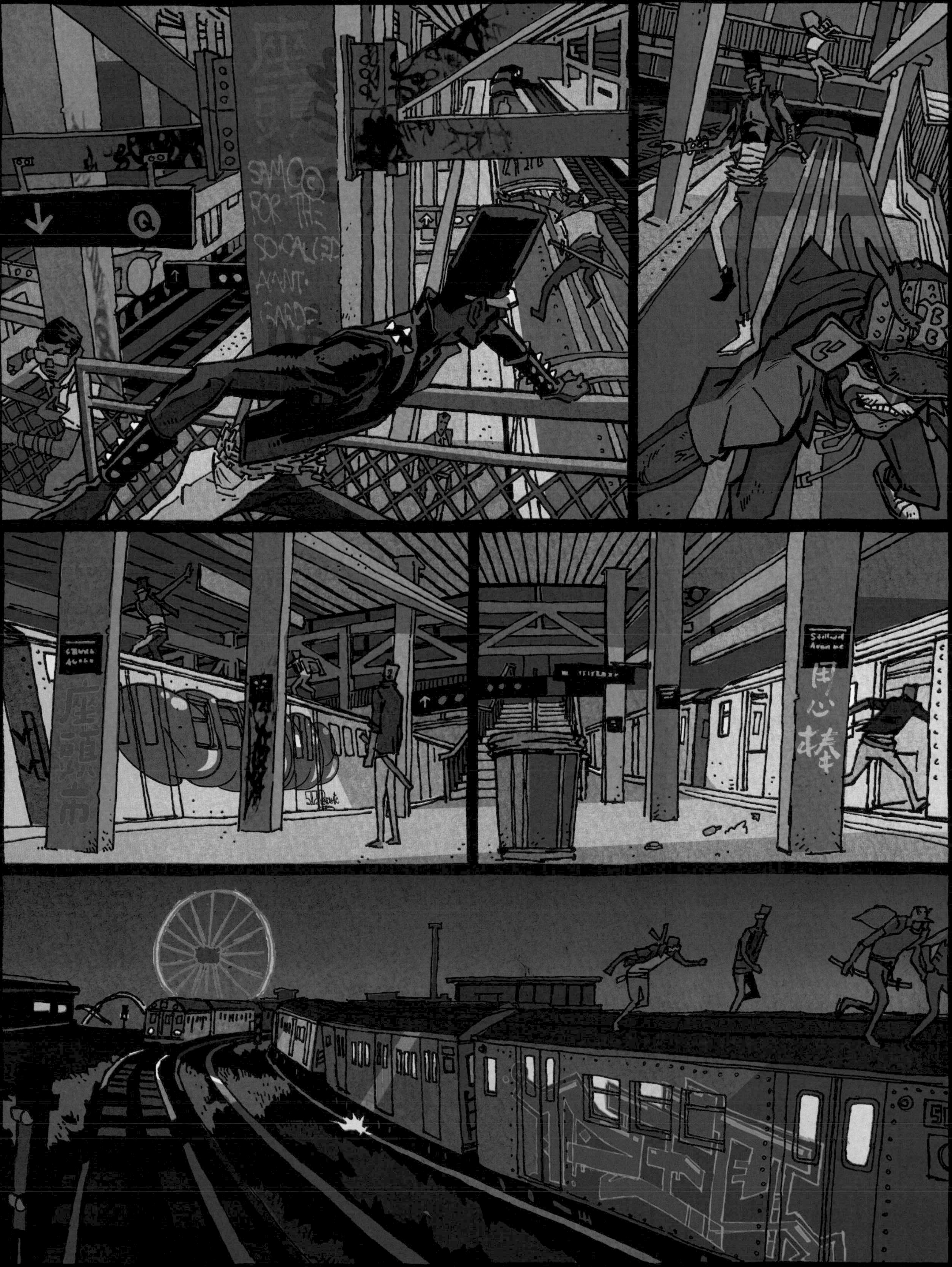
Q
SAMO©
FOR THE
SO-CALLED
AVANT-
GARDE
座頭市
用心棒

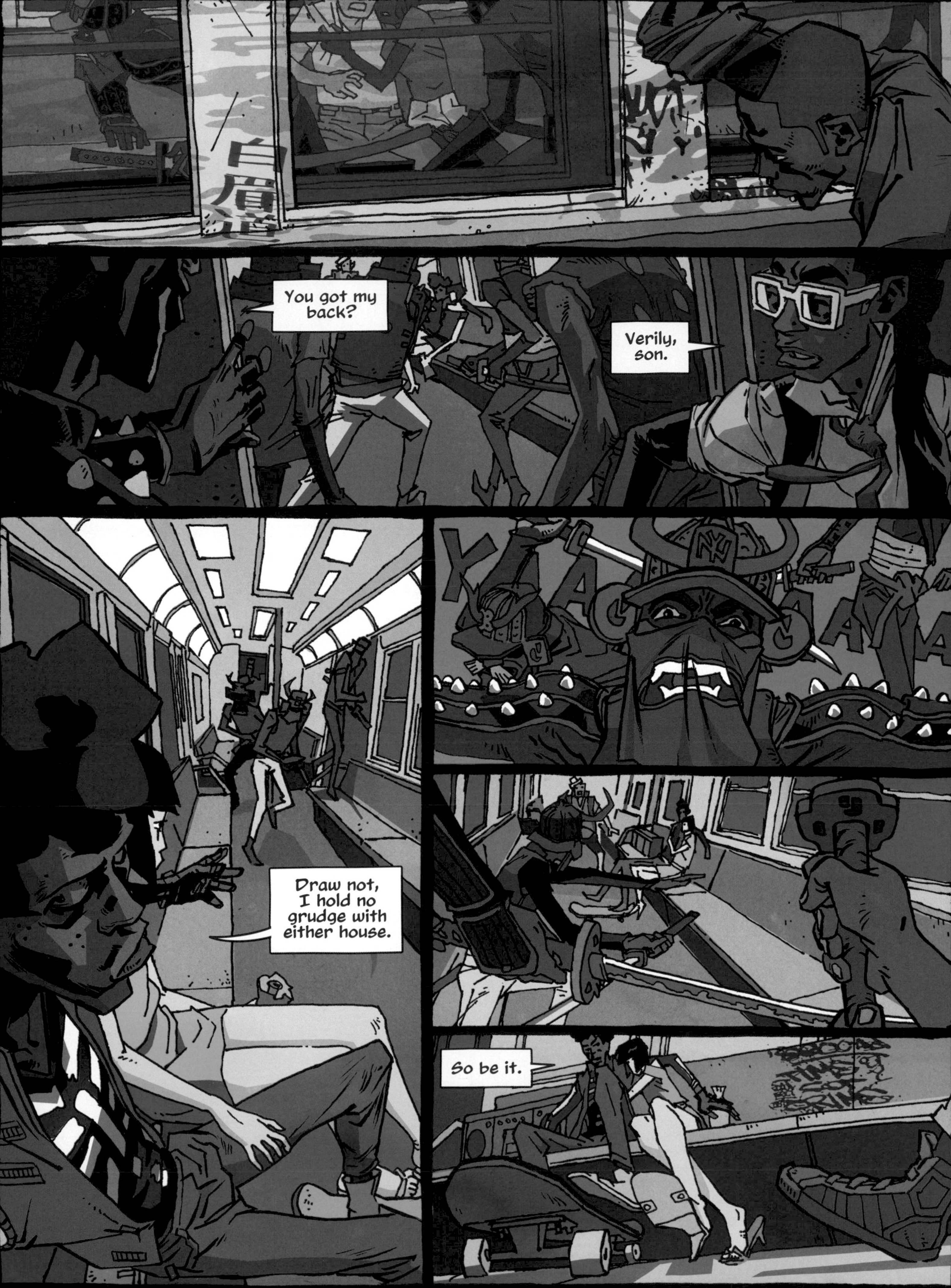
You got my back?
Verily, son.
Draw not, I hold no grudge with either house.
So be it.

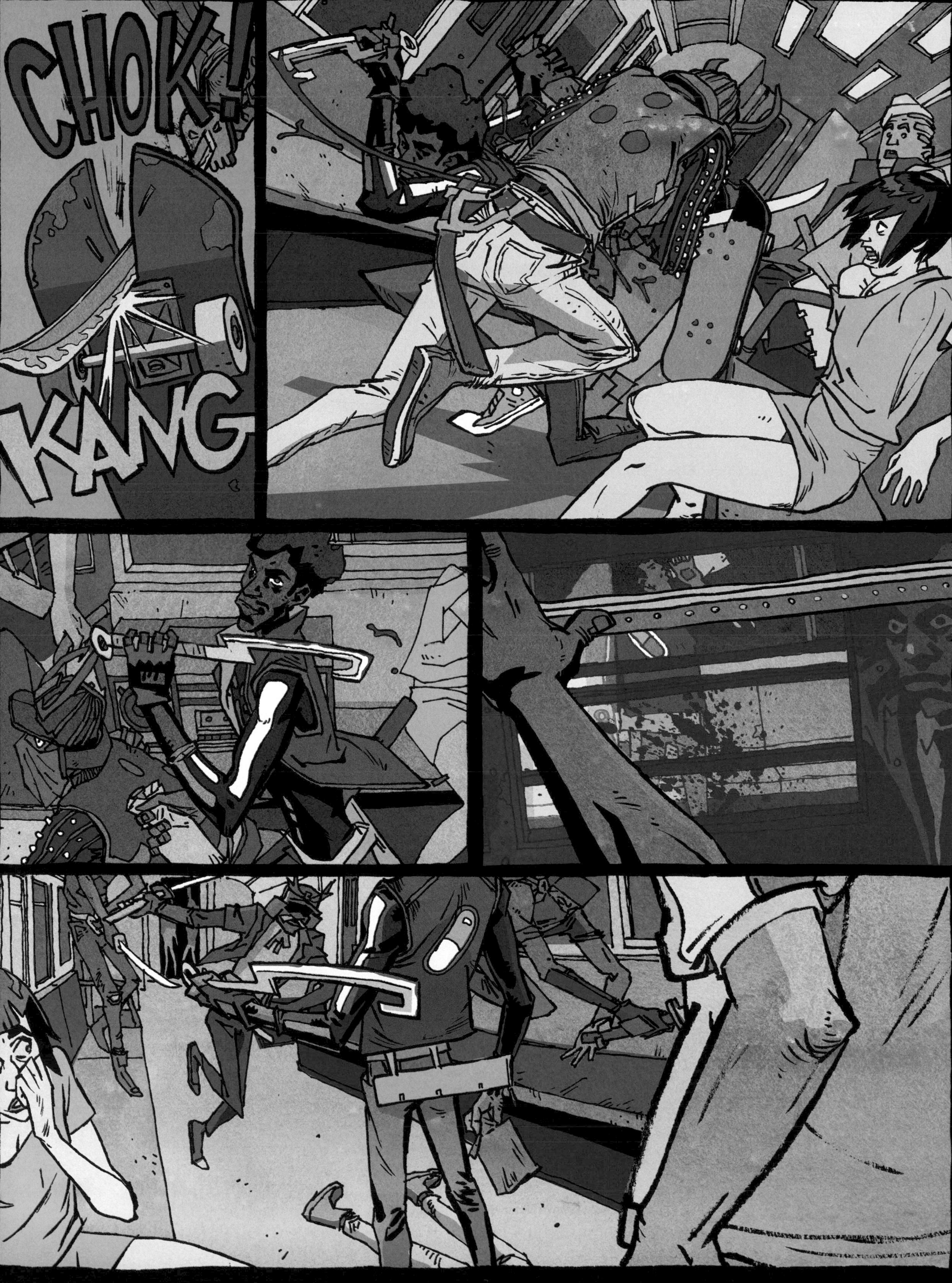
CHOK!
KANG

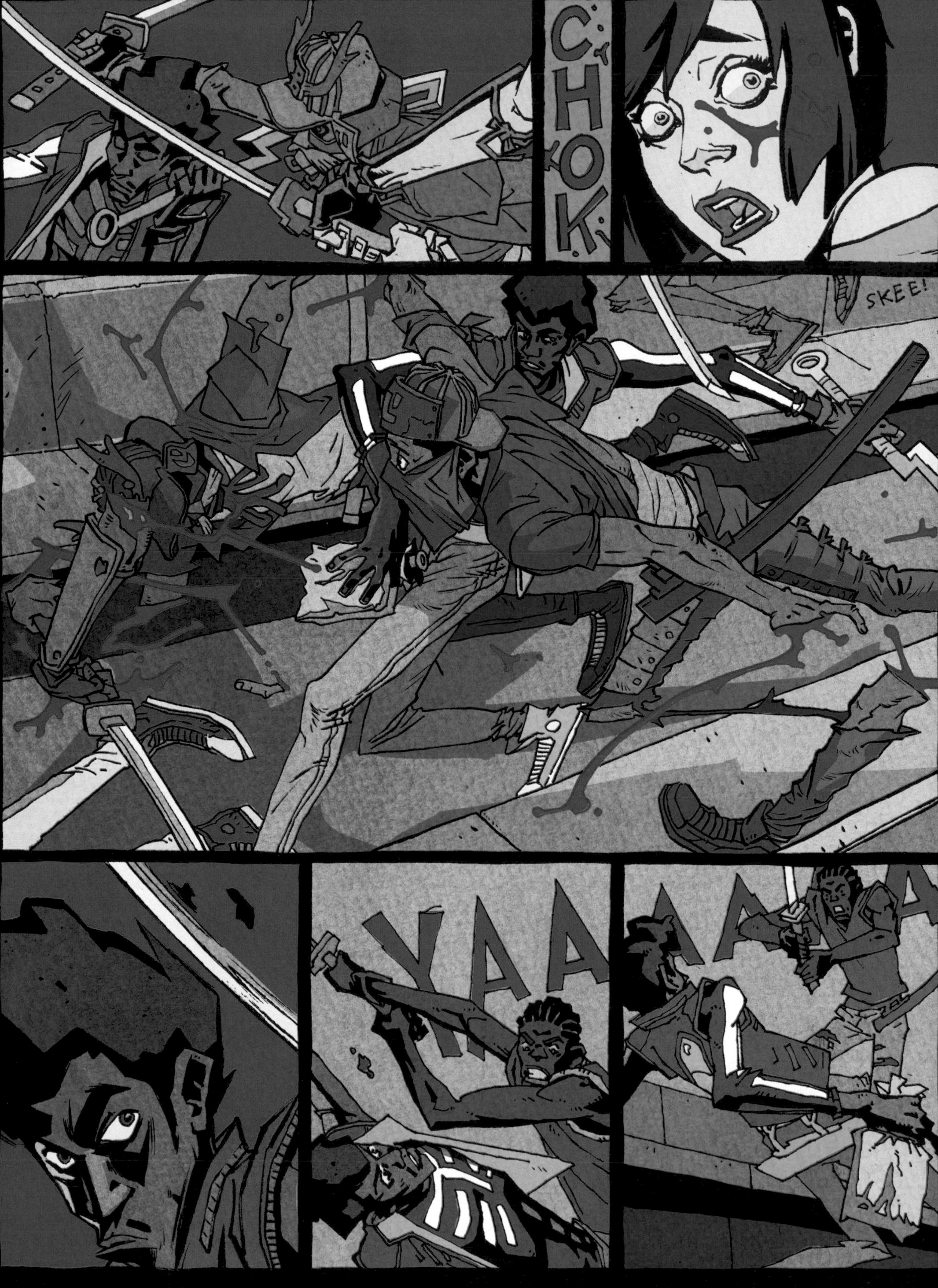

CHOK
SKEE!
YAAAA

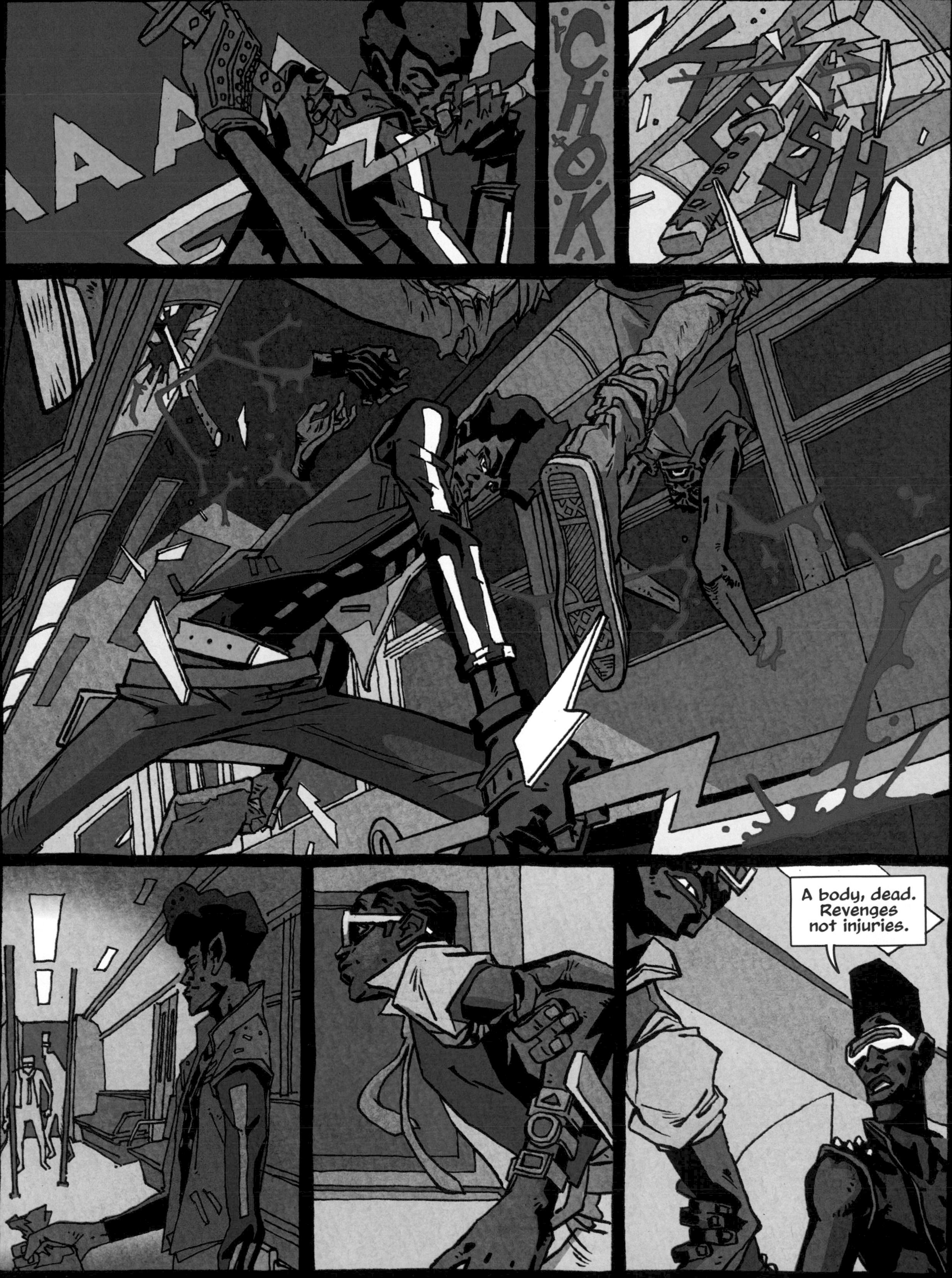
AAAAA
CHOK
!
A body, dead. Revenges not injuries.

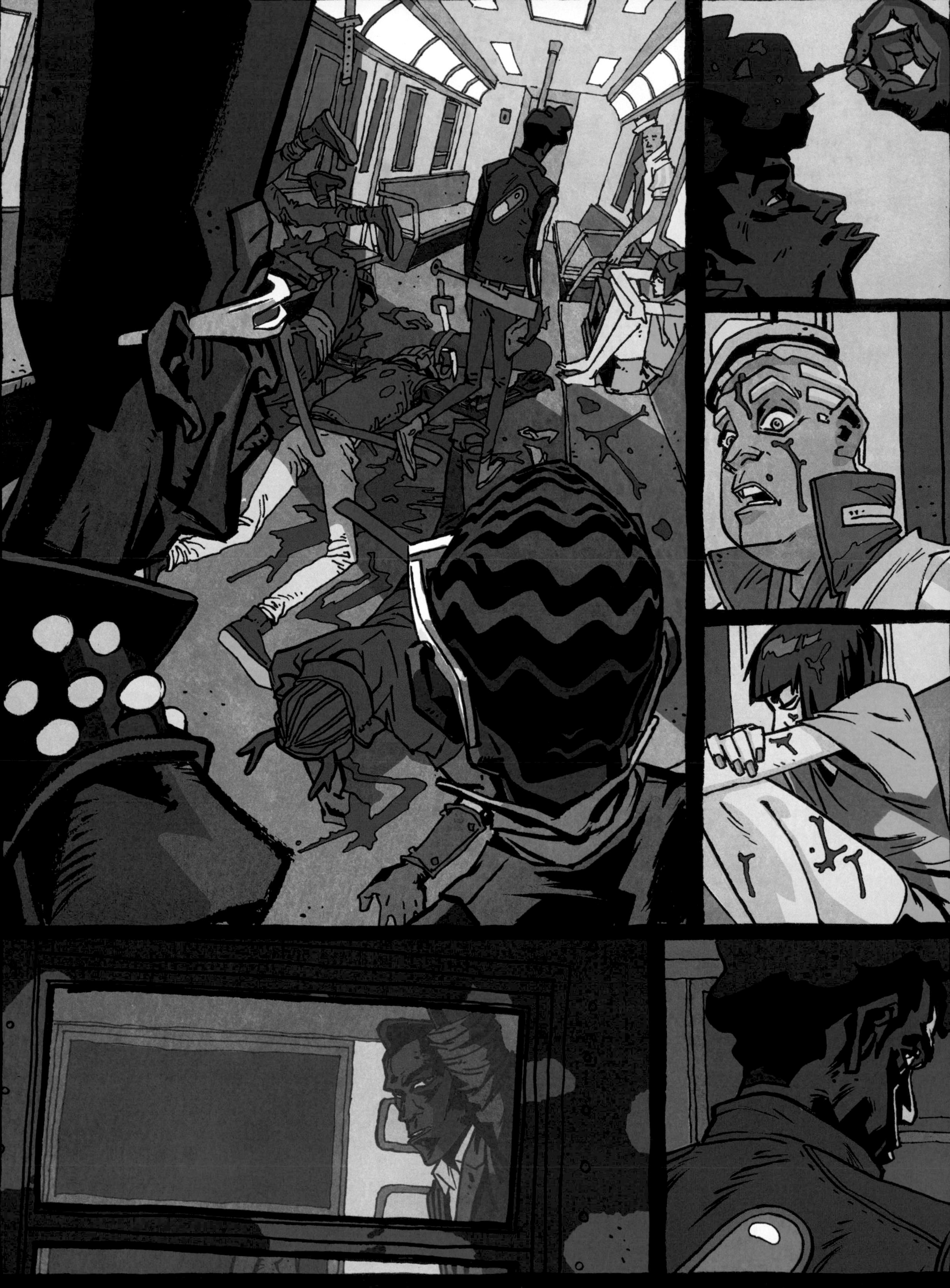

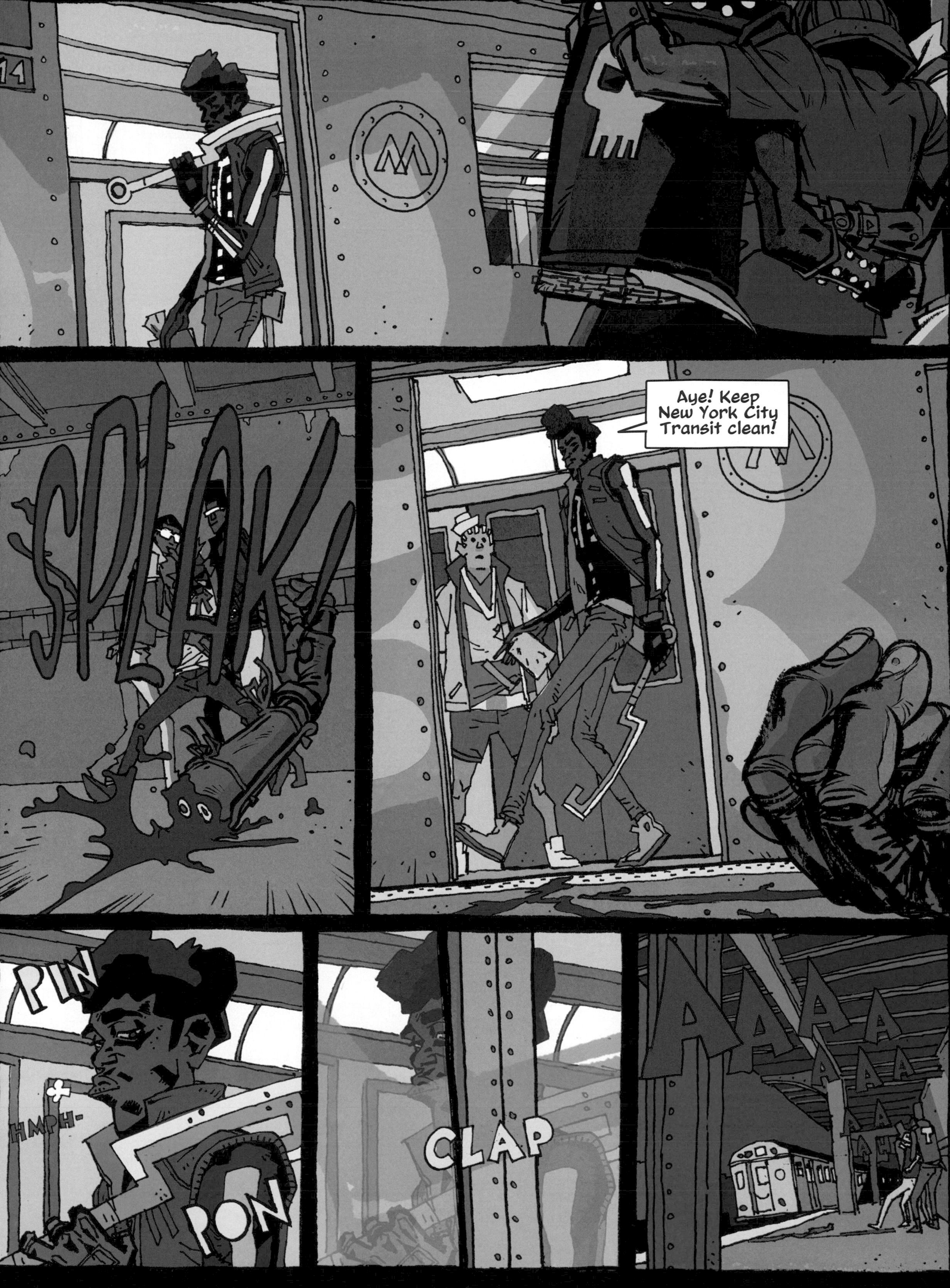
SPLAK!
Aye! Keep New York City Transit clean!
PIN
HMPH-
PON
CLAP
AAAAAAAAAH!

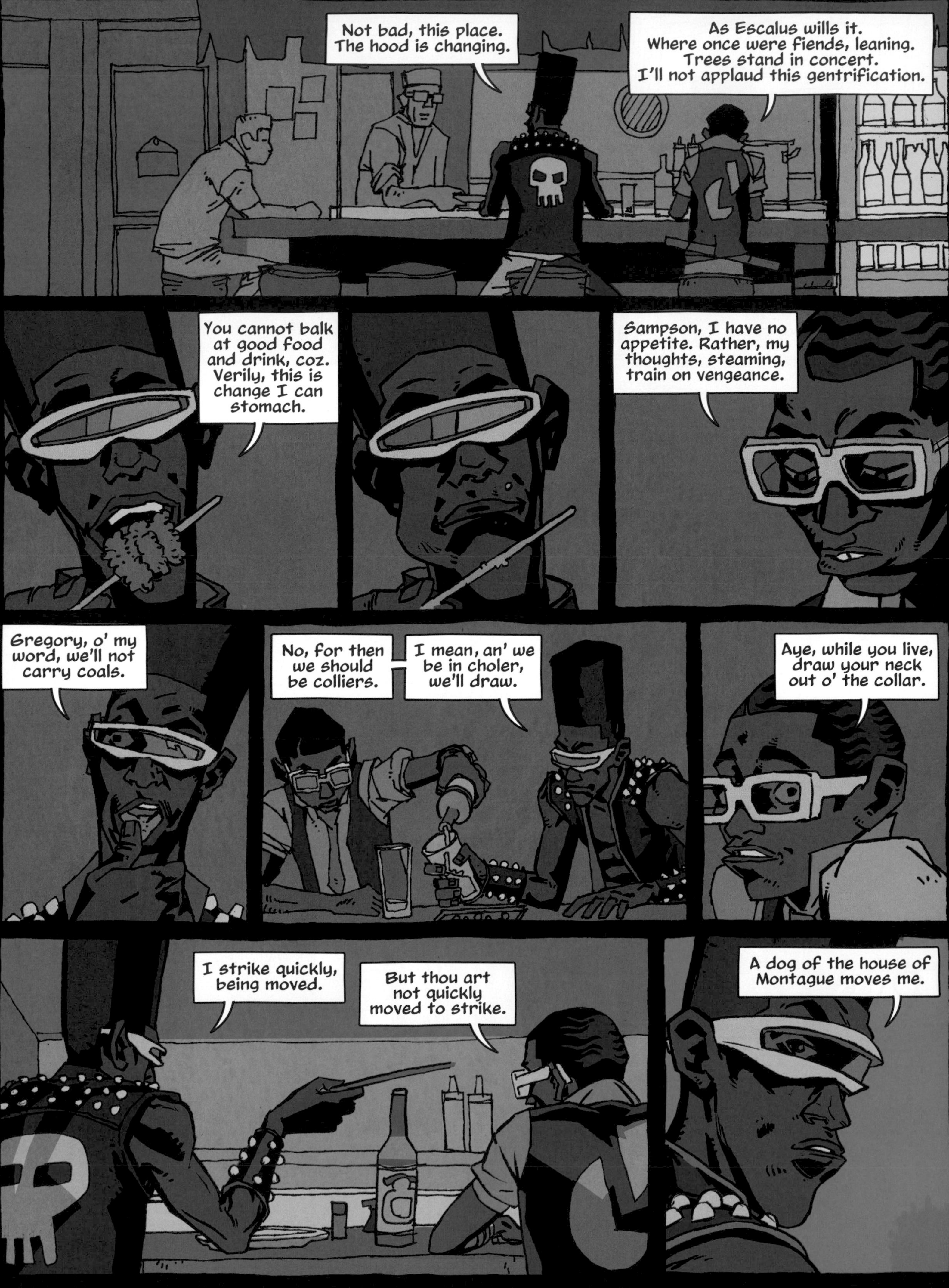
Not bad, this place. The hood is changing.
As Escalus wills it. Where once were fiends, leaning. Trees stand in concert. I'll not applaud this gentrification.
You cannot balk at good food and drink, coz. Verily, this is change I can stomach.
Sampson, I have no appetite. Rather, my thoughts, steaming, train on vengeance.
Gregory, o' my word, we'll not carry coals.
No, for then we should be colliers.
I mean, an' we be in choler, we'll draw.
Aye, while you live, draw your neck out o' the collar.
I strike quickly, being moved.
But thou art not quickly moved to strike.
A dog of the house of Montague moves me.

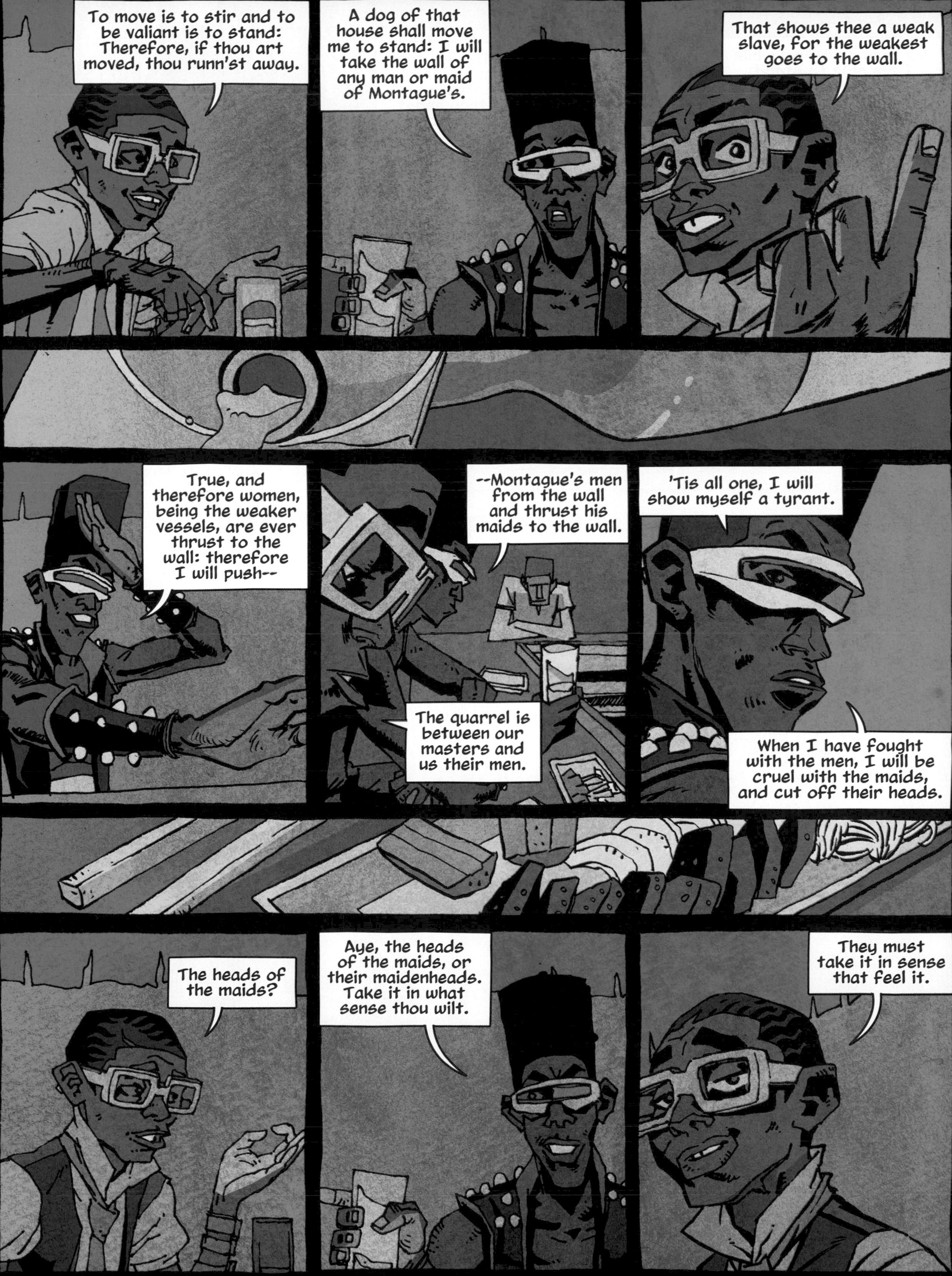
To move is to stir and to be valiant is to stand: Therefore, if thou art moved, thou runn'st away.
A dog of that house shall move me to stand: I will take the wall of any man or maid of Montague's.
That shows thee a weak slave, for the weakest goes to the wall.
True, and therefore women, being the weaker vessels, are ever thrust to the wall: therefore I will push--
--Montague's men from the wall and thrust his maids to the wall.
The quarrel is between our masters and us their men.
'Tis all one, I will show myself a tyrant.
When I have fought with the men, I will be cruel with the maids, and cut off their heads.
The heads of the maids?
Aye, the heads of the maids, or their maidenheads. Take it in what sense thou wilt.
They must take it in sense that feel it.

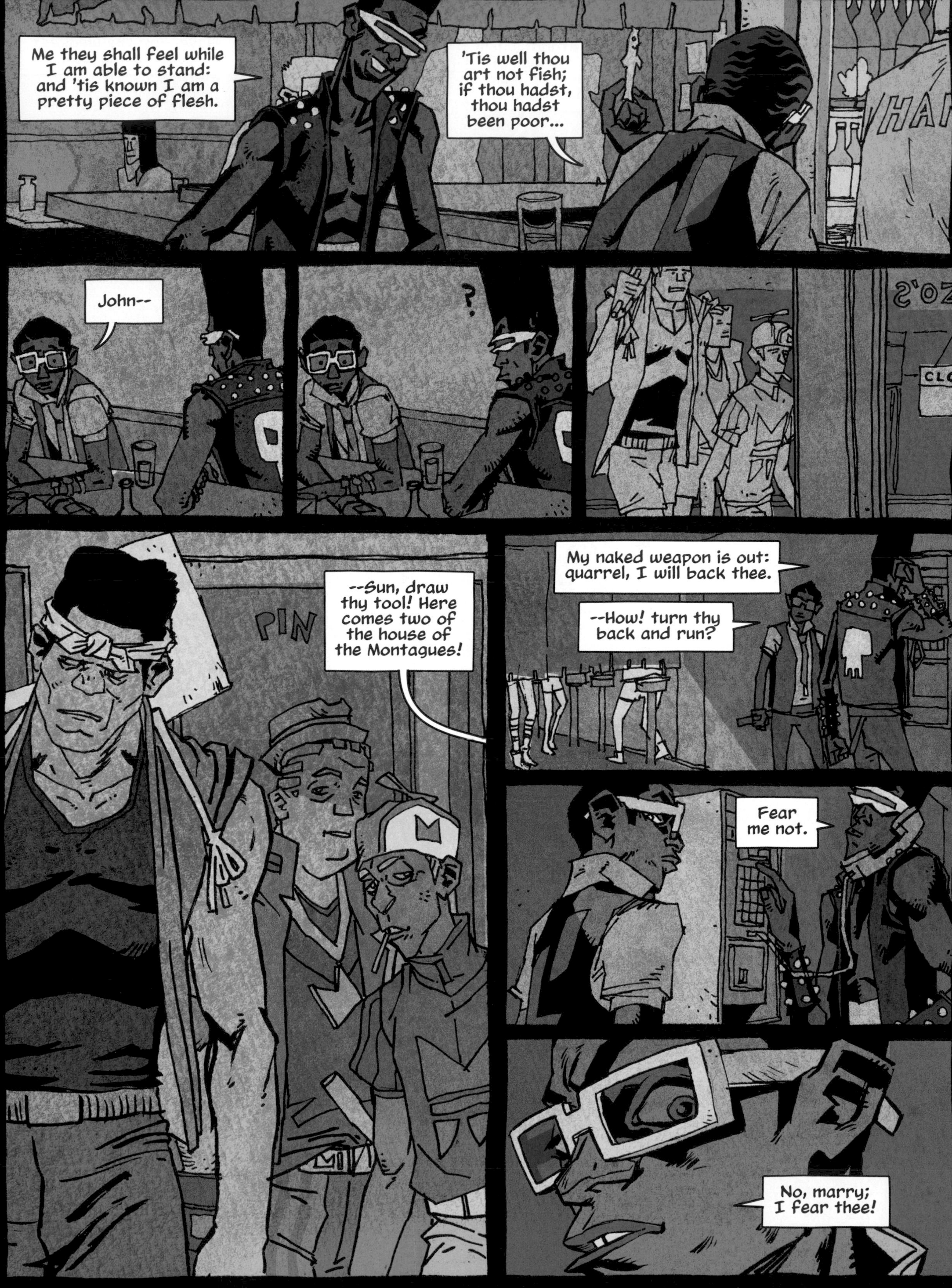
Me they shall feel while I am able to stand: and 'tis known I am a pretty piece of flesh.
'Tis well thou art not fish; if thou hadst, thou hadst been poor...
John--
?
ZO'S
CLO
PIN
--Sun, draw thy tool! Here comes two of the house of the Montagues!
My naked weapon is out: quarrel, I will back thee.
--How! turn thy back and run?
Fear me not.
No, marry; I fear thee!

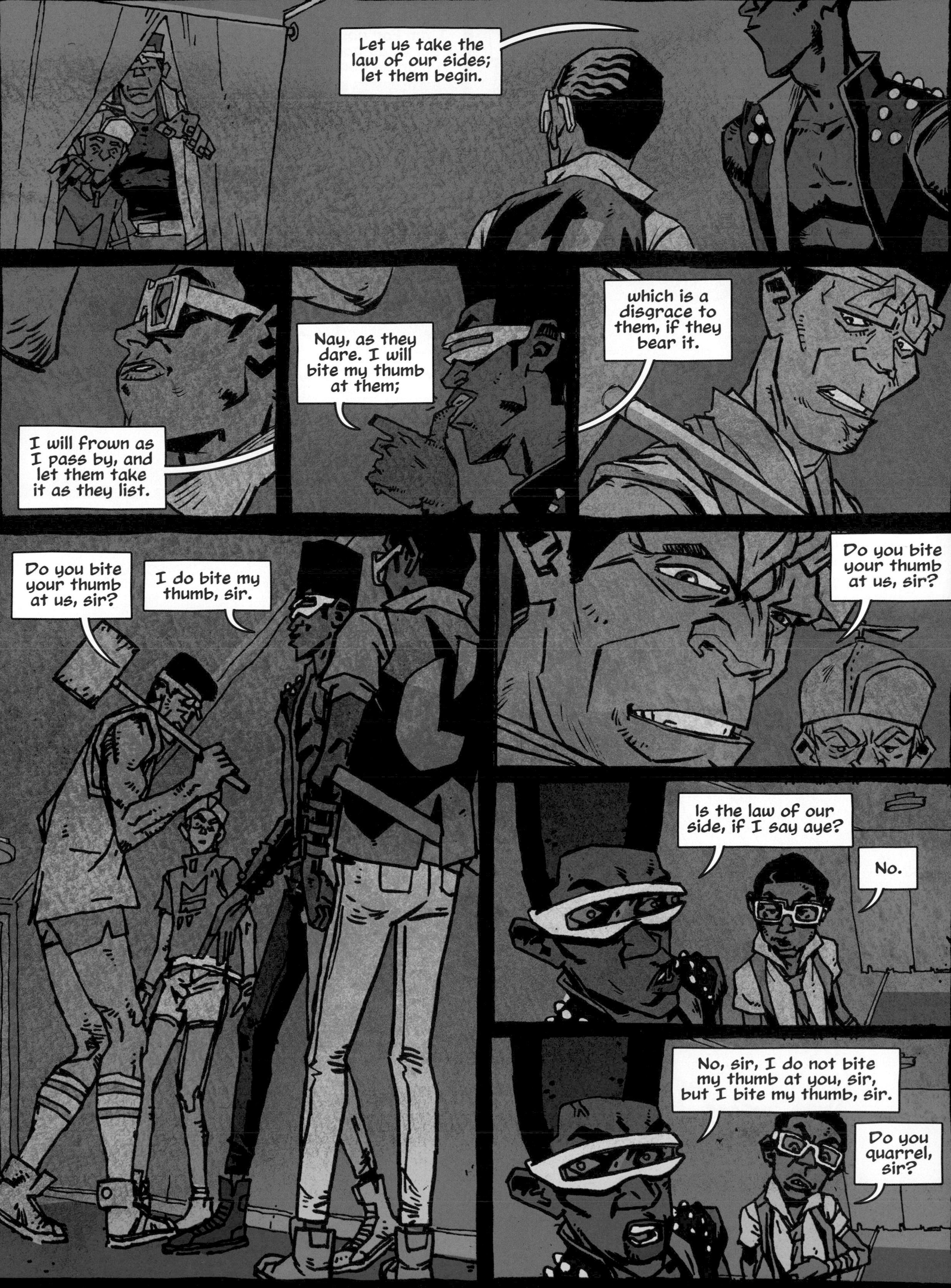
Let us take the law of our sides; let them begin.
I will frown as I pass by, and let them take it as they list.
Nay, as they dare. I will bite my thumb at them;
which is a disgrace to them, if they bear it.
Do you bite your thumb at us, sir?
I do bite my thumb, sir.
Do you bite your thumb at us, sir?
Is the law of our side, if I say aye?
No.
No, sir, I do not bite my thumb at you, sir, but I bite my thumb, sir.
Do you quarrel, sir?

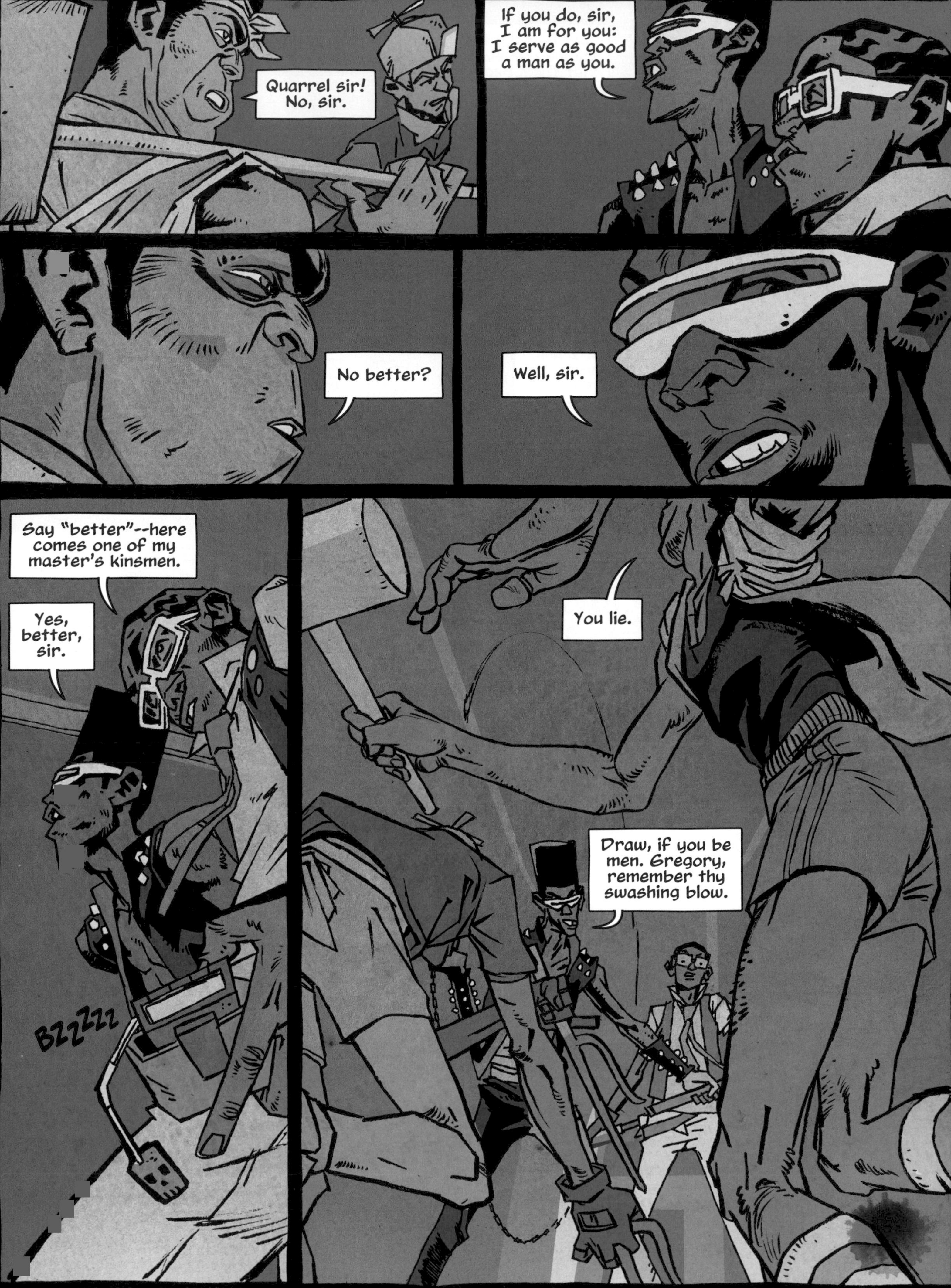
Quarrel sir! No, sir.
If you do, sir, I am for you: I serve as good a man as you.
No better?
Well, sir.
Say "better"--here comes one of my master's kinsmen.
Yes, better, sir.
BZZZZZ
You lie.
Draw, if you be men. Gregory, remember thy swashing blow.

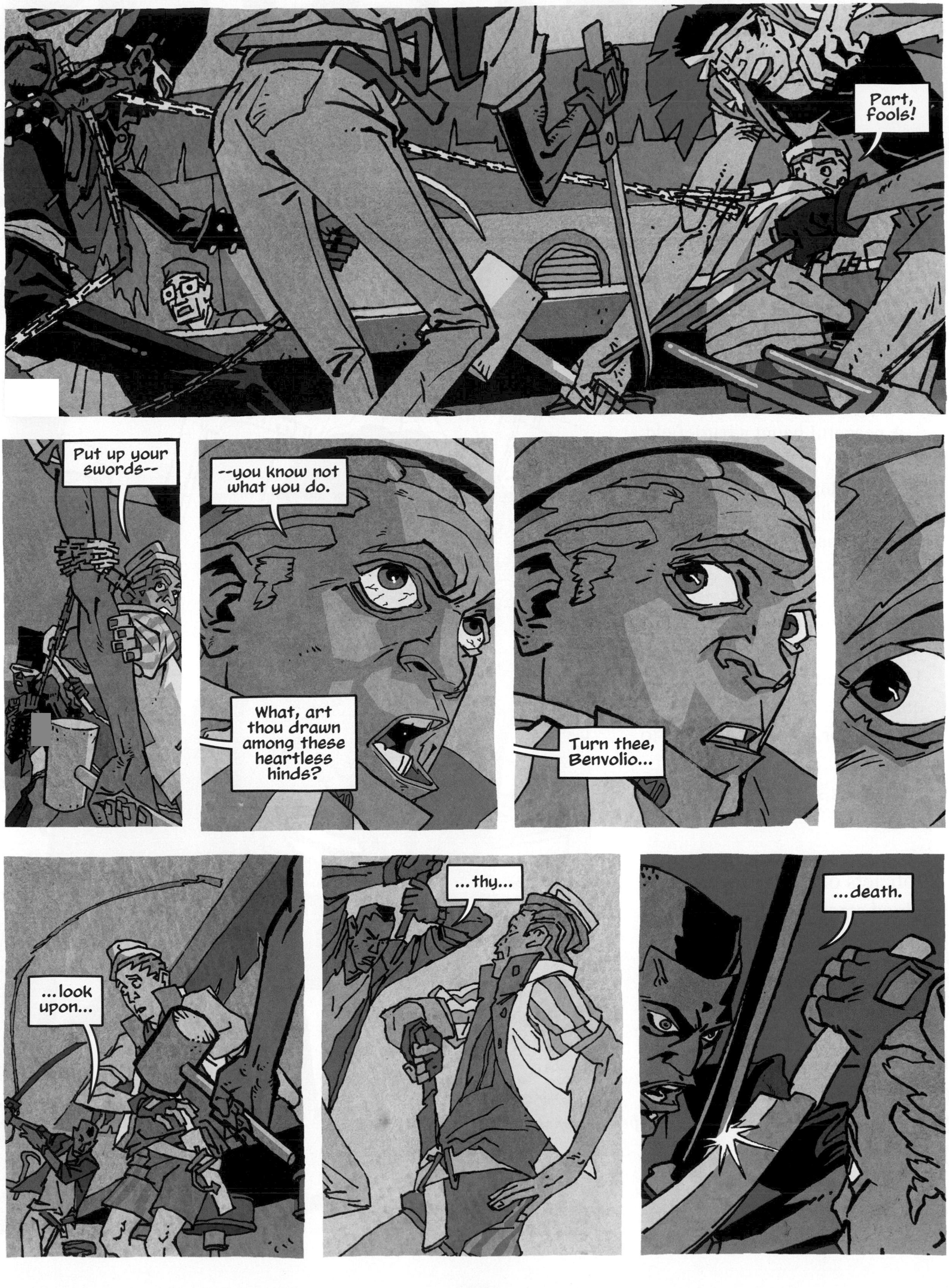
Part, fools!
Put up your swords--
--you know not what you do.
What, art thou drawn among these heartless hinds?
Turn thee, Benvolio...
...look upon...
...thy...
...death.

# A Thrice Disturbed Peac

**-Edward de Vere**

A Thrice Disturbed Peace
Gang violence again did make
A peaceful haunt a battlefield
yesterday
As Montague and Capulet
crossed blades
Over a sushi bar in crown
heights.

Three civil brawls, bred of an airy
word,
Have thrice disturb'd the quiet of
our streets.
Our Mayor, Escalus had this to
say:
Rebellious subjects, enemies to
peace,

Profaners of this neighbour-
stained steel,--
Throw your mistemper'd weapons to the ground,
And hear the sentence of your
moved mayor.
If ever you disturb our streets
again,
Your lives shall pay the forfeit of
the peace.

**contd. on page 3a.**

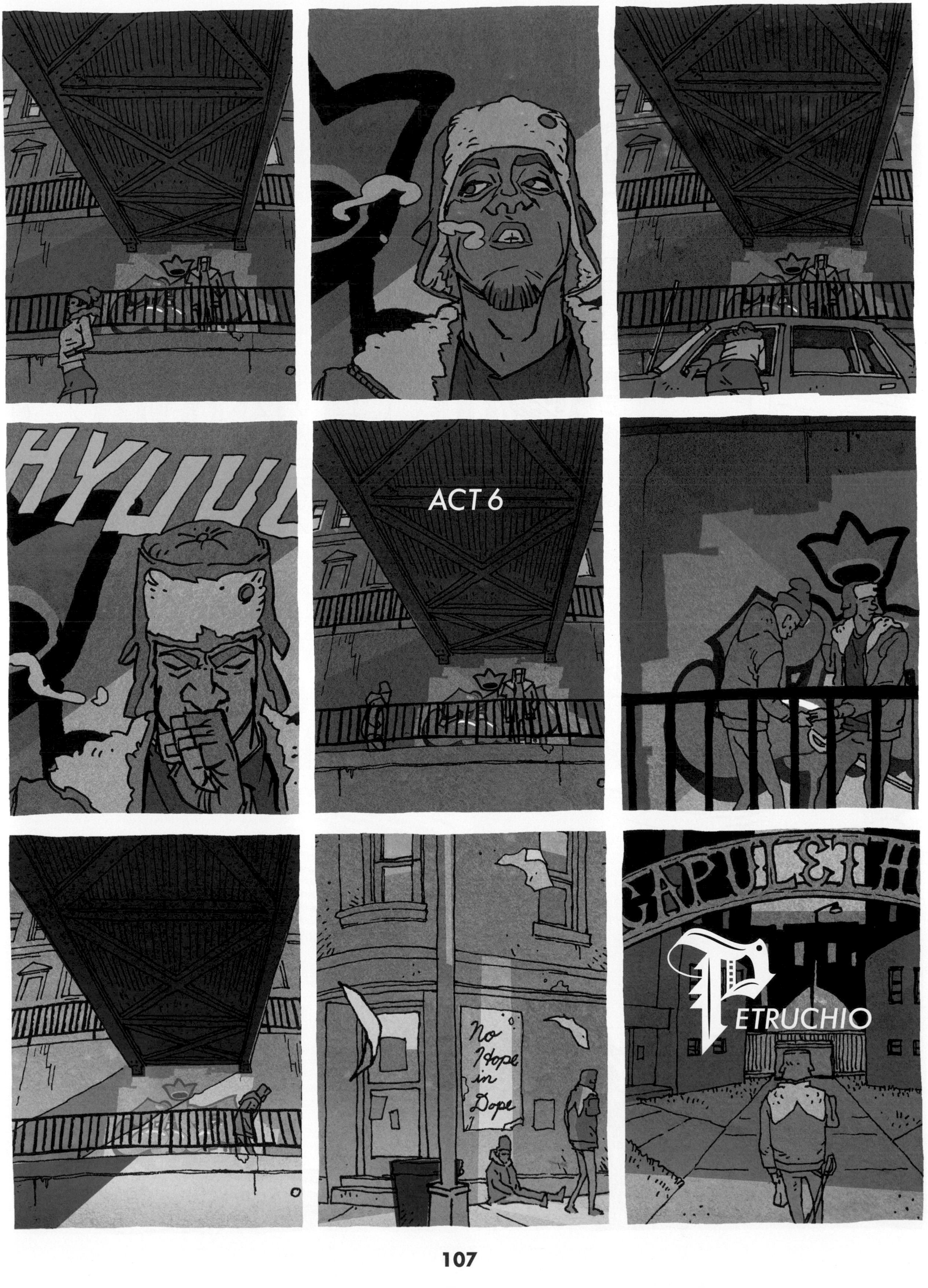
ACT 6
No Hope in Dope
PETRUCHIO

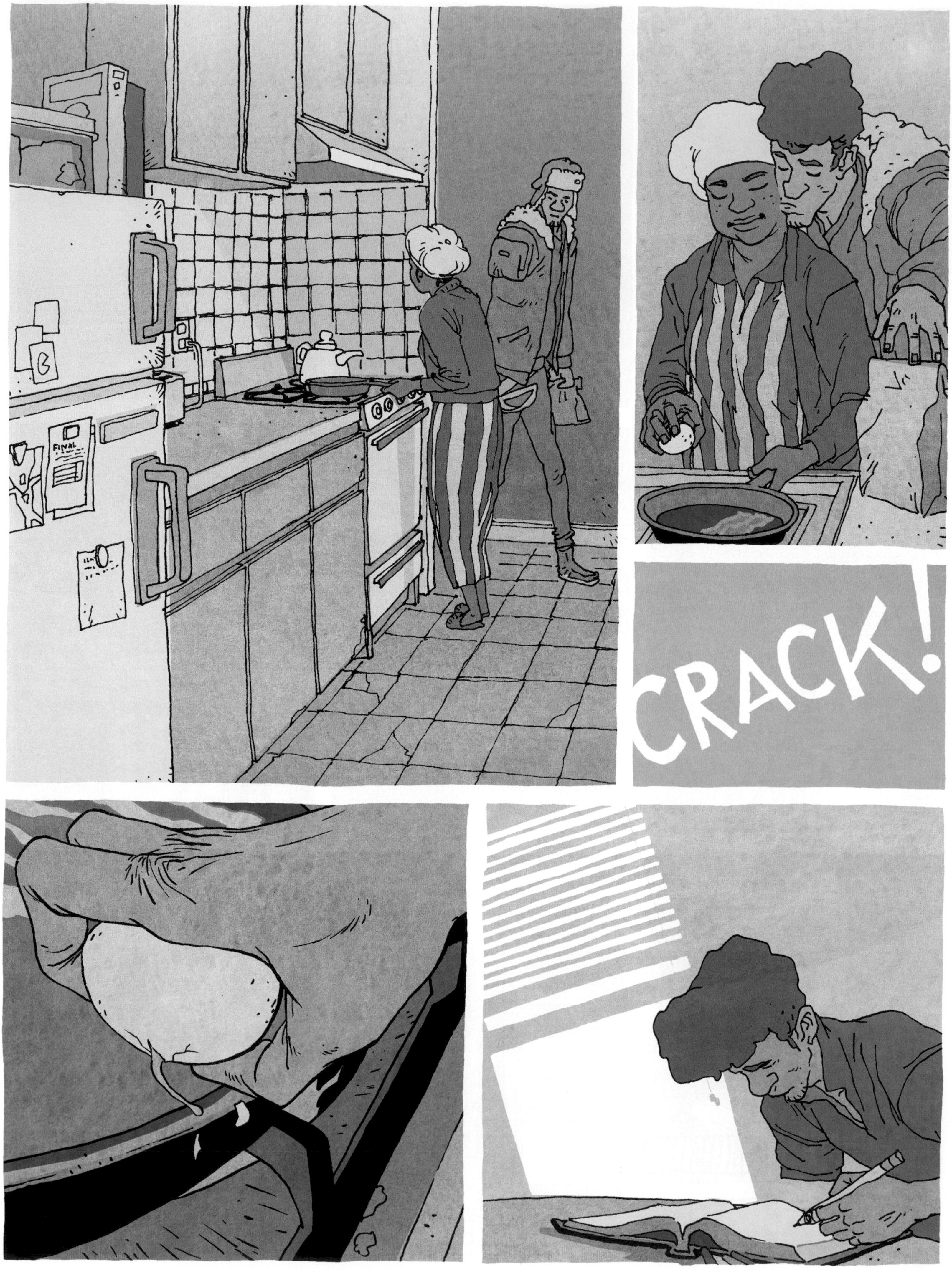
B
FINAL
CRACK!

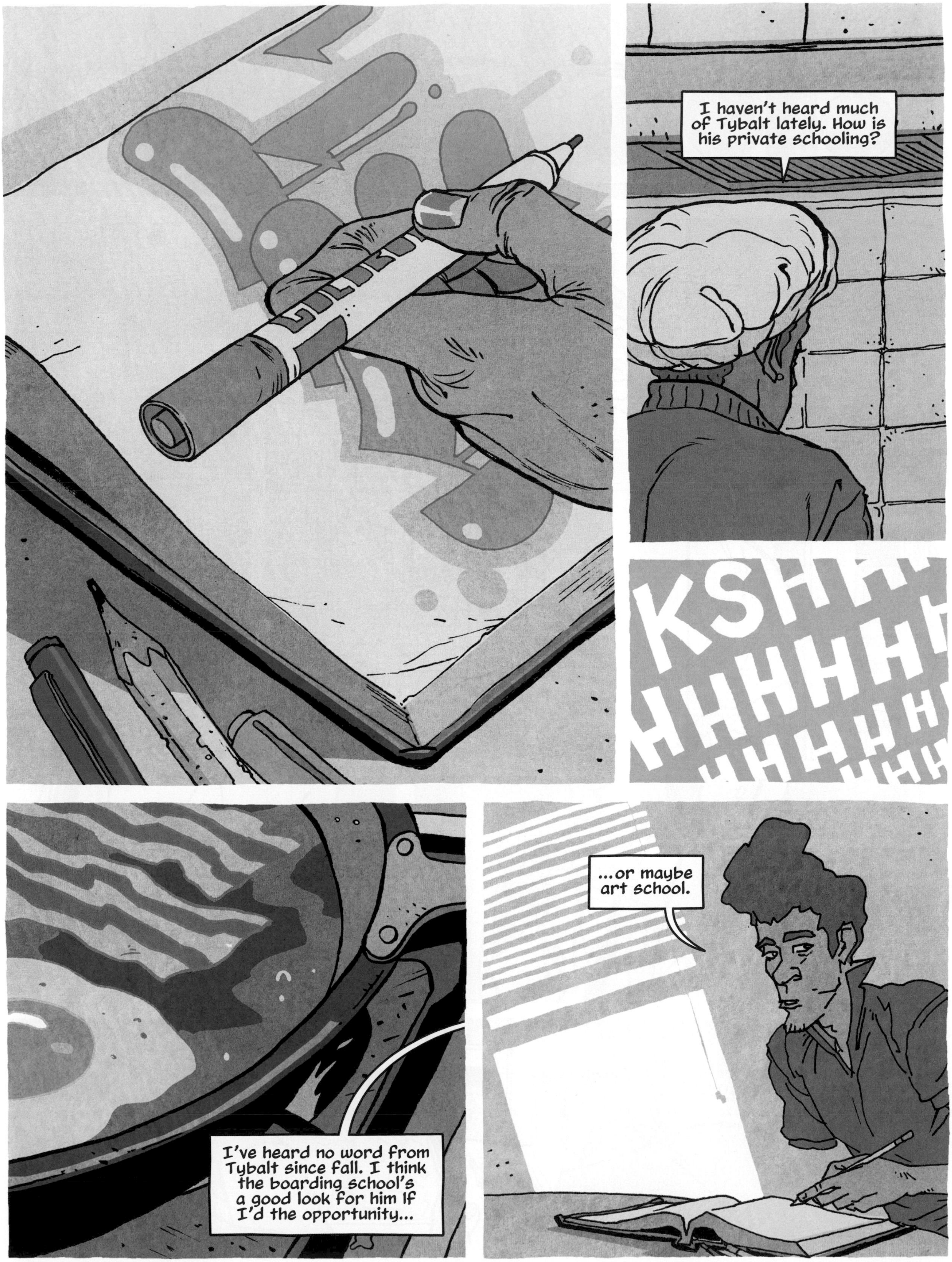
I haven't heard much of Tybalt lately. How is his private schooling?
KSHHHHHHHHHHHHHHHHHHH
I've heard no word from Tybalt since fall. I think the boarding school's a good look for him If I'd the opportunity...
...or maybe art school.

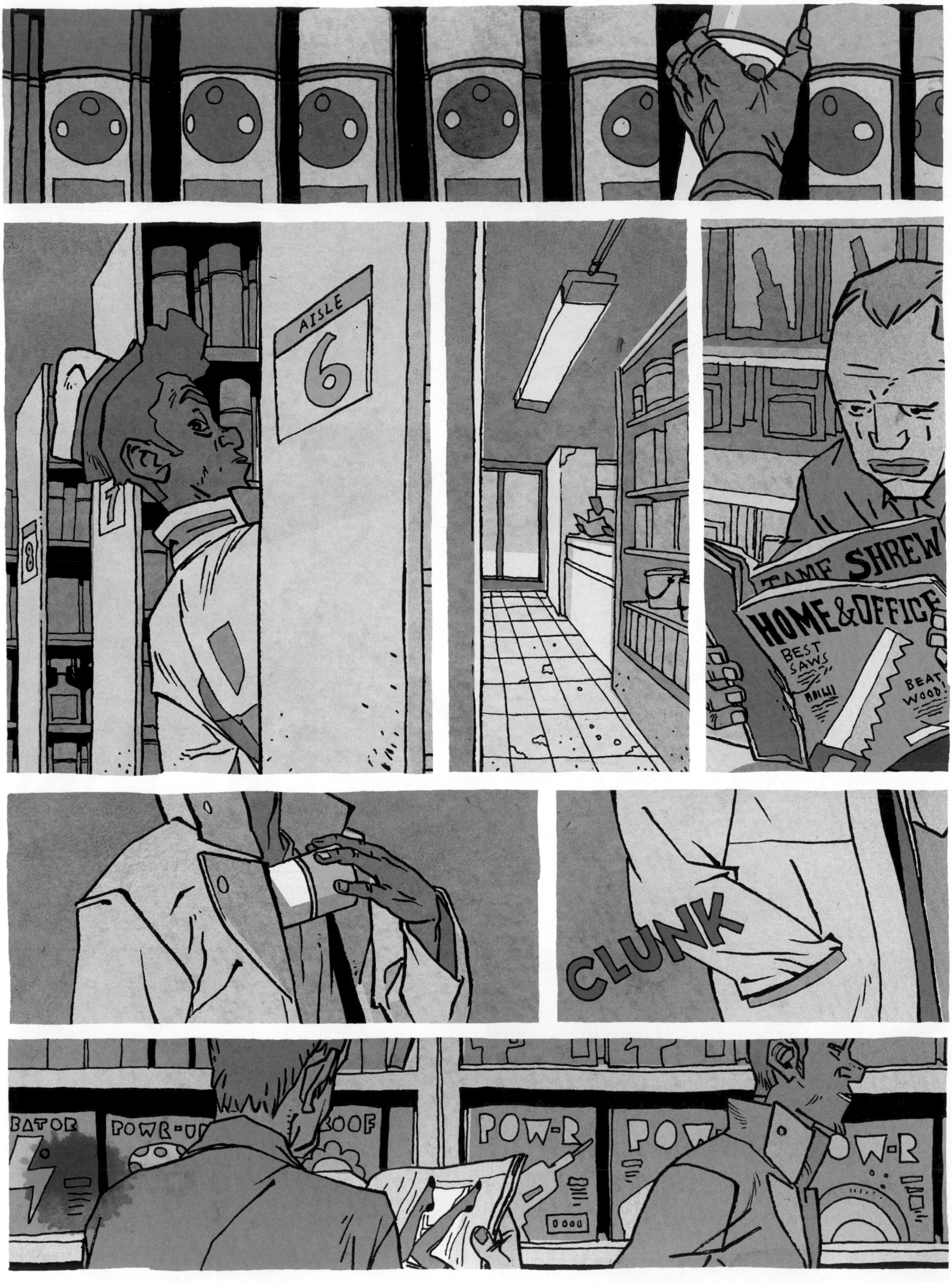
AISLE
6
TAME SHREW
HOME&OFFICE
BEST SAWS
BEAT WOOD!
CLUNK
POW-R
POW-R

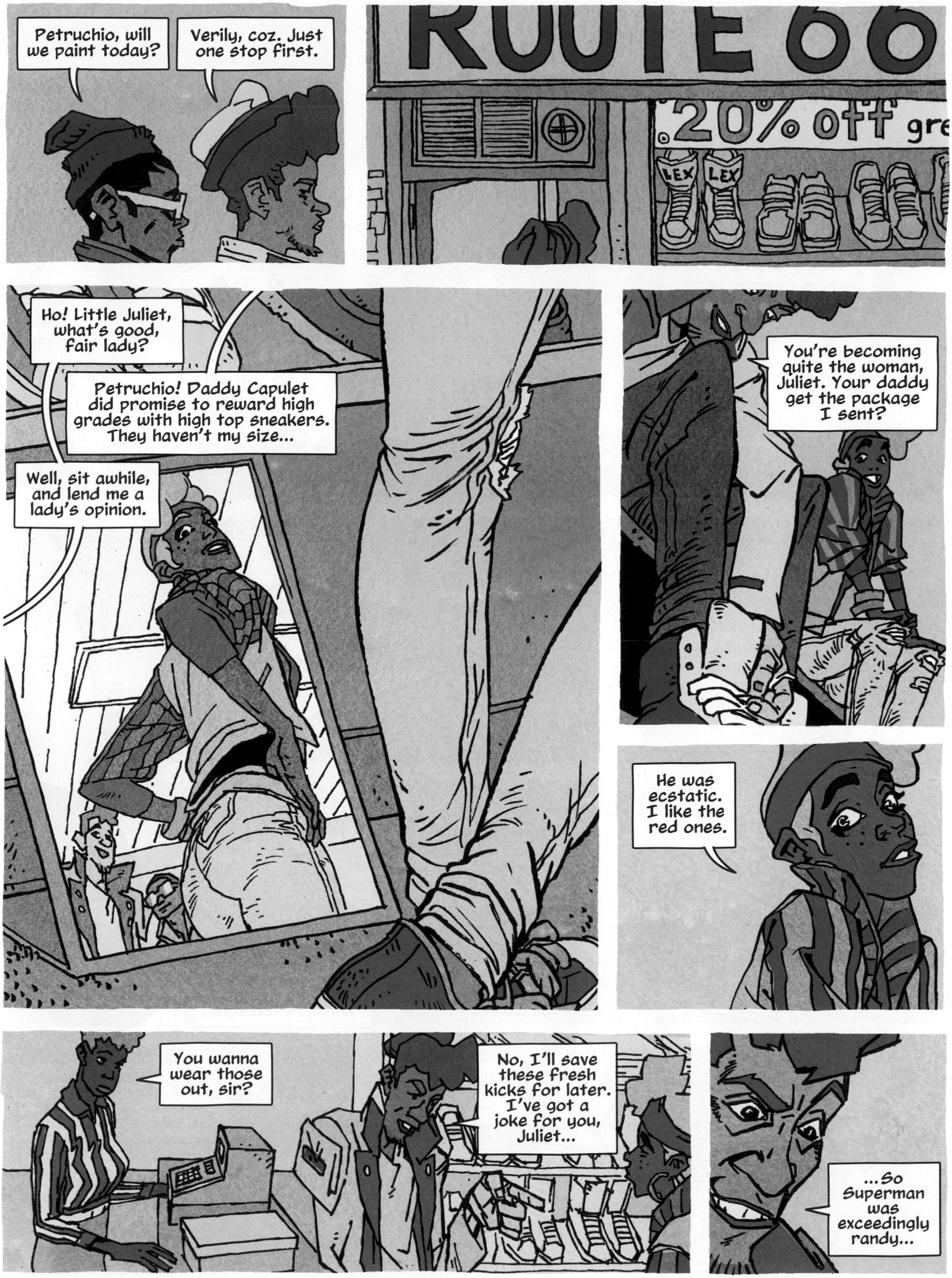
Petruchio, will we paint today?
Verily, coz. Just one stop first.
ROUTE 66
20% off gre
LEX LEX
Ho! Little Juliet, what's good, fair lady?
Petruchio! Daddy Capulet did promise to reward high grades with high top sneakers. They haven't my size...
Well, sit awhile, and lend me a lady's opinion.
You're becoming quite the woman, Juliet. Your daddy get the package I sent?
He was ecstatic. I like the red ones.
You wanna wear those out, sir?
No, I'll save these fresh kicks for later. I've got a joke for you, Juliet...
...So Superman was exceedingly randy...

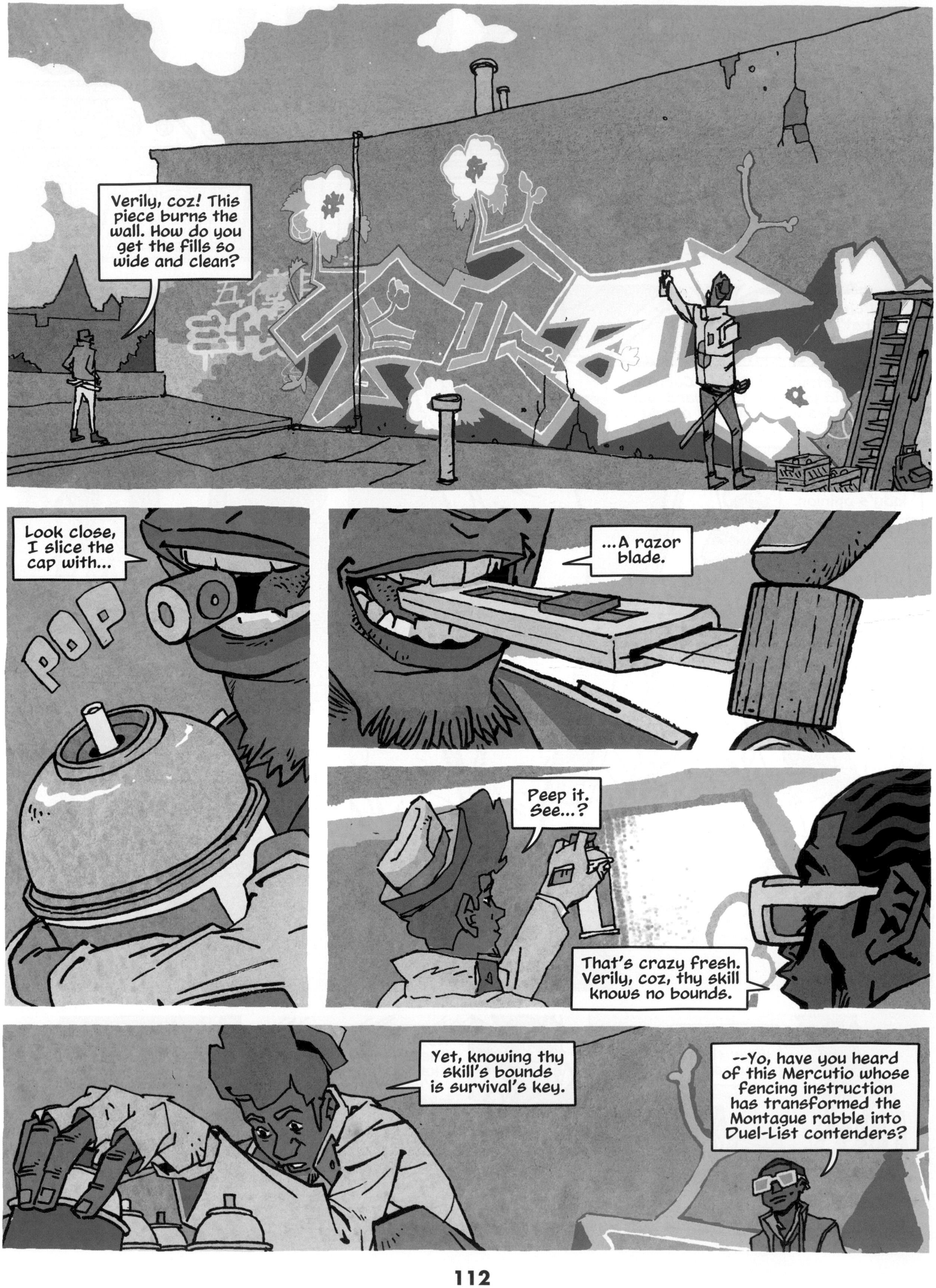

Verily, coz! This piece burns the wall. How do you get the fills so wide and clean?
Look close, I slice the cap with...
POP
...A razor blade.
Peep it. See...?
That's crazy fresh. Verily, coz, thy skill knows no bounds.
Yet, knowing thy skill's bounds is survival's key.
--Yo, have you heard of this Mercutio whose fencing instruction has transformed the Montague rabble into Duel-List contenders?

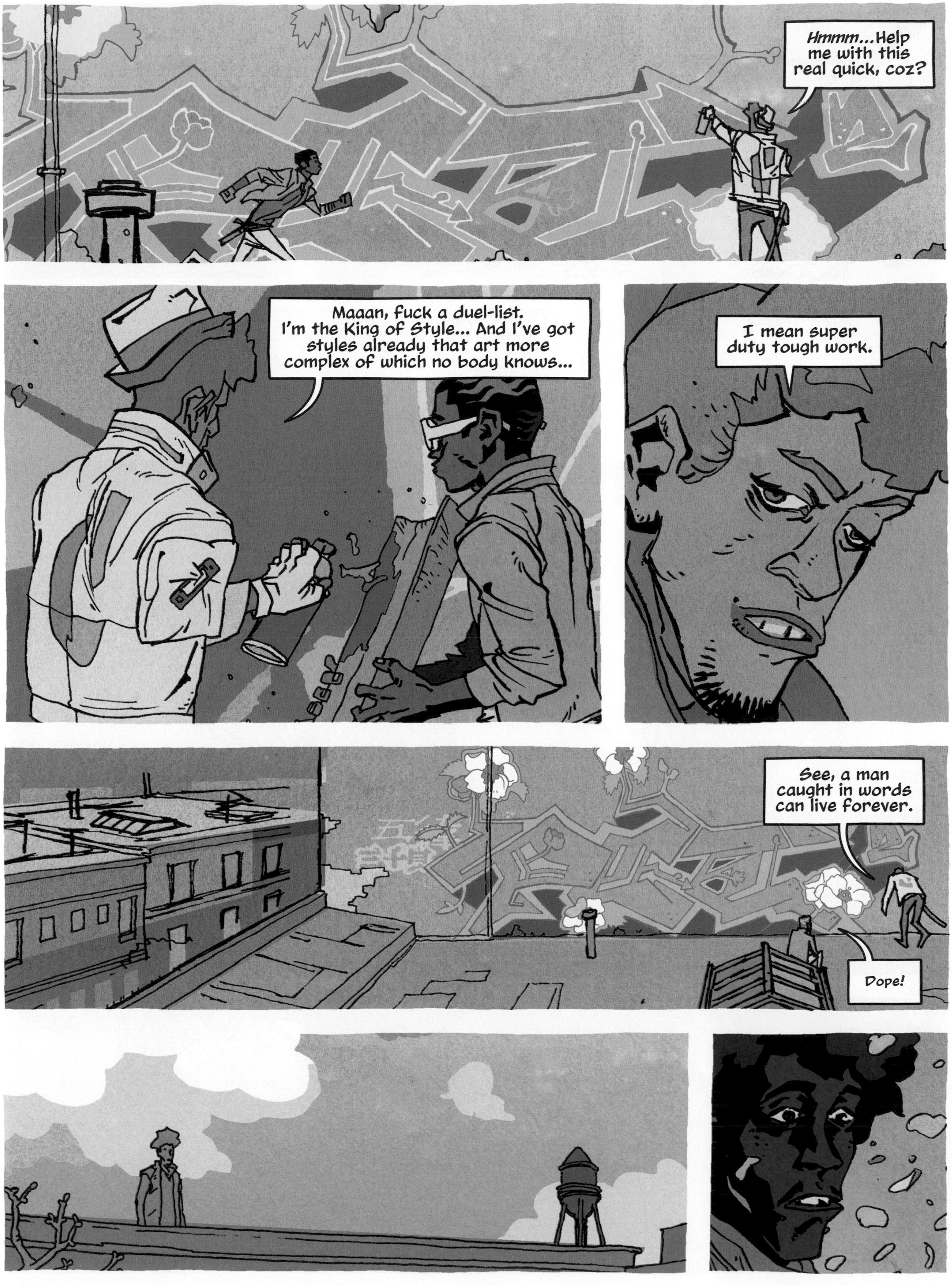
Hmmm...Help me with this real quick, coz?
Maaan, fuck a duel-list. I'm the King of Style... And I've got styles already that art more complex of which no body knows...
I mean super duty tough work.
See, a man caught in words can live forever.
Dope!

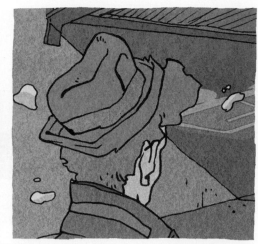
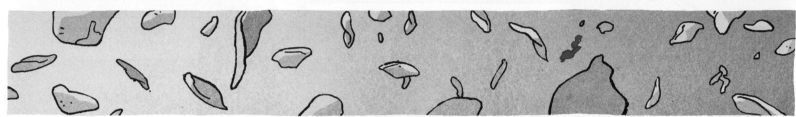

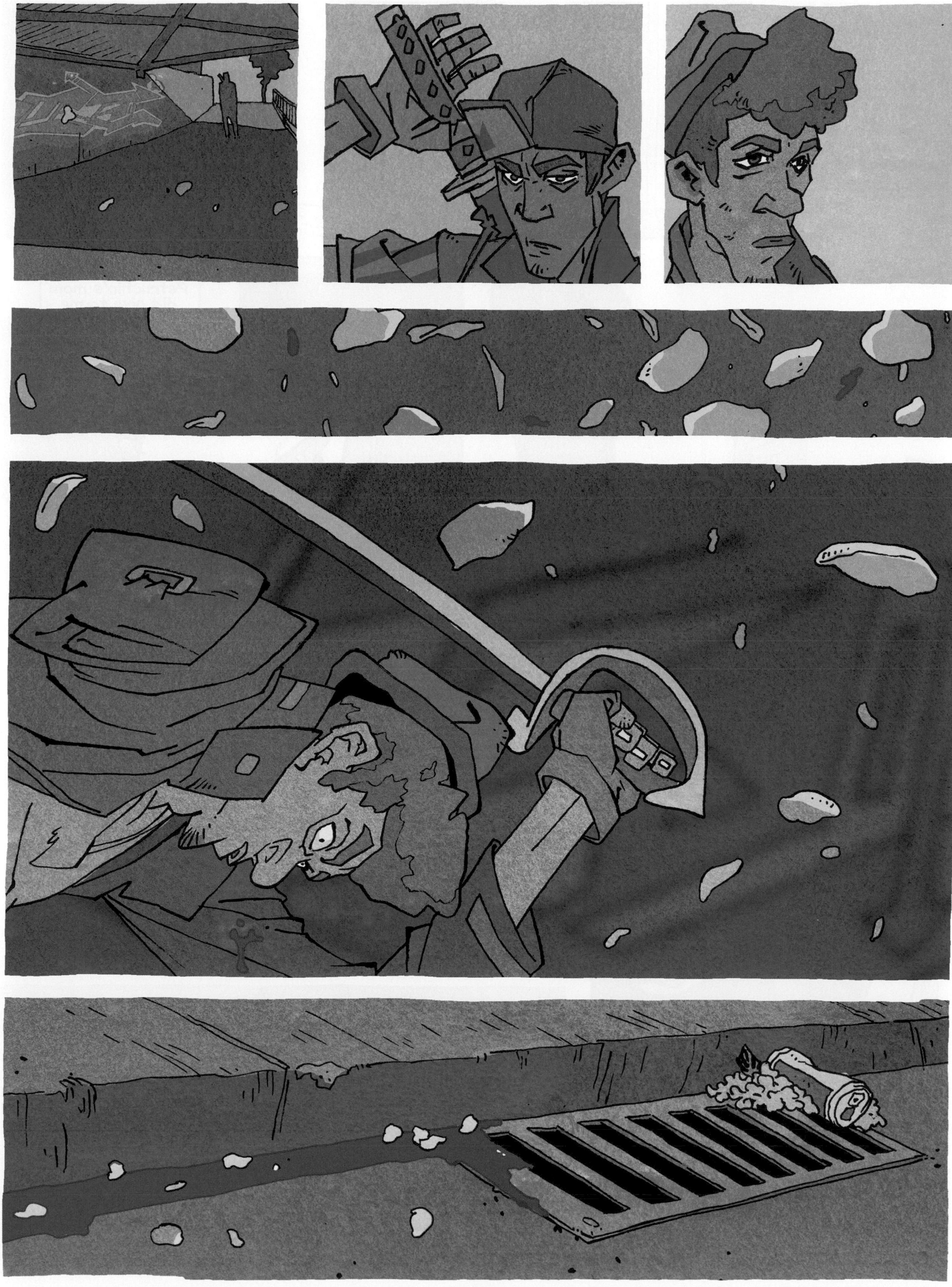

Tybalt.

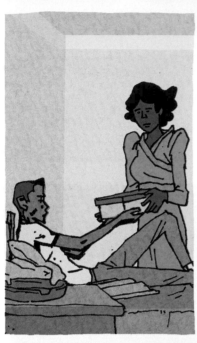

Petruchio's mom did give to me to give to you.

I'm working late, till ten or eleven.

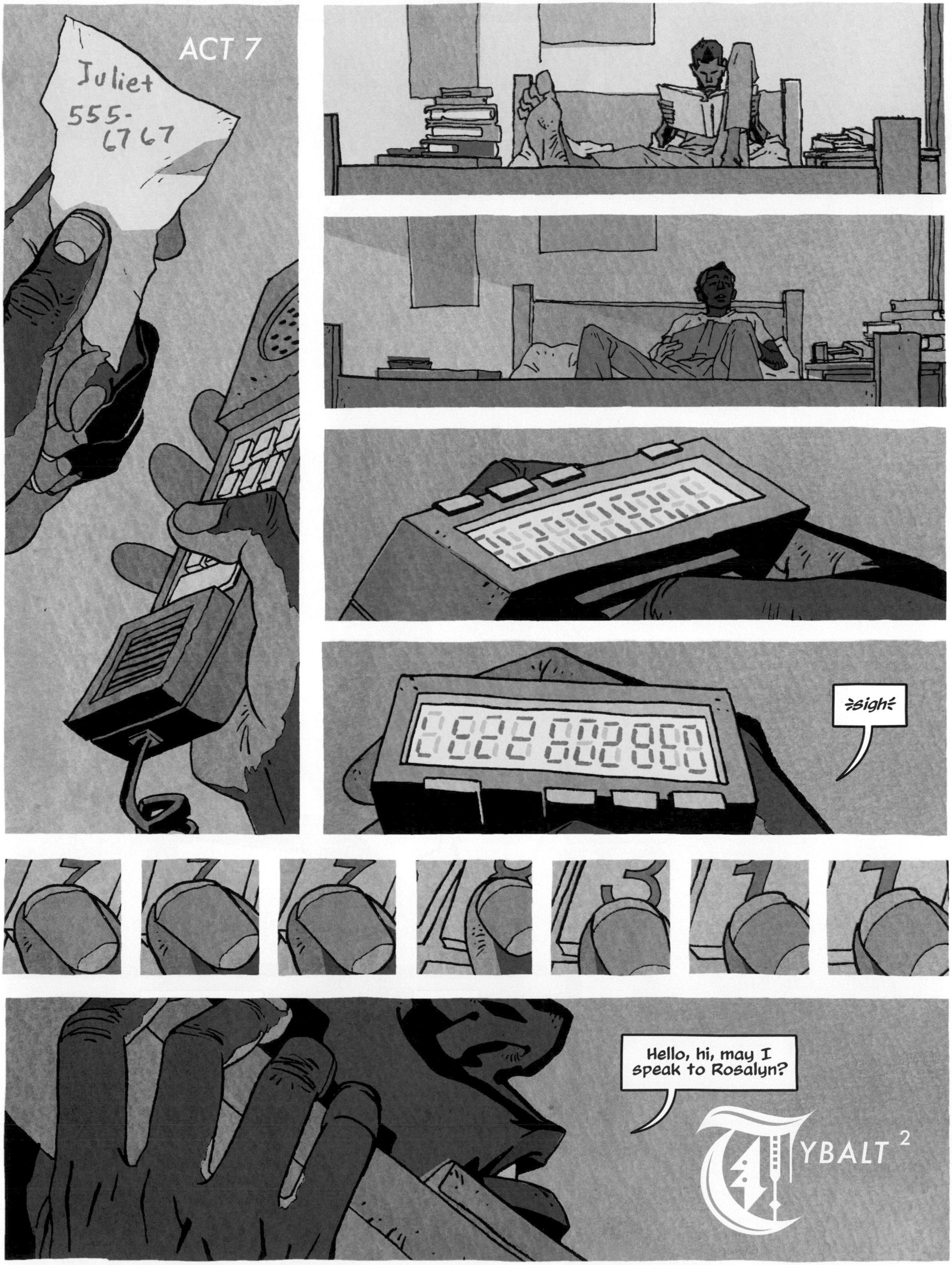
ACT 7
Juliet
555-
6767
sigh
Hello, hi, may I speak to Rosalyn?
TYBALT 2

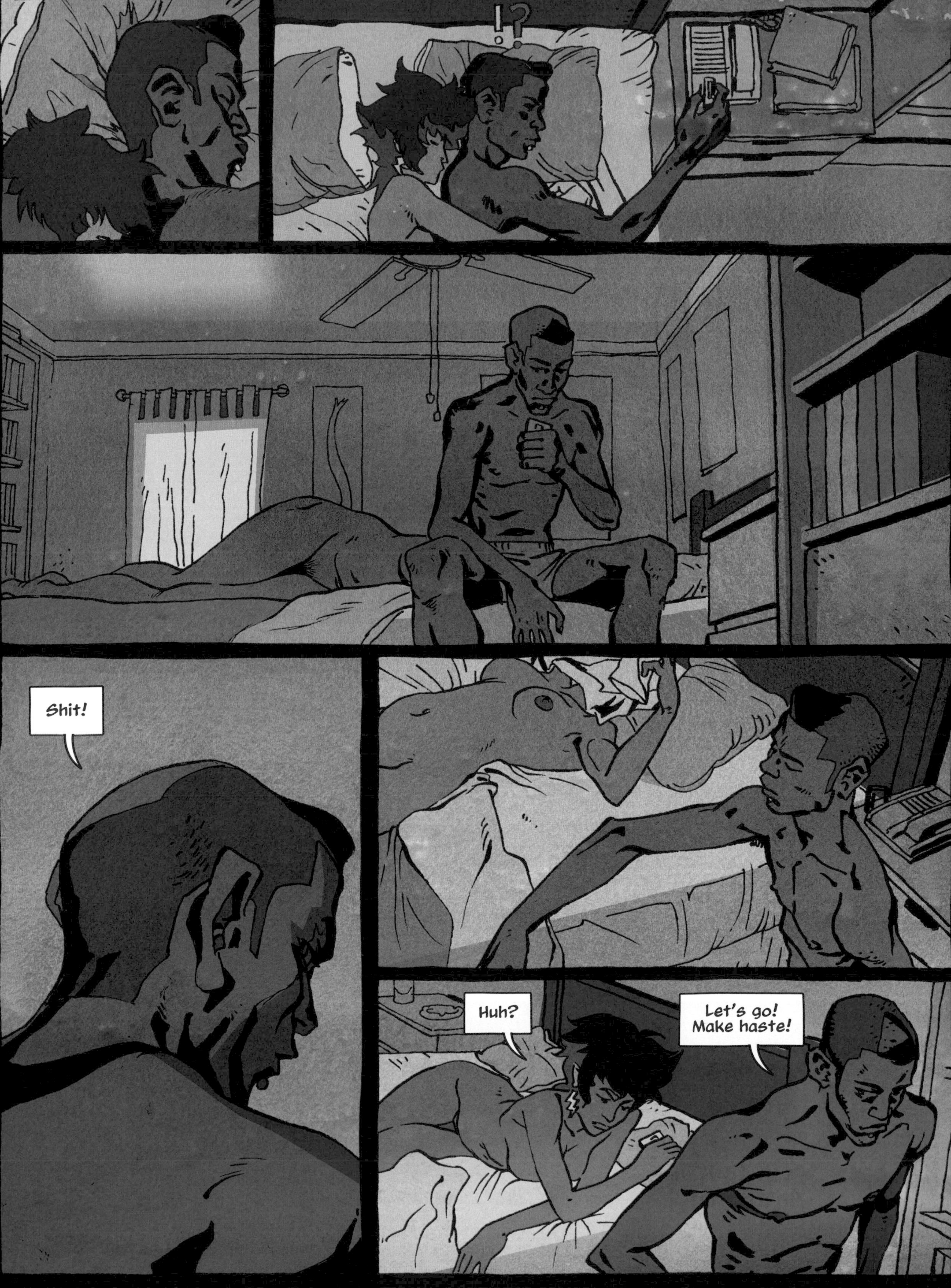
!?
Shit!
Huh?
Let's go!
Make haste!

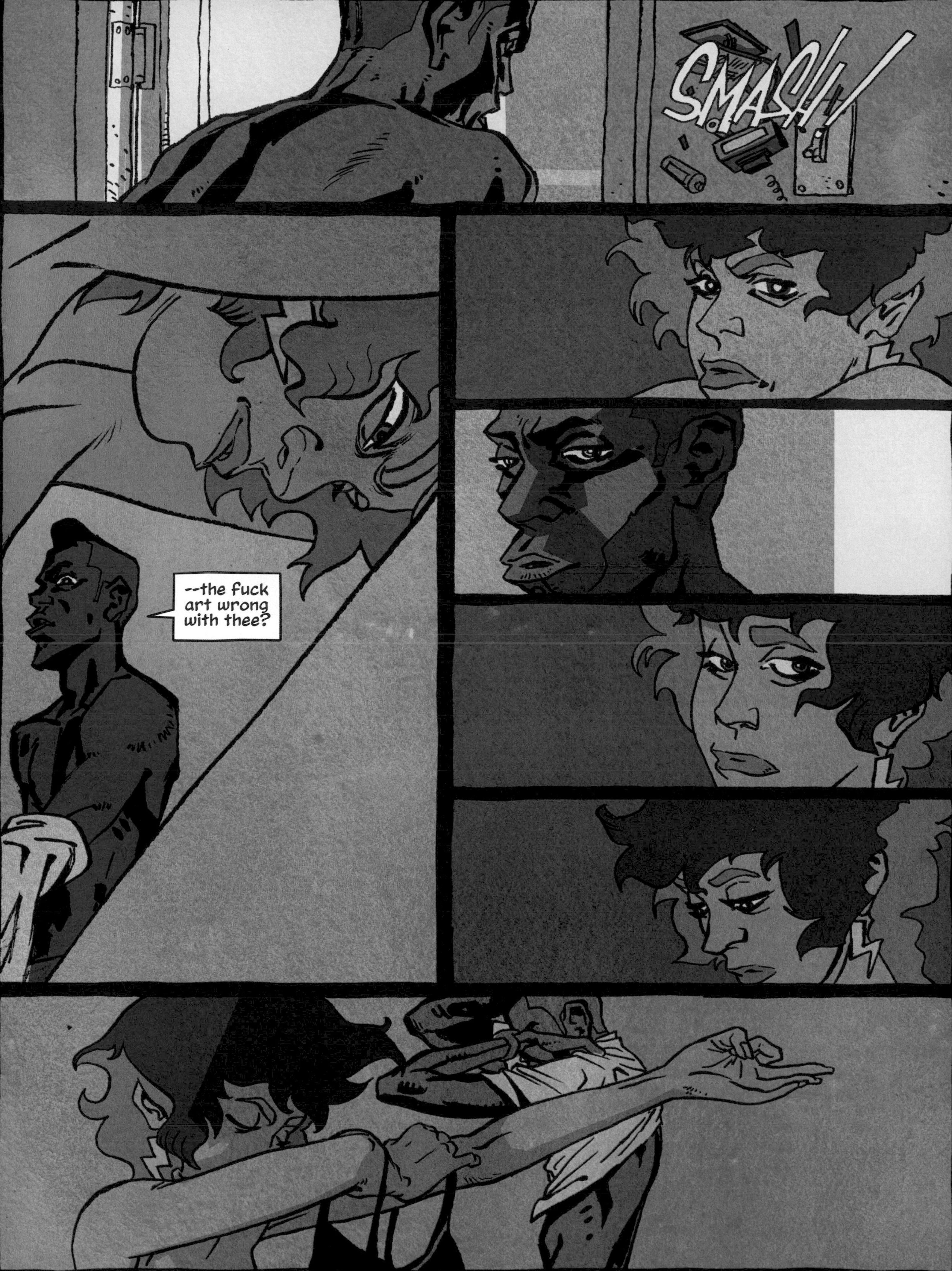
SMASH!
--the fuck art wrong with thee?

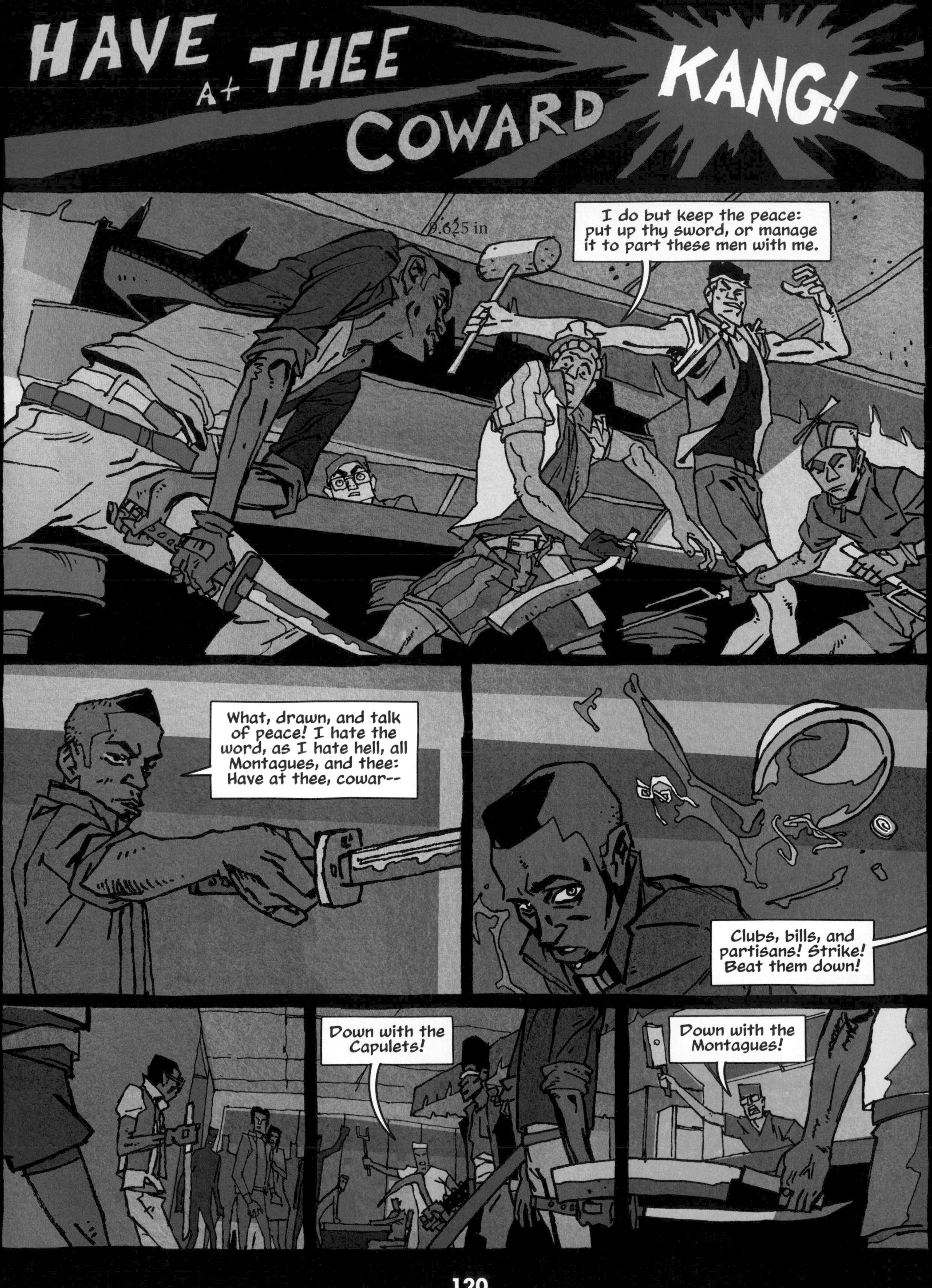
HAVE AT THEE COWARD
KANG!
I do but keep the peace: put up thy sword, or manage it to part these men with me.
What, drawn, and talk of peace! I hate the word, as I hate hell, all Montagues, and thee: Have at thee, cowar--
Clubs, bills, and partisans! Strike! Beat them down!
Down with the Capulets!
Down with the Montagues!

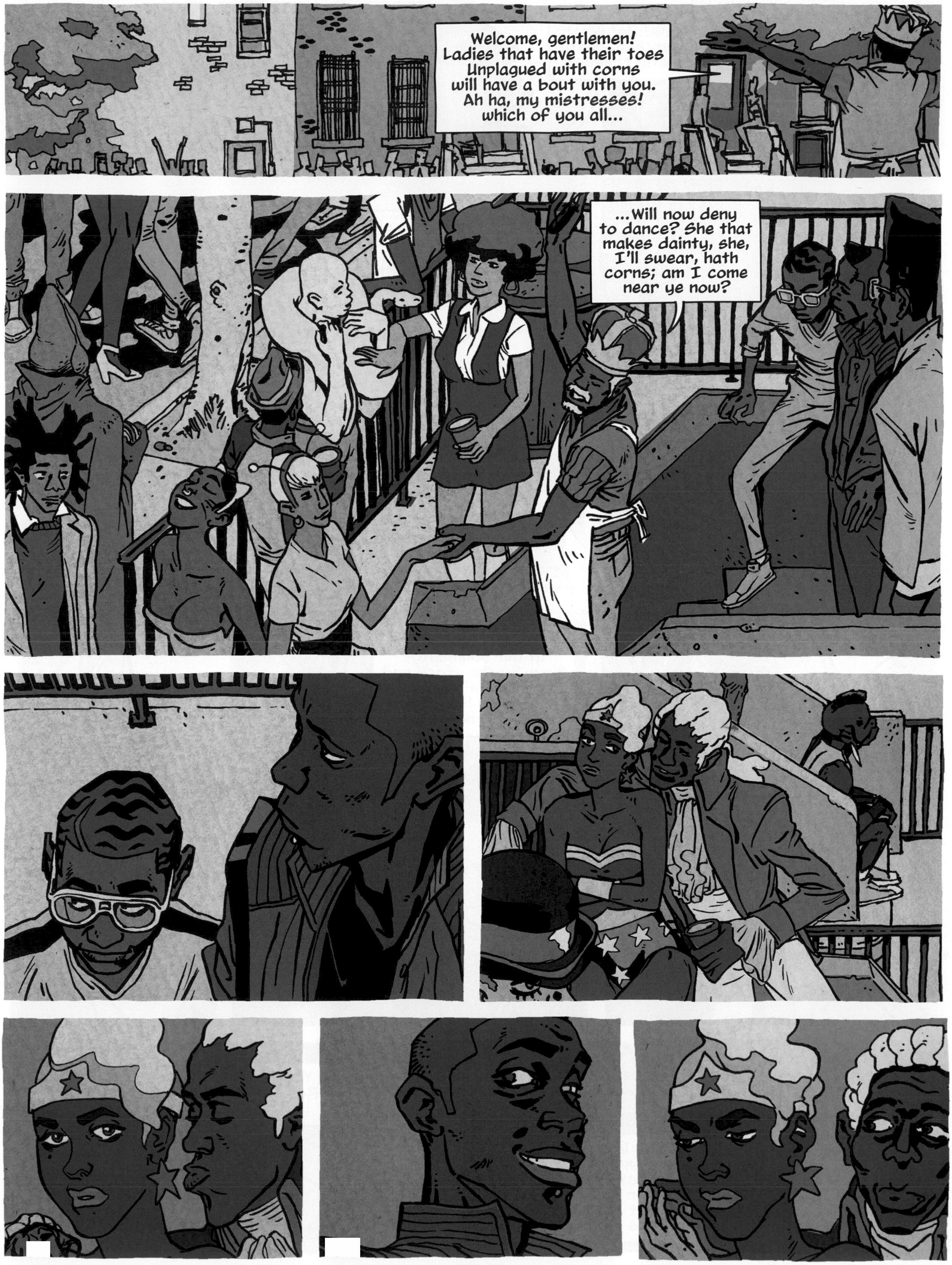
Welcome, gentlemen! Ladies that have their toes Unplagued with corns will have a bout with you. Ah ha, my mistresses! which of you all...
...Will now deny to dance? She that makes dainty, she, I'll swear, hath corns; am I come near ye now?

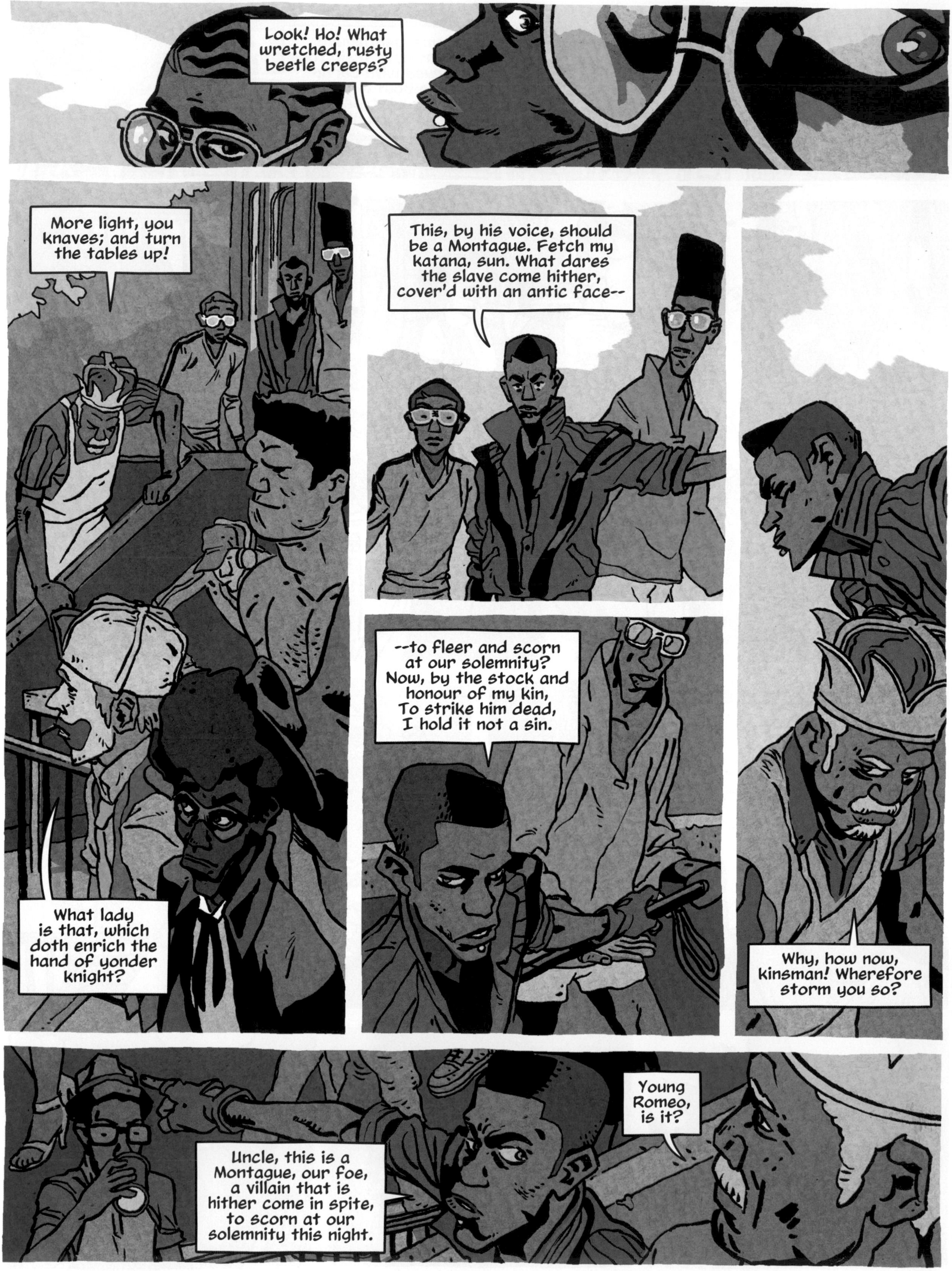

Look! Ho! What wretched, rusty beetle creeps?
More light, you knaves; and turn the tables up!
What lady is that, which doth enrich the hand of yonder knight?
This, by his voice, should be a Montague. Fetch my katana, sun. What dares the slave come hither, cover'd with an antic face--
--to fleer and scorn at our solemnity? Now, by the stock and honour of my kin, To strike him dead, I hold it not a sin.
Why, how now, kinsman! Wherefore storm you so?
Uncle, this is a Montague, our foe, a villain that is hither come in spite, to scorn at our solemnity this night.
Young Romeo, is it?

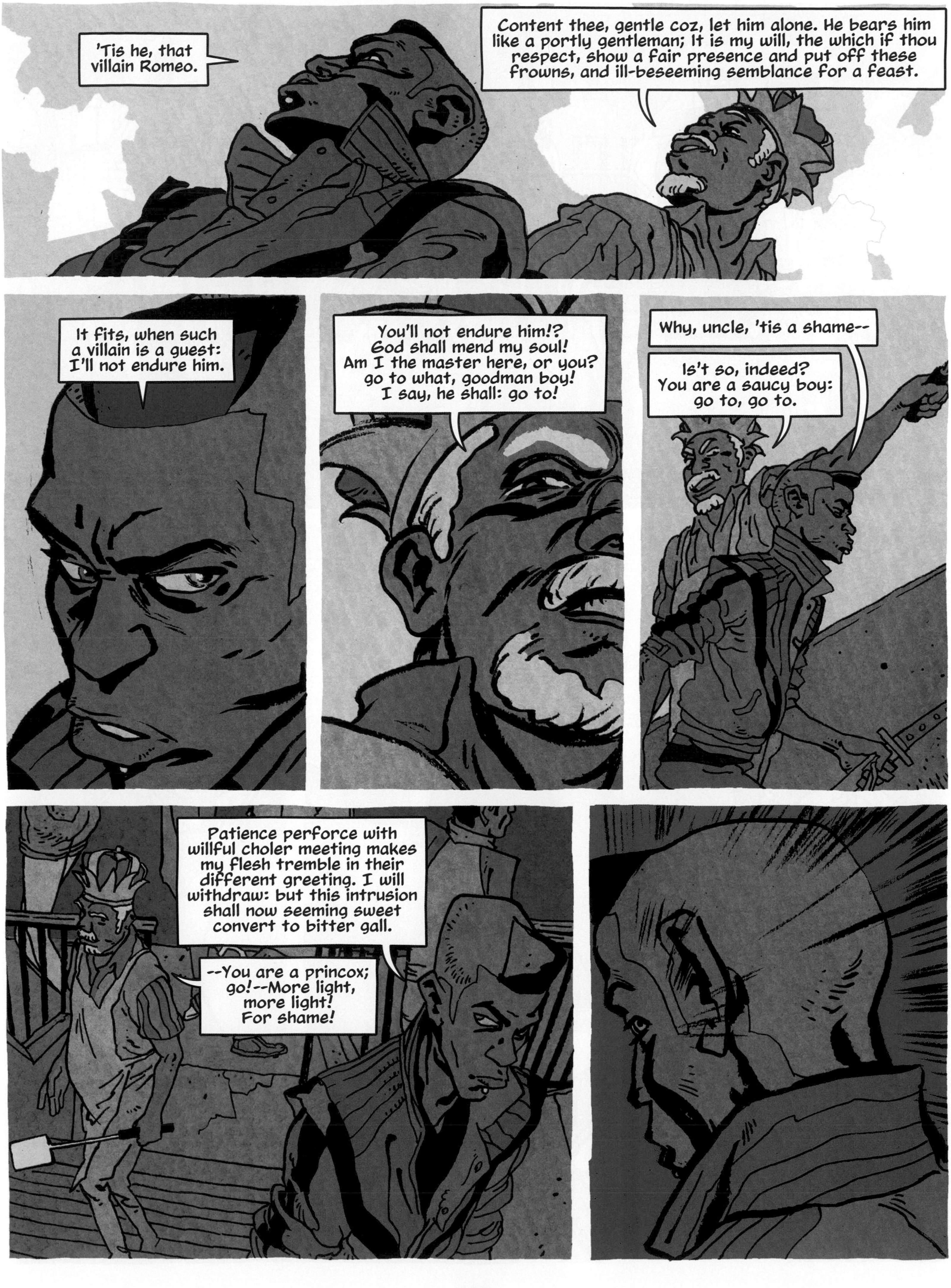
'Tis he, that villain Romeo.
Content thee, gentle coz, let him alone. He bears him like a portly gentleman; It is my will, the which if thou respect, show a fair presence and put off these frowns, and ill-beseeming semblance for a feast.
It fits, when such a villain is a guest: I'll not endure him.
You'll not endure him!? God shall mend my soul! Am I the master here, or you? go to what, goodman boy! I say, he shall: go to!
Why, uncle, 'tis a shame--
Is't so, indeed? You are a saucy boy: go to, go to.
Patience perforce with willful choler meeting makes my flesh tremble in their different greeting. I will withdraw: but this intrusion shall now seeming sweet convert to bitter gall.
--You are a princox; go!--More light, more light! For shame!

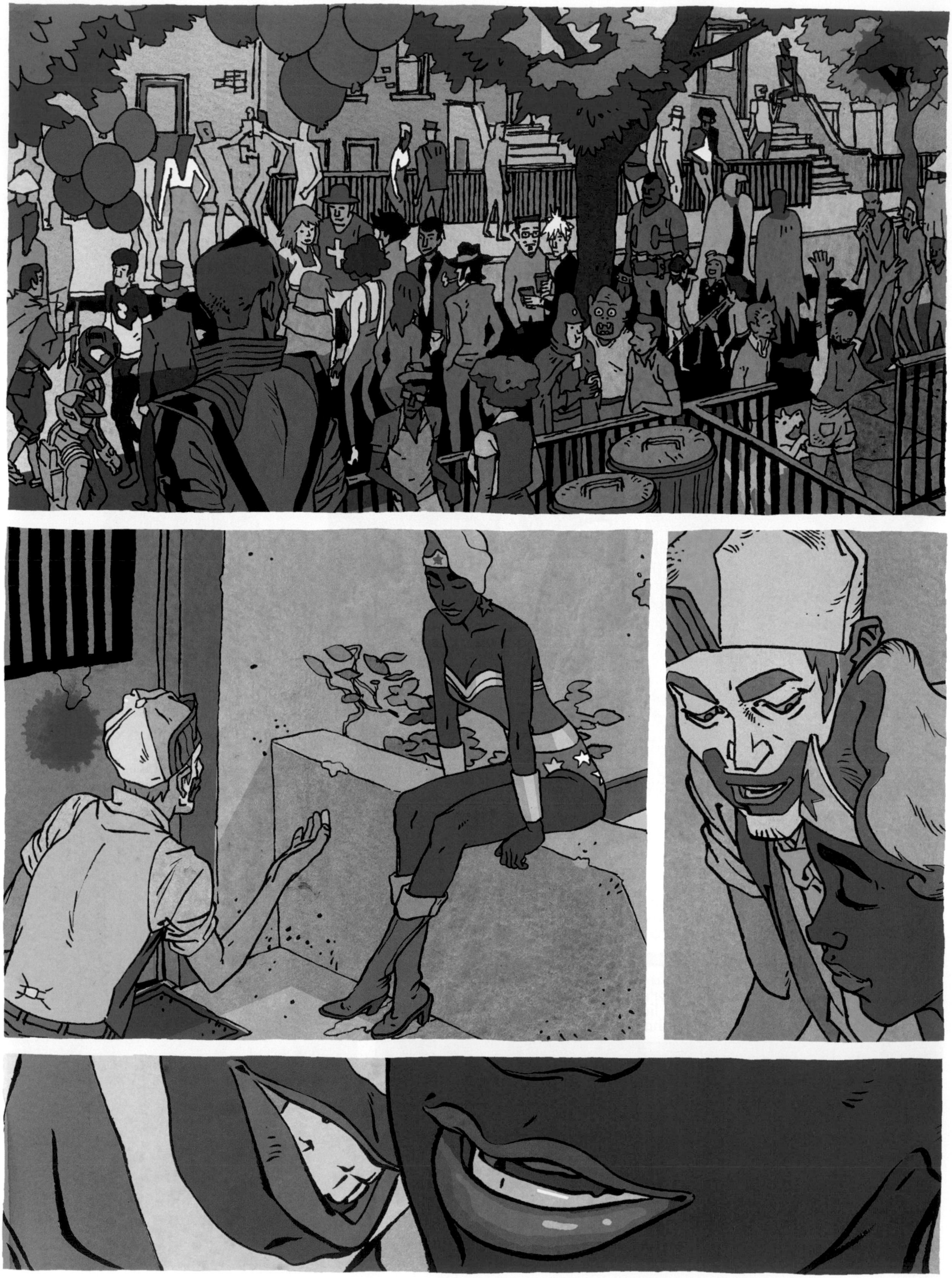

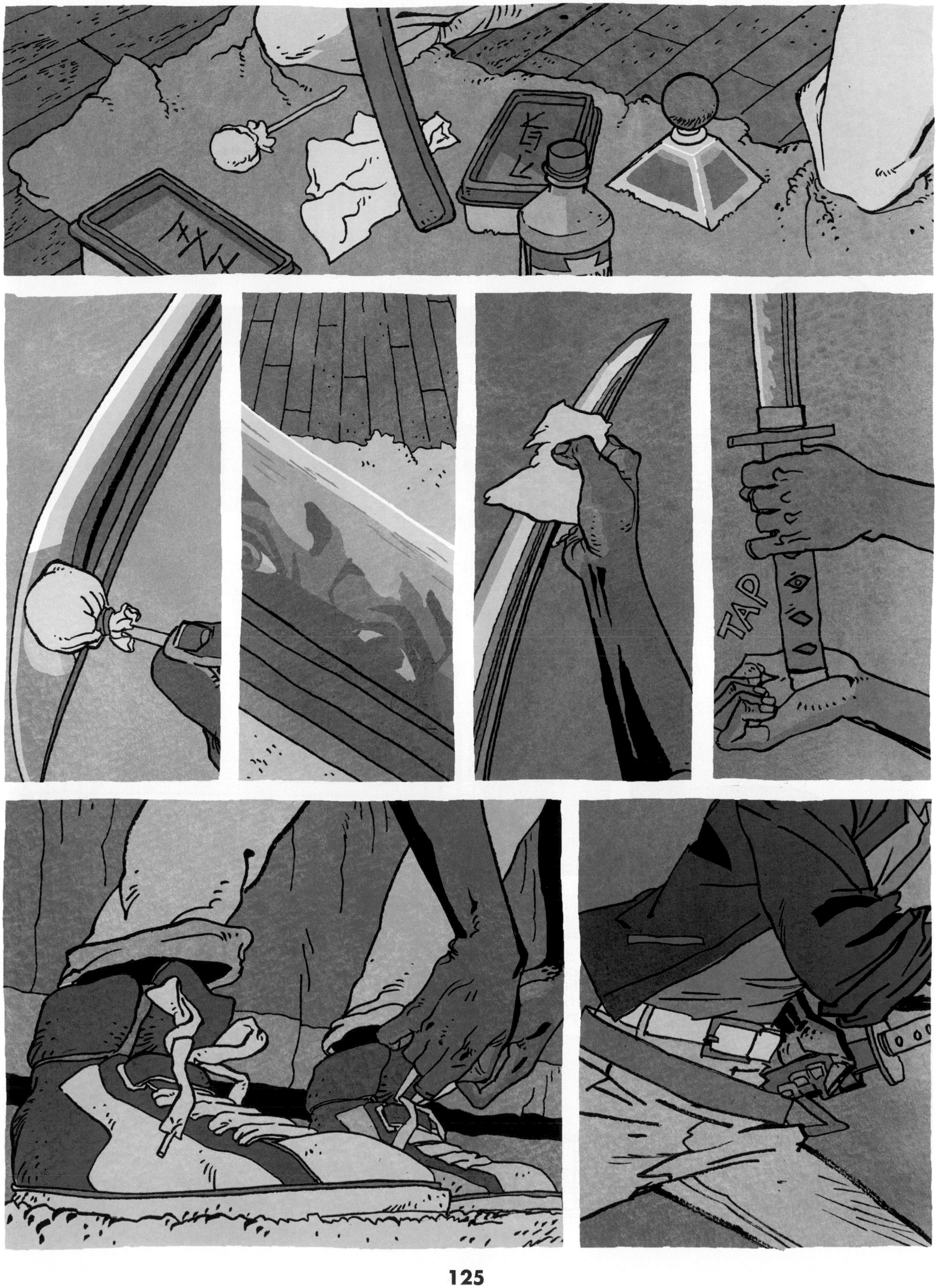
TAP

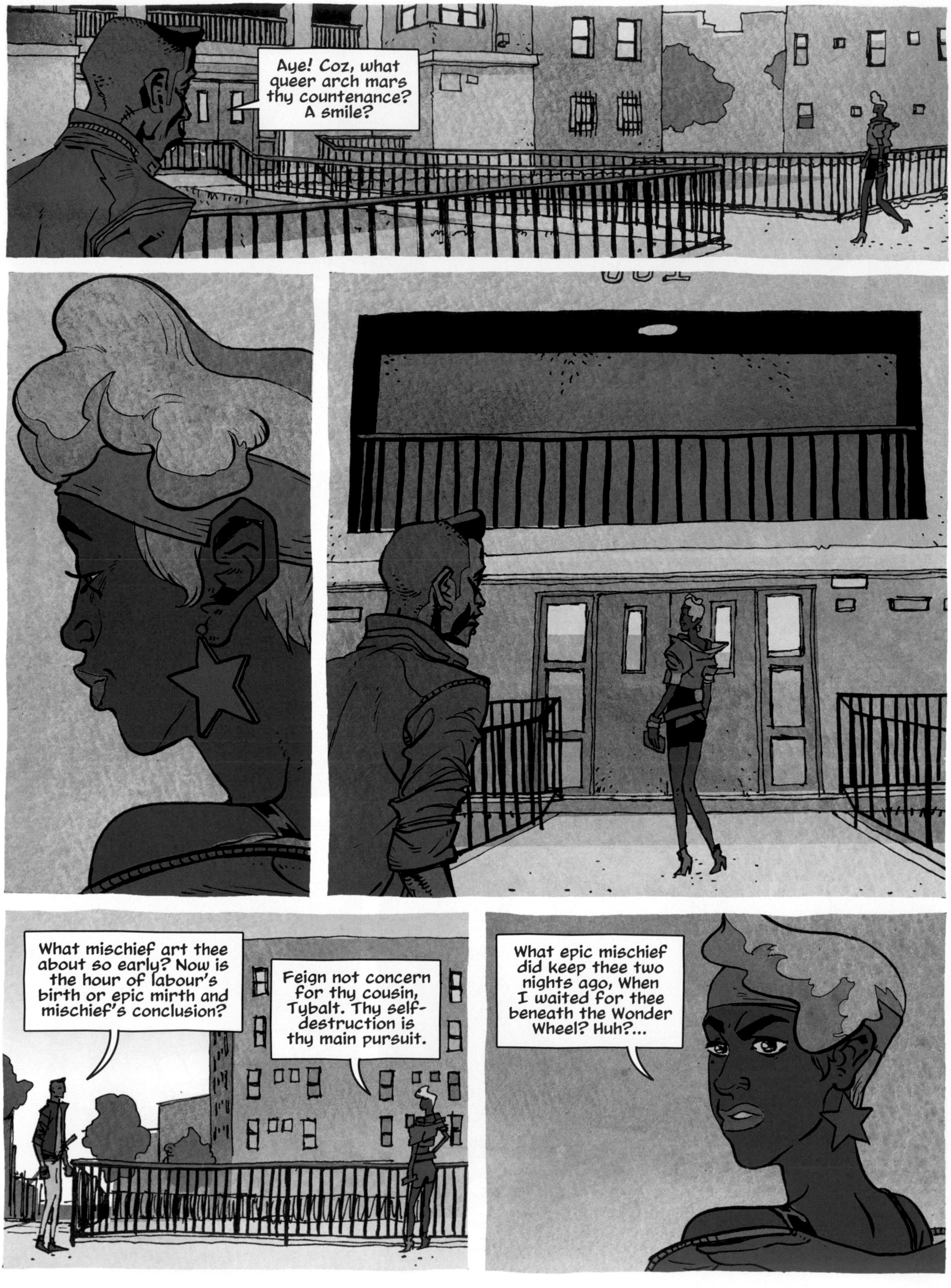
Aye! Coz, what queer arch mars thy countenance? A smile?
What mischief art thee about so early? Now is the hour of labour's birth or epic mirth and mischief's conclusion?
Feign not concern for thy cousin, Tybalt. Thy self-destruction is thy main pursuit.
What epic mischief did keep thee two nights ago, When I waited for thee beneath the Wonder Wheel? Huh?...

Romeo!

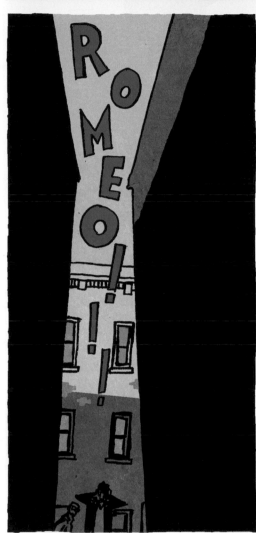

R
O
M
E
O
!

Gentlemen, good den: a word with one of you.

And but one word with one of us? Couple it with something--

--Make it a word and a blow.

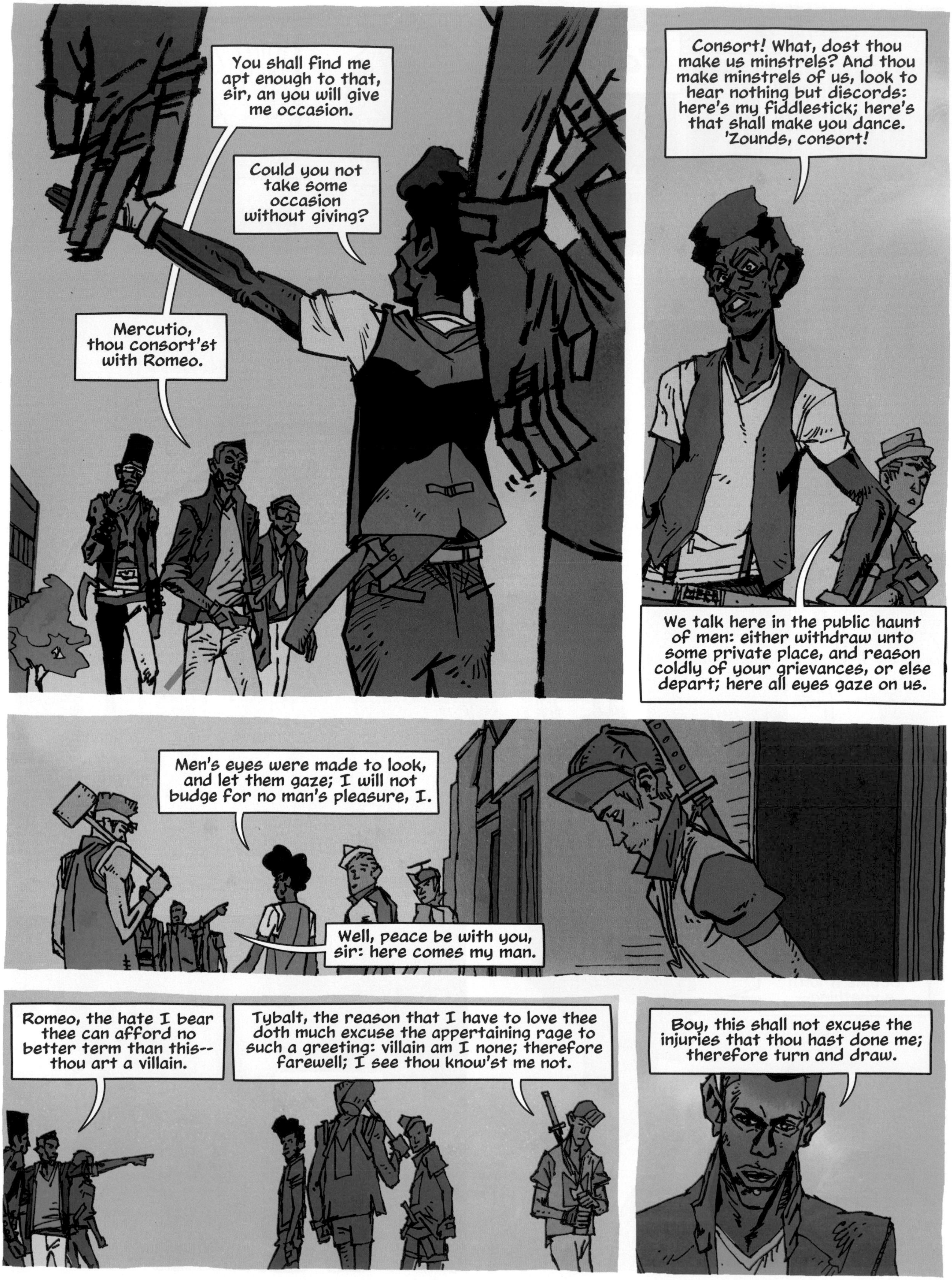

Mercutio, thou consort'st with Romeo.
Consort! What, dost thou make us minstrels? And thou make minstrels of us, look to hear nothing but discords: here's my fiddlestick; here's that shall make you dance. 'Zounds, consort!
You shall find me apt enough to that, sir, an you will give me occasion.
Could you not take some occasion without giving?
We talk here in the public haunt of men: either withdraw unto some private place, and reason coldly of your grievances, or else depart; here all eyes gaze on us.
Men's eyes were made to look, and let them gaze; I will not budge for no man's pleasure, I.
Well, peace be with you, sir: here comes my man.
Romeo, the hate I bear thee can afford no better term than this--thou art a villain.
Tybalt, the reason that I have to love thee doth much excuse the appertaining rage to such a greeting: villain am I none; therefore farewell; I see thou know'st me not.
Boy, this shall not excuse the injuries that thou hast done me; therefore turn and draw.

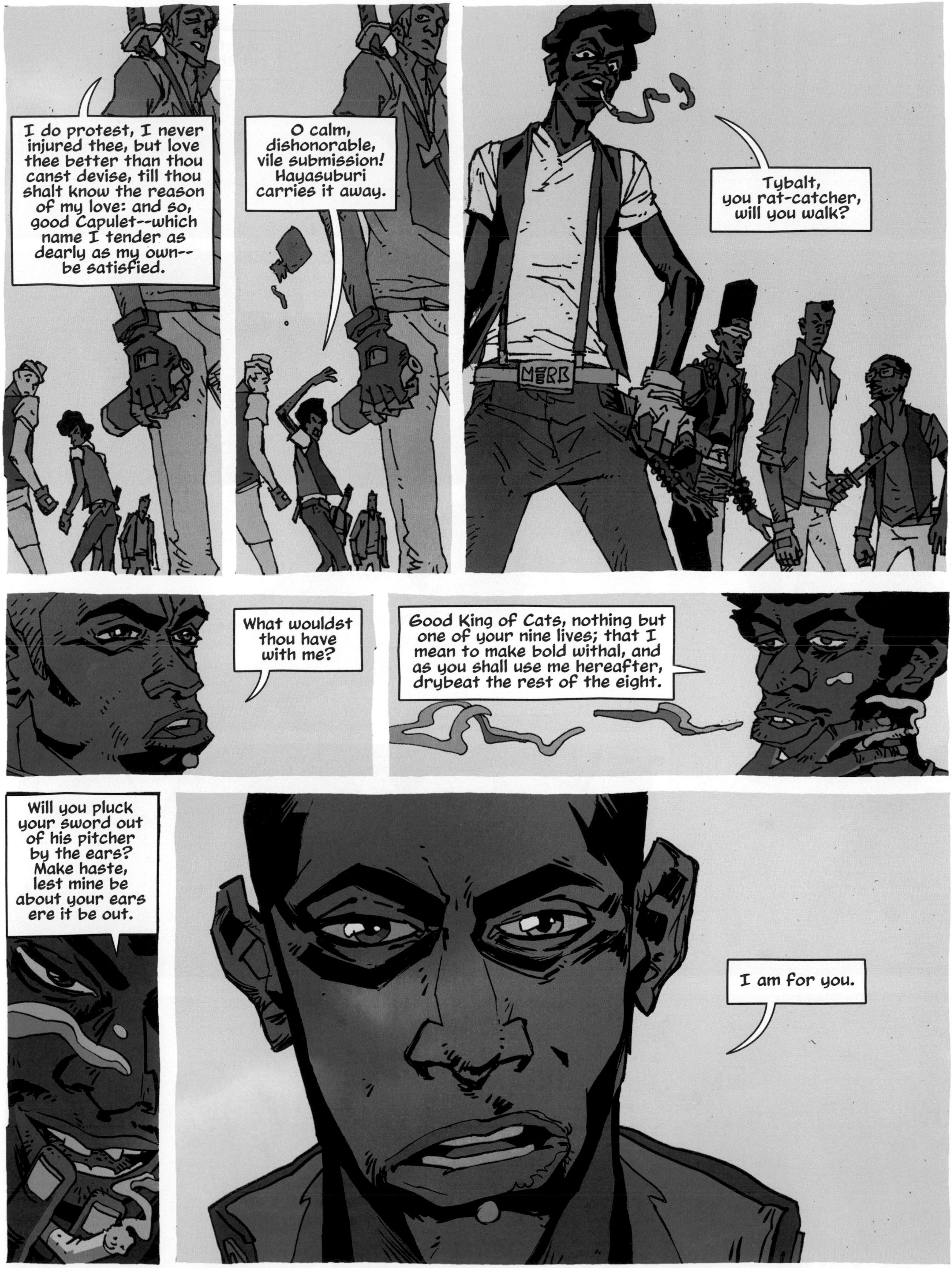
I do protest, I never injured thee, but love thee better than thou canst devise, till thou shalt know the reason of my love: and so, good Capulet--which name I tender as dearly as my own--be satisfied.
O calm, dishonorable, vile submission! Hayasuburi carries it away.
Tybalt, you rat-catcher, will you walk?
What wouldst thou have with me?
Good King of Cats, nothing but one of your nine lives; that I mean to make bold withal, and as you shall use me hereafter, drybeat the rest of the eight.
Will you pluck your sword out of his pitcher by the ears? Make haste, lest mine be about your ears ere it be out.
I am for you.

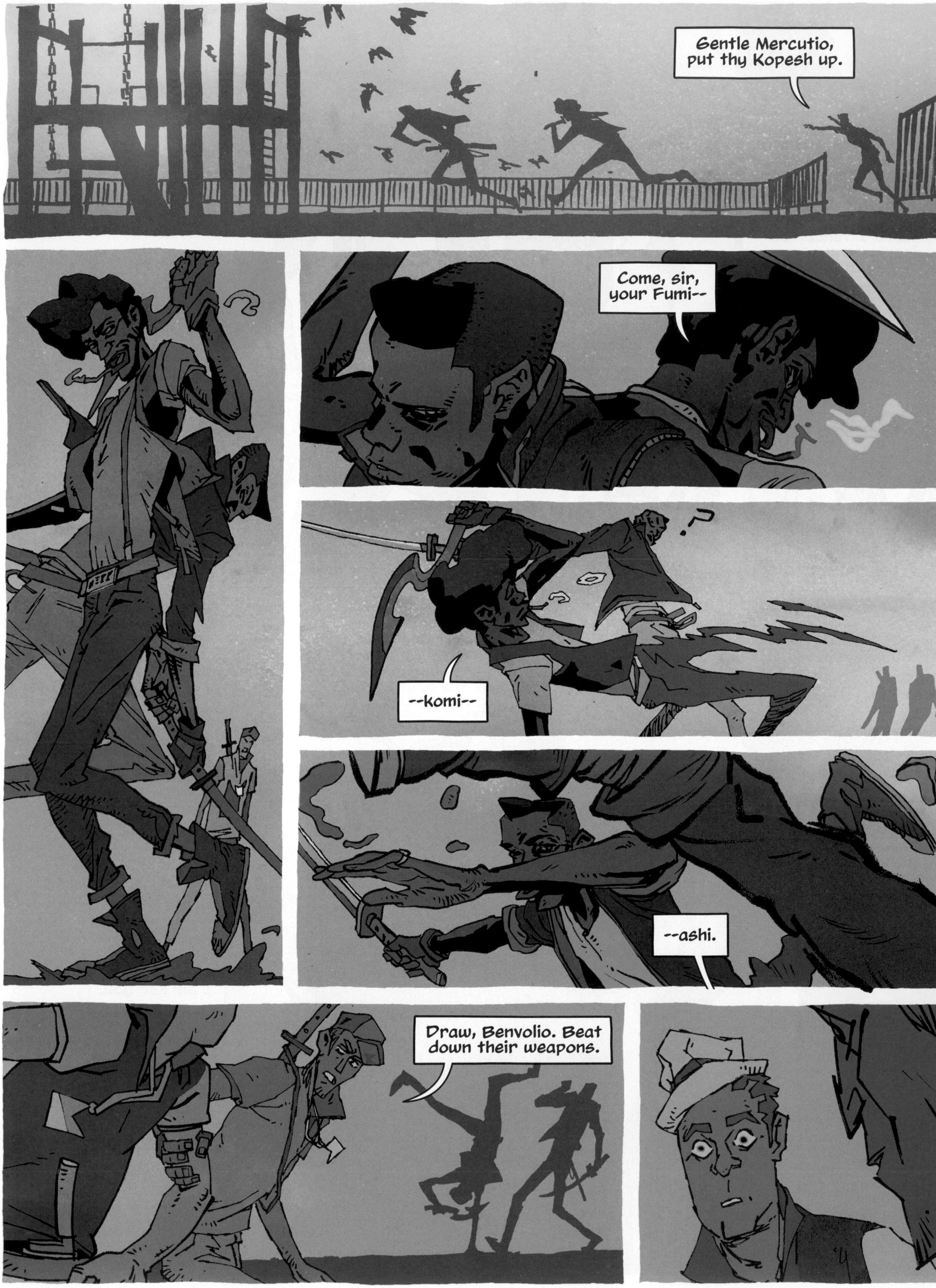
Gentle Mercutio, put thy Kopesh up.
Come, sir, your Fumi--
--komi--
--ashi.
Draw, Benvolio. Beat down their weapons.

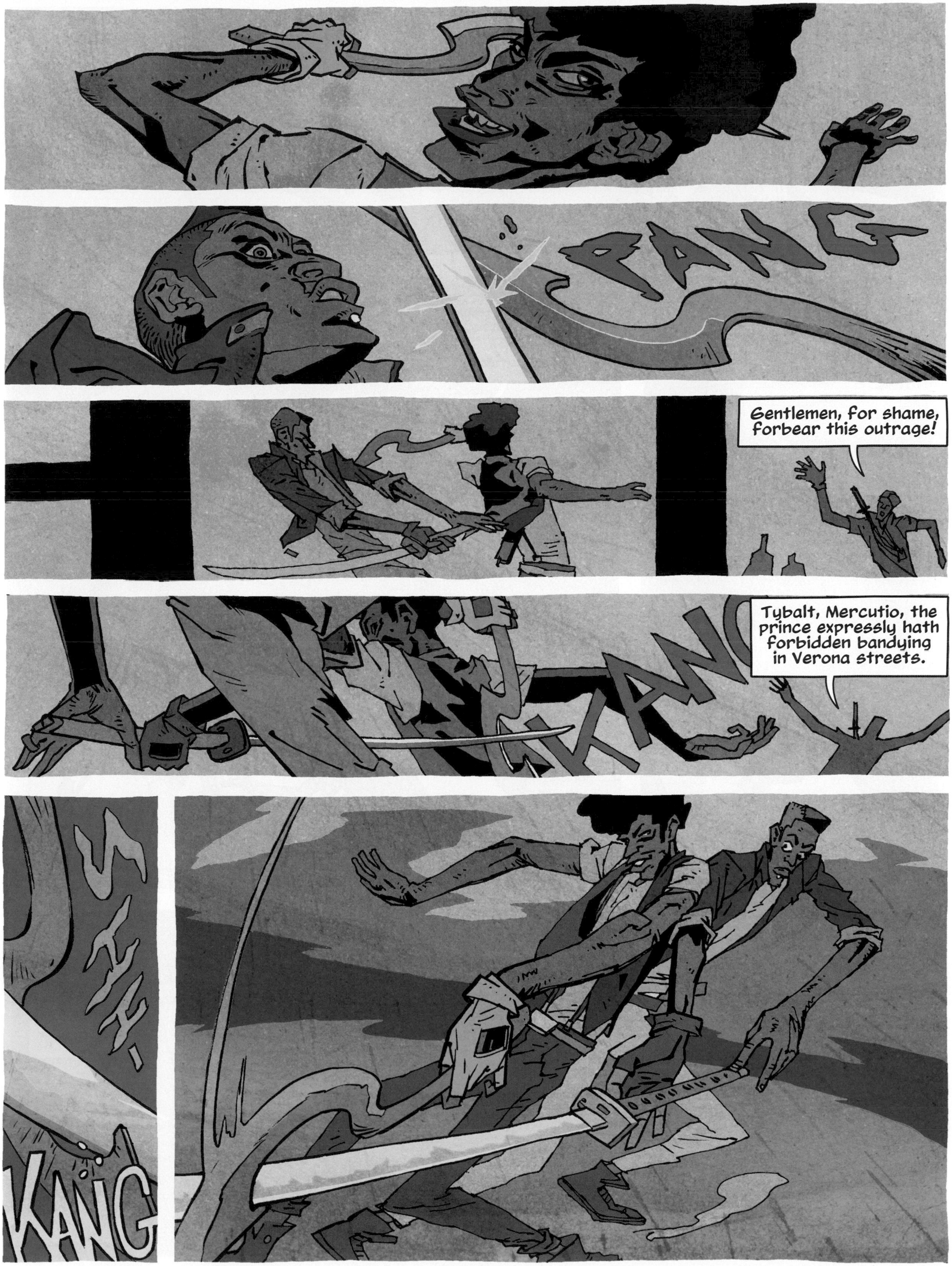
PANG
Gentlemen, for shame, forbear this outrage!
Tybalt, Mercutio, the prince expressly hath forbidden bandying in Verona streets.
KANG
SHH-
KANG

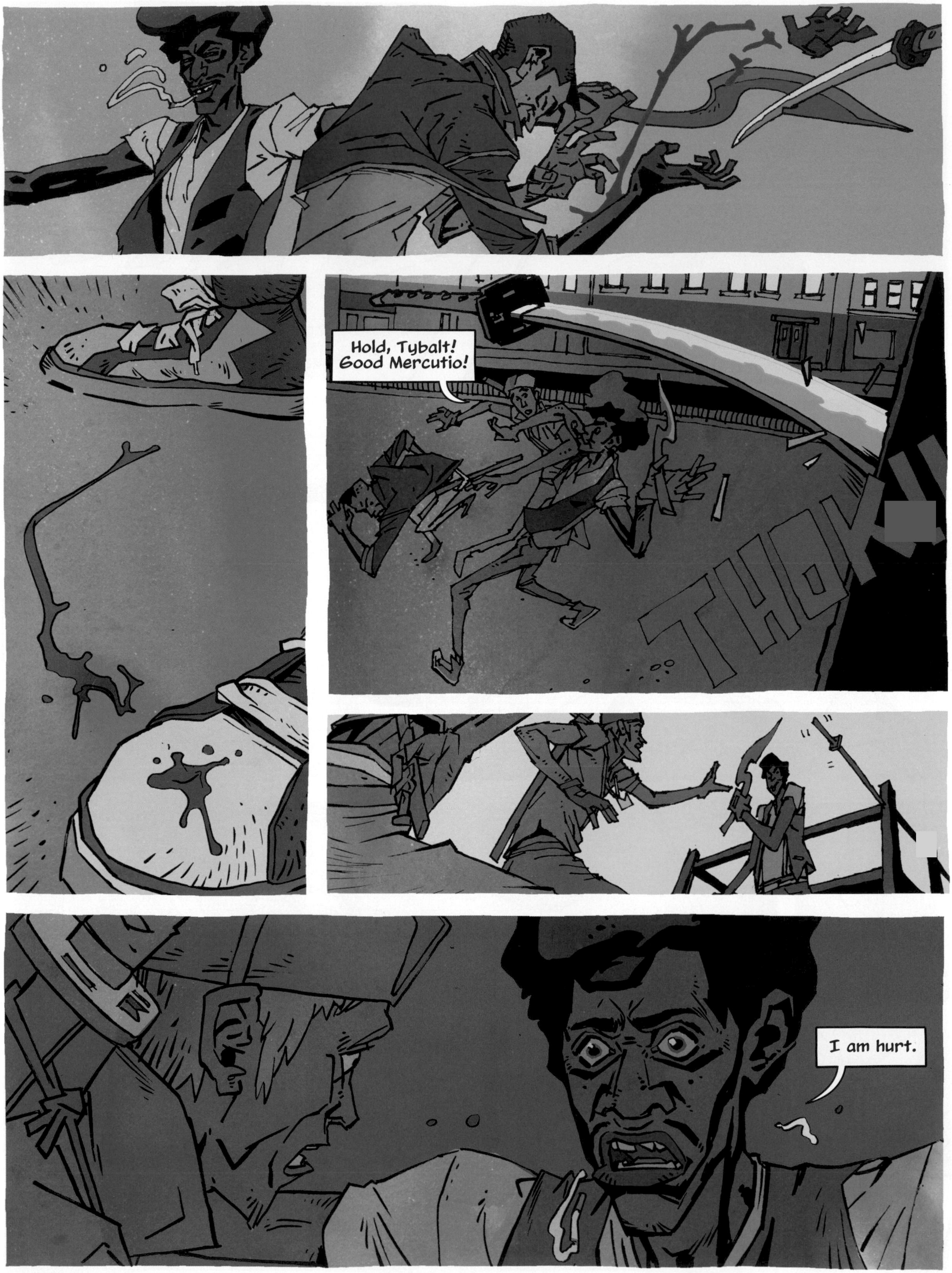
Hold, Tybalt! Good Mercutio!
THOK
I am hurt.

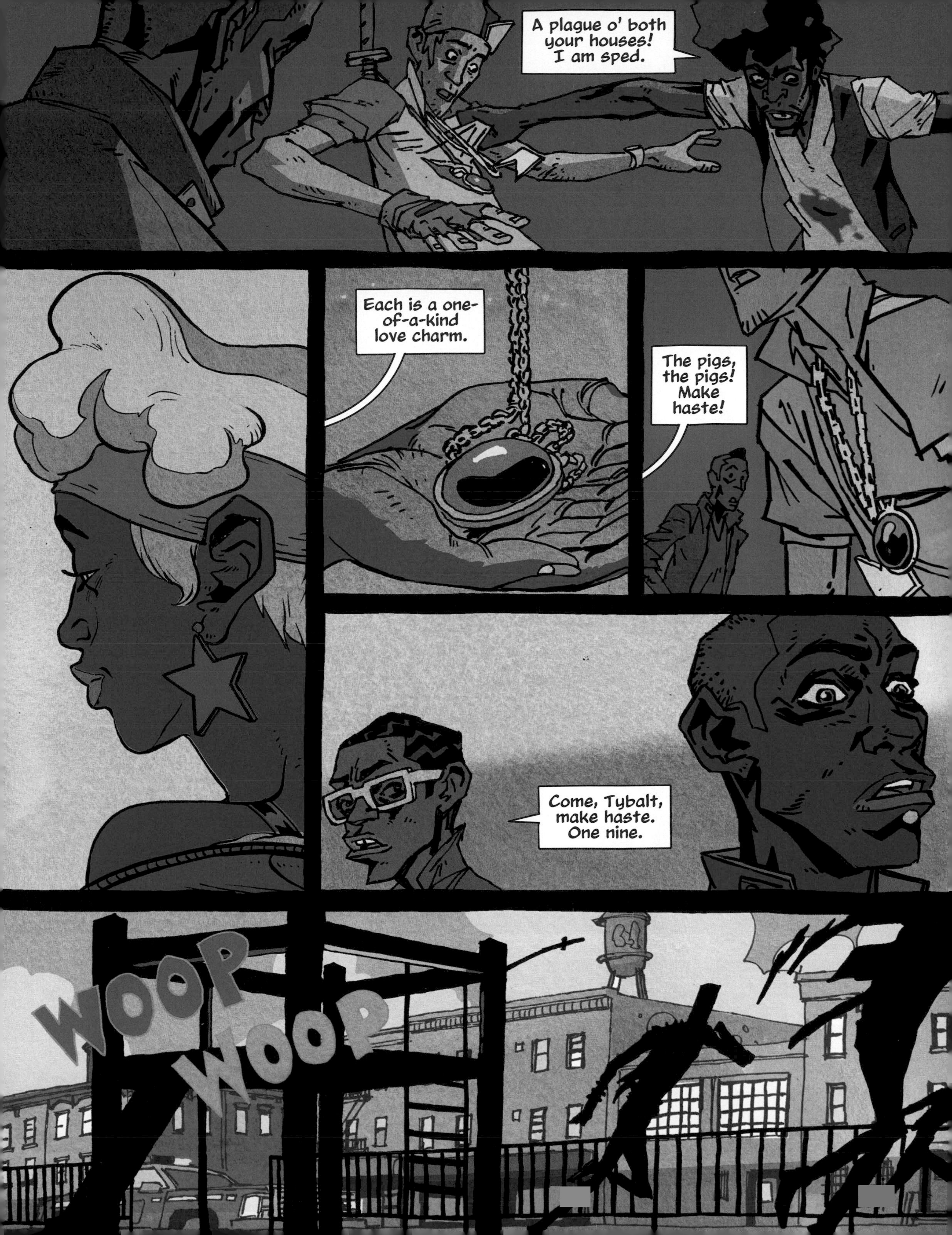
A plague o' both your houses! I am sped.
Each is a one-of-a-kind love charm.
The pigs, the pigs! Make haste!
Come, Tybalt, make haste. One nine.
WOOP WOOP

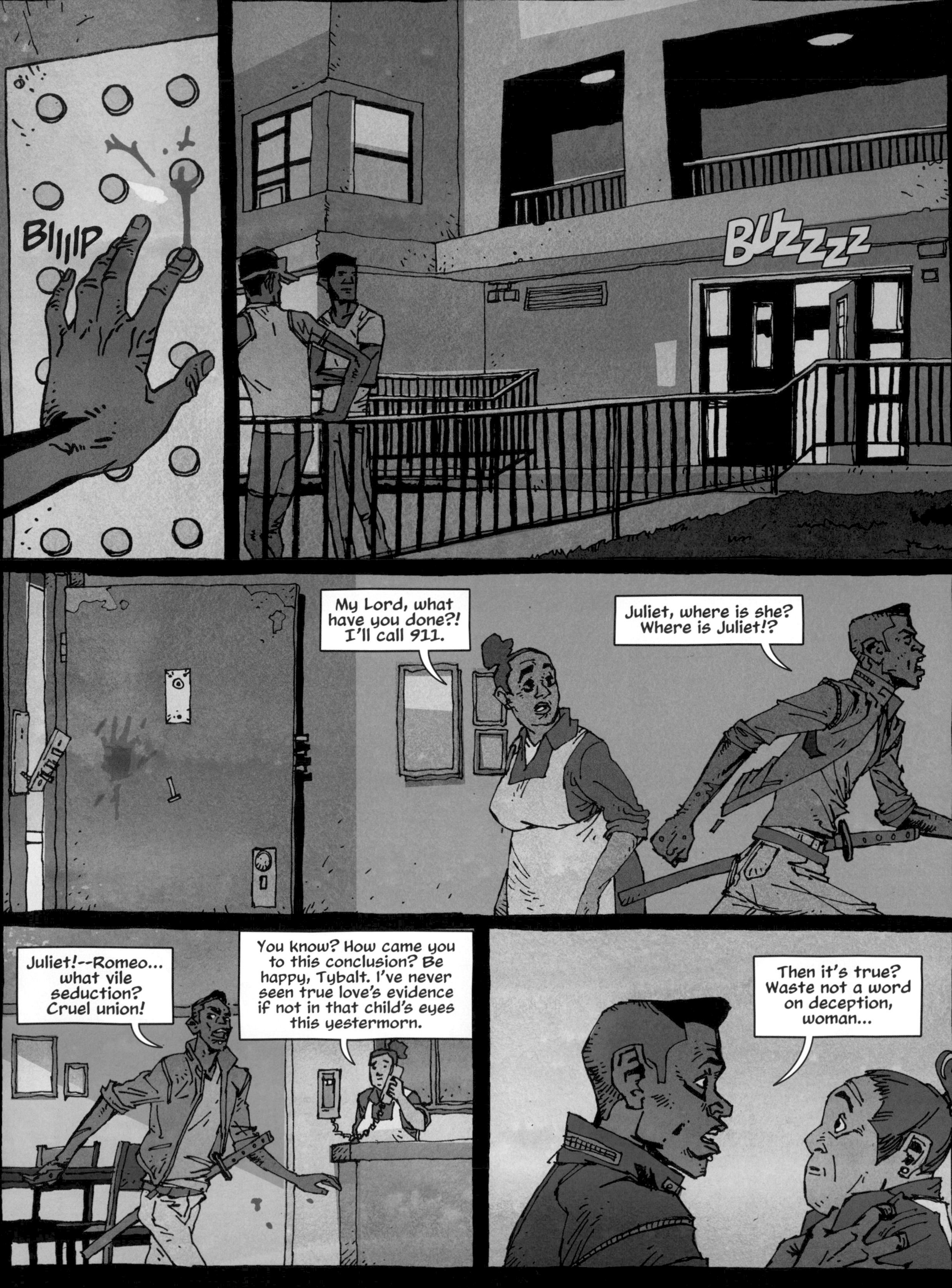
BIIIIP
BUZZZZ
My Lord, what have you done?! I'll call 911.
Juliet, where is she? Where is Juliet!?
Juliet!--Romeo... what vile seduction? Cruel union!
You know? How came you to this conclusion? Be happy, Tybalt. I've never seen true love's evidence if not in that child's eyes this yestermorn.
Then it's true? Waste not a word on deception, woman...

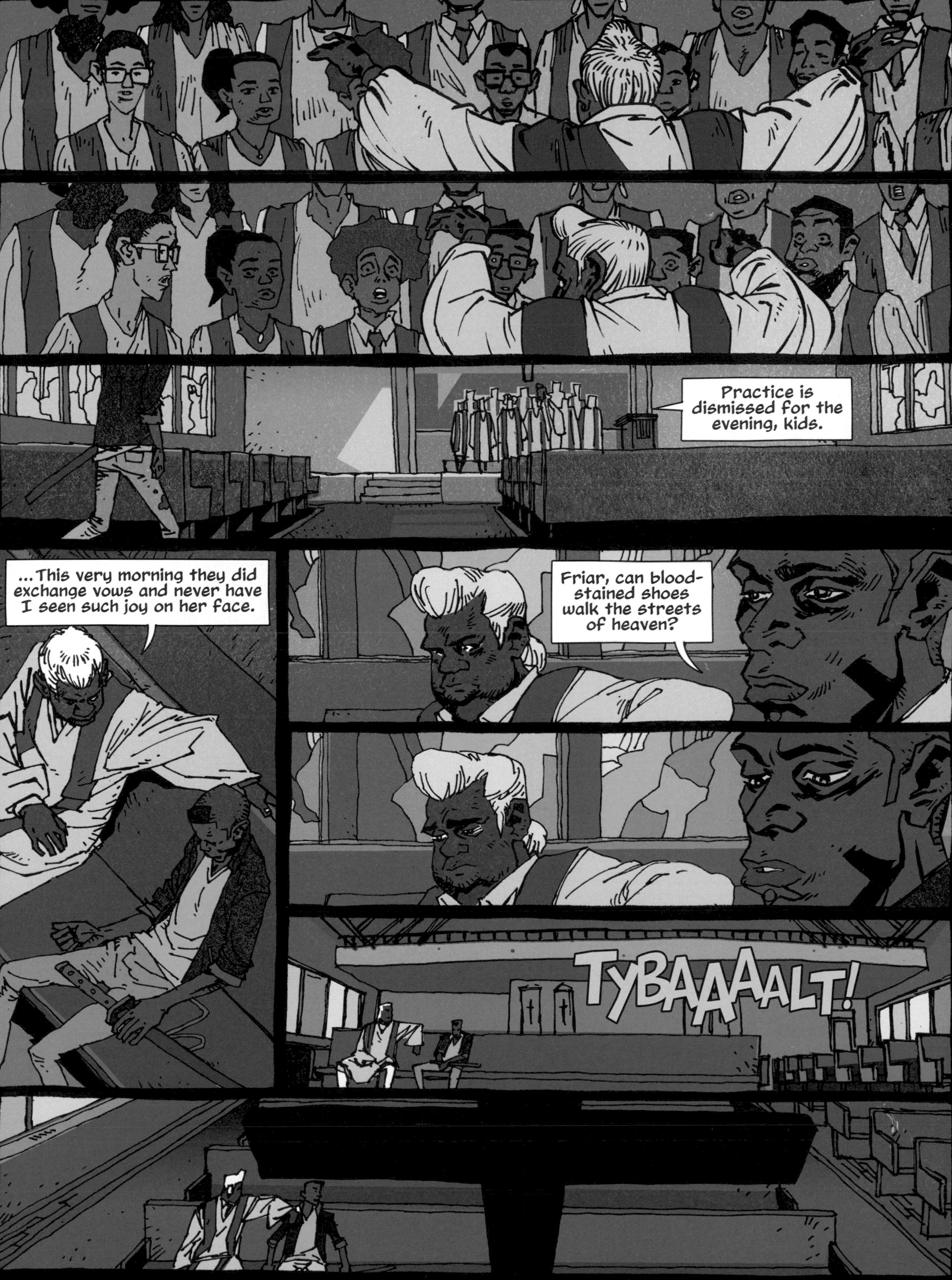
Practice is dismissed for the evening, kids.
...This very morning they did exchange vows and never have I seen such joy on her face.
Friar, can blood-stained shoes walk the streets of heaven?
TYBAAAAALT!

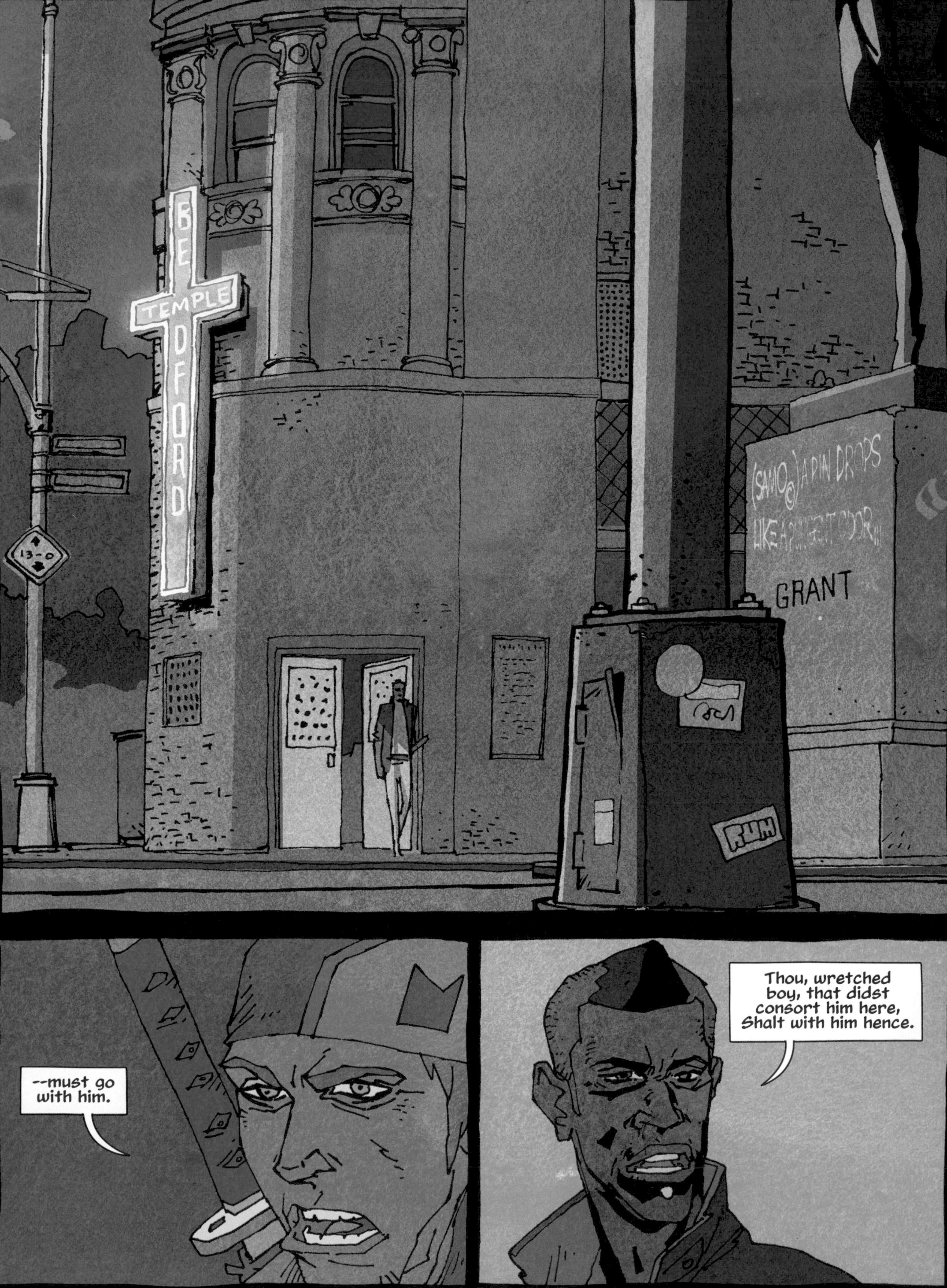
TEMPLE
BEDFORD
(SAMO©) A PIN DROPS LIKE A PUNGENT ODOR!!!
GRANT
RUM
--must go with him.
Thou, wretched boy, that didst consort him here, Shalt with him hence.

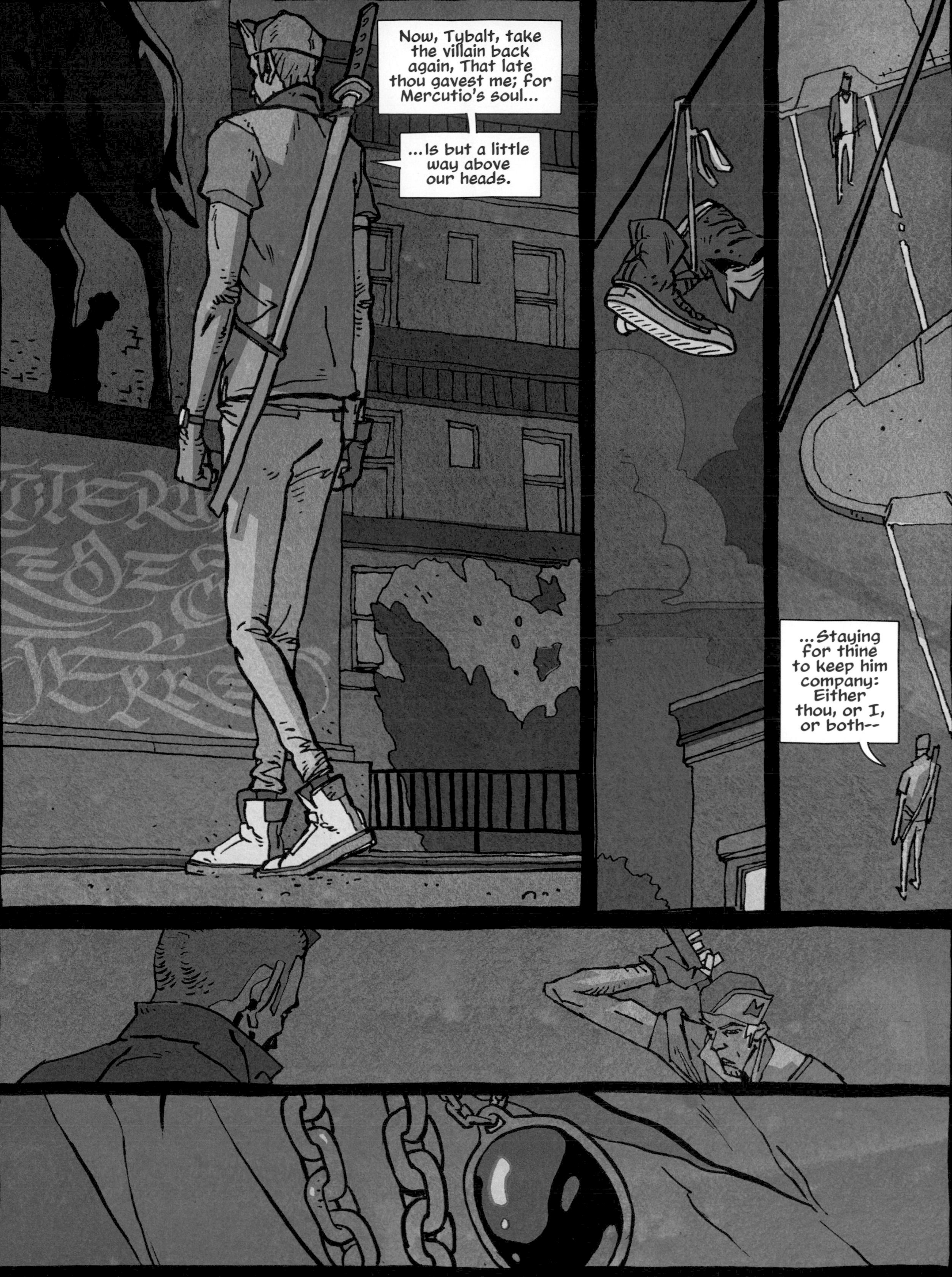
Now, Tybalt, take the villain back again, That late thou gavest me; for Mercutio's soul...
...Is but a little way above our heads.
...Staying for thine to keep him company: Either thou, or I, or both--

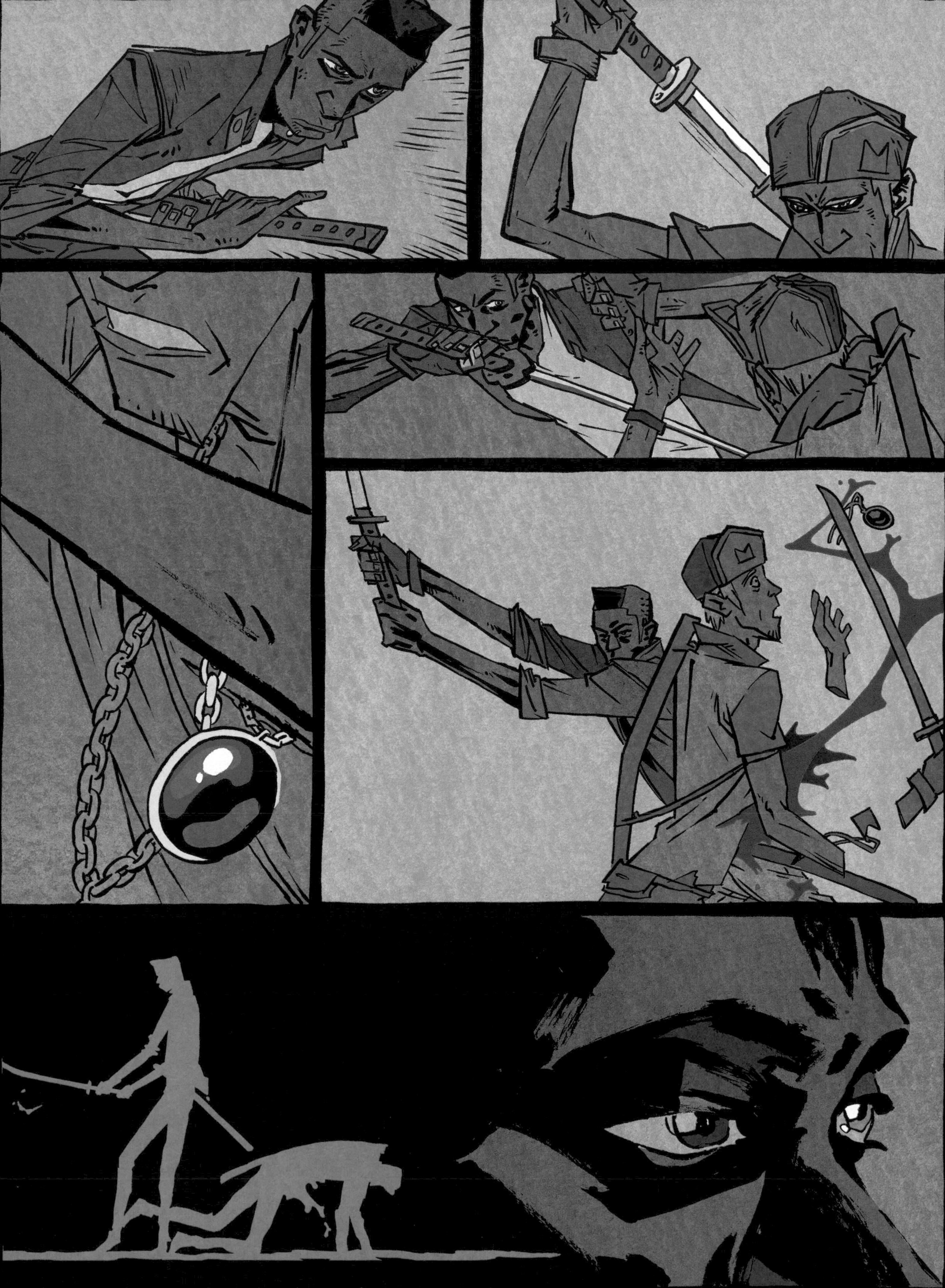

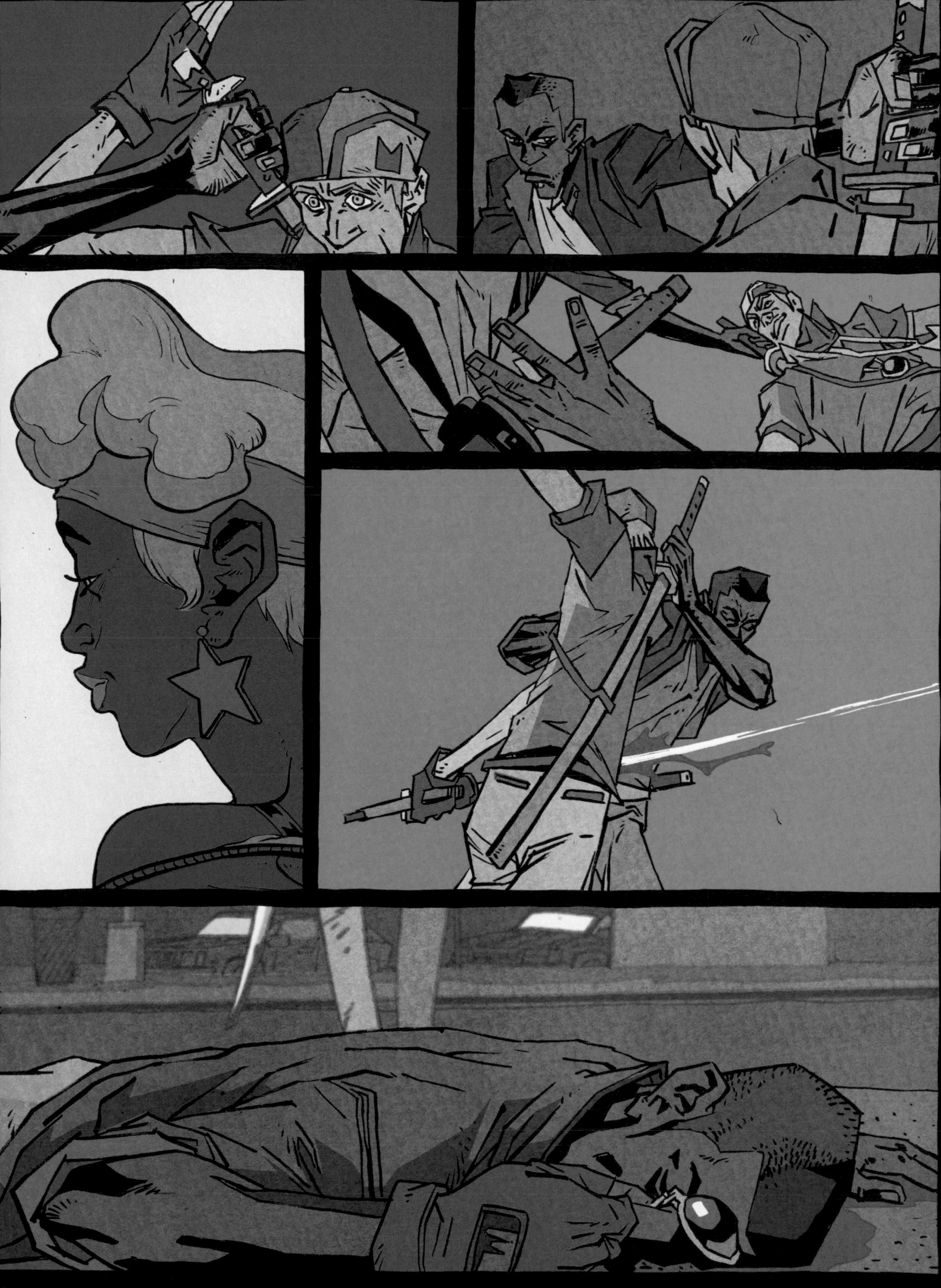

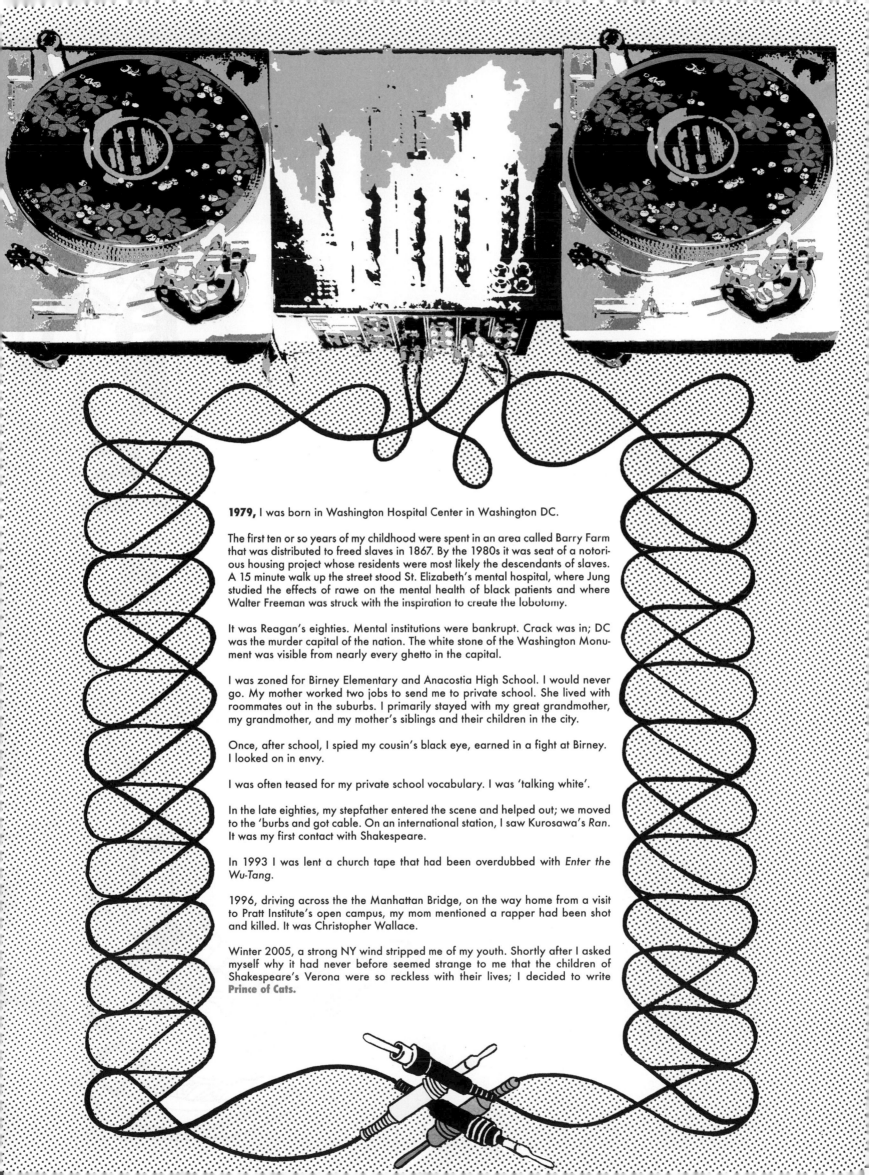

**1979,** I was born in Washington Hospital Center in Washington DC.

The first ten or so years of my childhood were spent in an area called Barry Farm that was distributed to freed slaves in 1867. By the 1980s it was seat of a notorious housing project whose residents were most likely the descendants of slaves. A 15 minute walk up the street stood St. Elizabeth's mental hospital, where Jung studied the effects of rawe on the mental health of black patients and where Walter Freeman was struck with the inspiration to create the lobotomy.

It was Reagan's eighties. Mental institutions were bankrupt. Crack was in; DC was the murder capital of the nation. The white stone of the Washington Monument was visible from nearly every ghetto in the capital.

I was zoned for Birney Elementary and Anacostia High School. I would never go. My mother worked two jobs to send me to private school. She lived with roommates out in the suburbs. I primarily stayed with my great grandmother, my grandmother, and my mother's siblings and their children in the city.

Once, after school, I spied my cousin's black eye, earned in a fight at Birney. I looked on in envy.

I was often teased for my private school vocabulary. I was 'talking white'.

In the late eighties, my stepfather entered the scene and helped out; we moved to the 'burbs and got cable. On an international station, I saw Kurosawa's *Ran*. It was my first contact with Shakespeare.

In 1993 I was lent a church tape that had been overdubbed with *Enter the Wu-Tang*.

1996, driving across the the Manhattan Bridge, on the way home from a visit to Pratt Institute's open campus, my mom mentioned a rapper had been shot and killed. It was Christopher Wallace.

Winter 2005, a strong NY wind stripped me of my youth. Shortly after I asked myself why it had never before seemed strange to me that the children of Shakespeare's Verona were so reckless with their lives; I decided to write **Prince of Cats.**

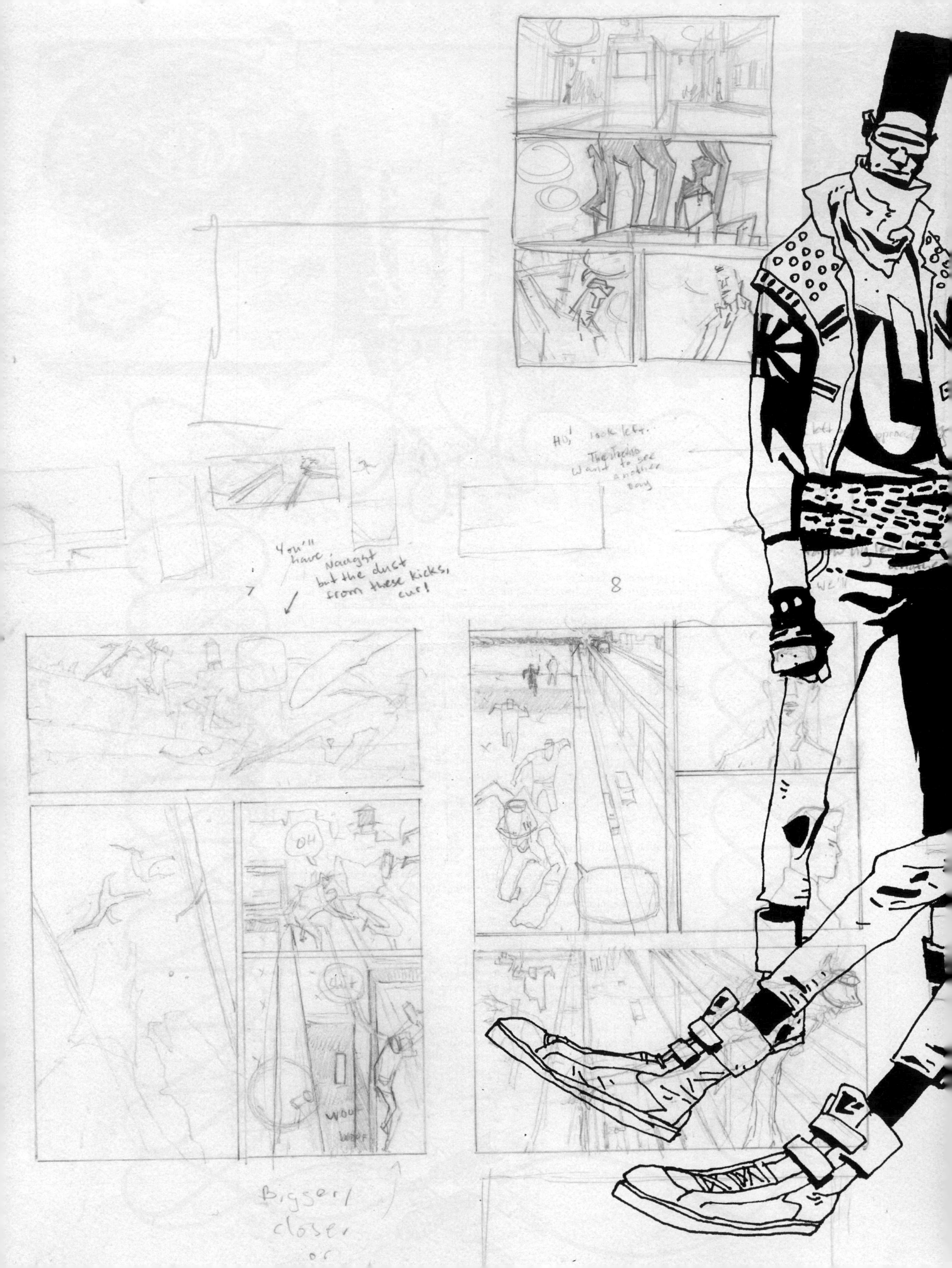
HO! look left.
Want to see another Day
You'll have Naught but the dust from these kicks, cur!
7
8
OH
WOOF
WOOF
Bigger/ closer, or

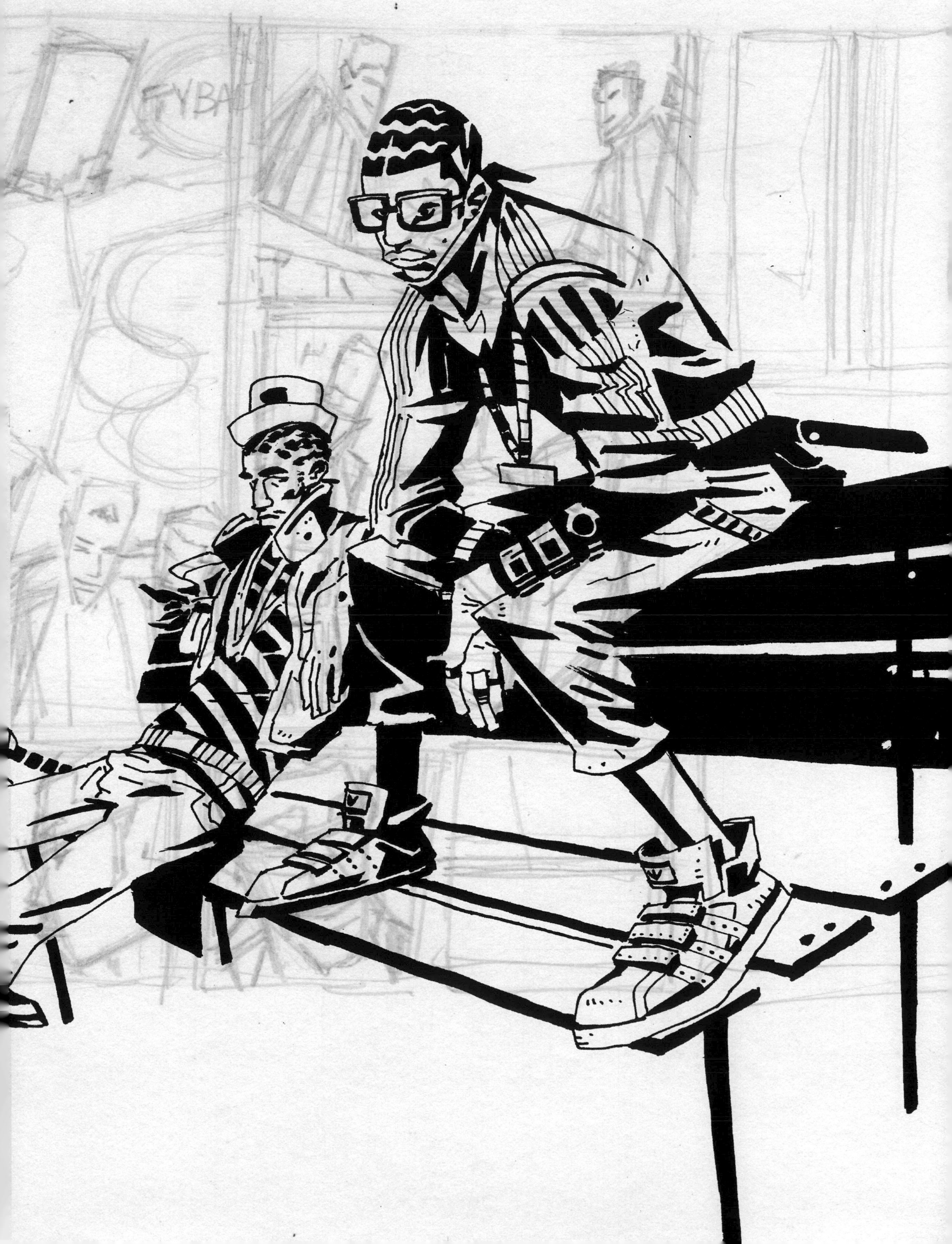

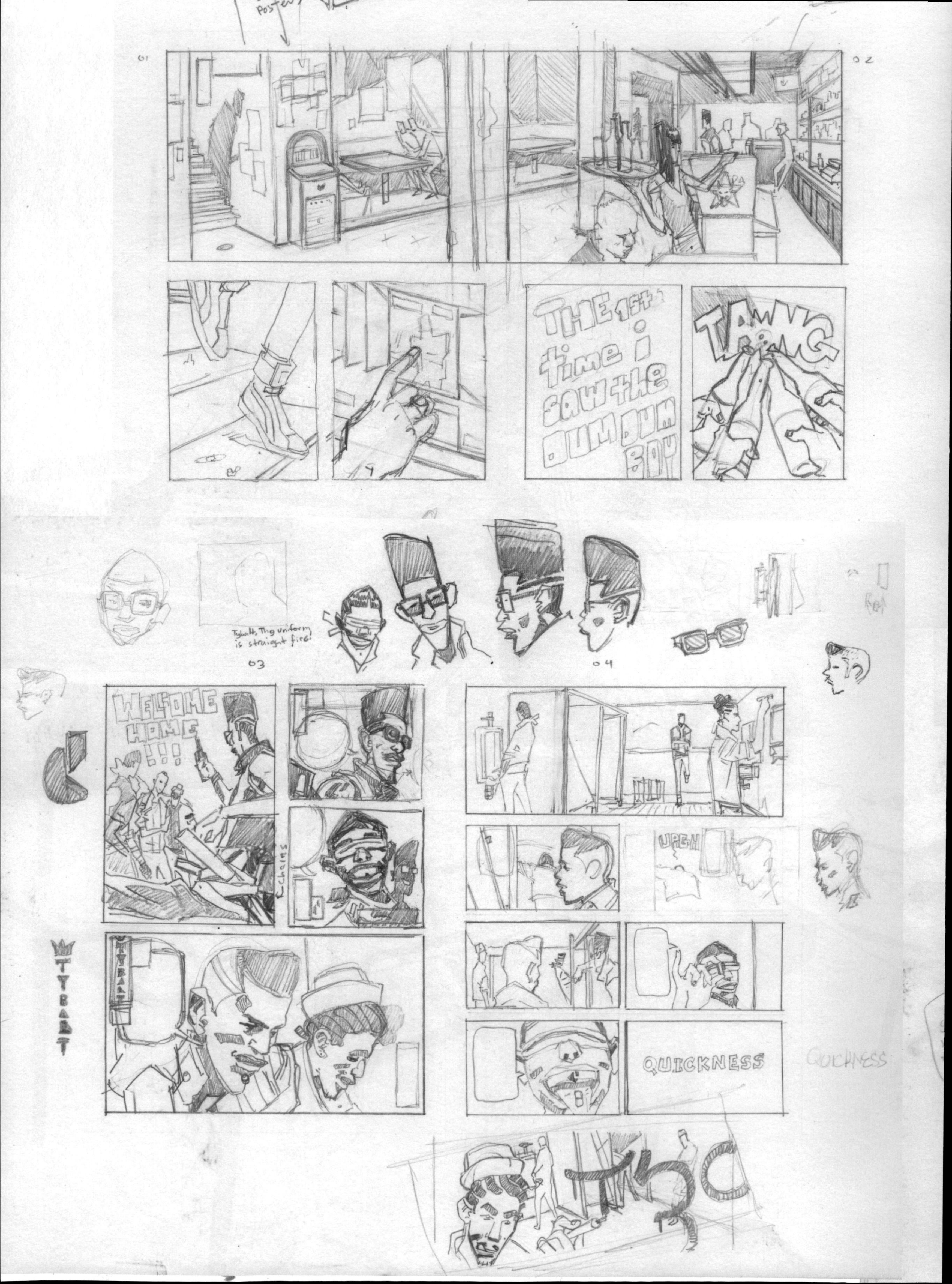

01
02
THE 1st time i saw the DUM DUM BOY
TANG
Tybalt, Thg uniform is straight fire!
03
04
WELCOME HOME !!!
QUICKNESS
QUICKNESS
TYBALT

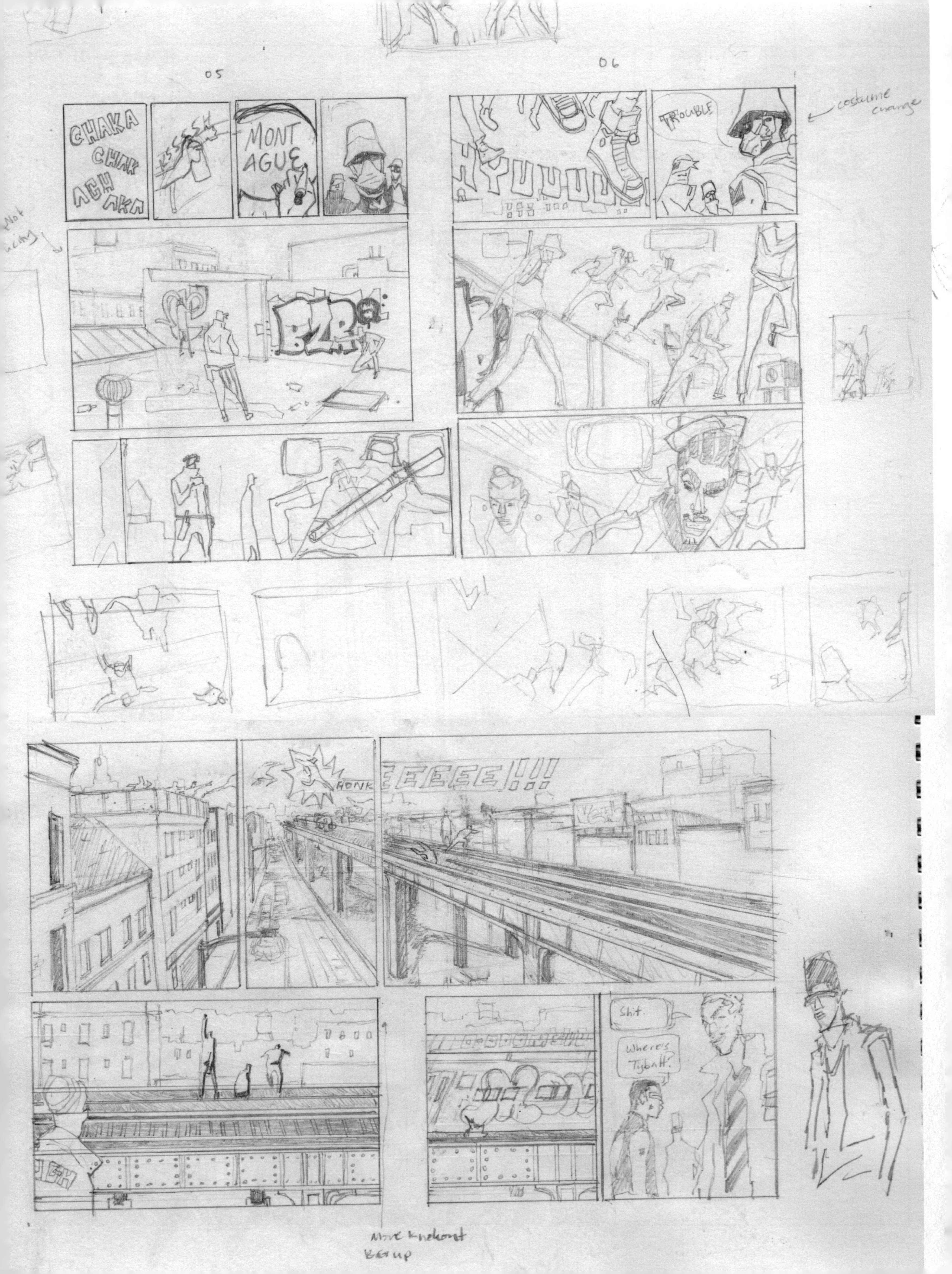

05
06
CHAKA
CHAK
ACH
AKA
MONT
AGUE
TROUBLE
costume change
HONK
EEEEE!!!
Shit.
Where's Tybalt?

POC 006

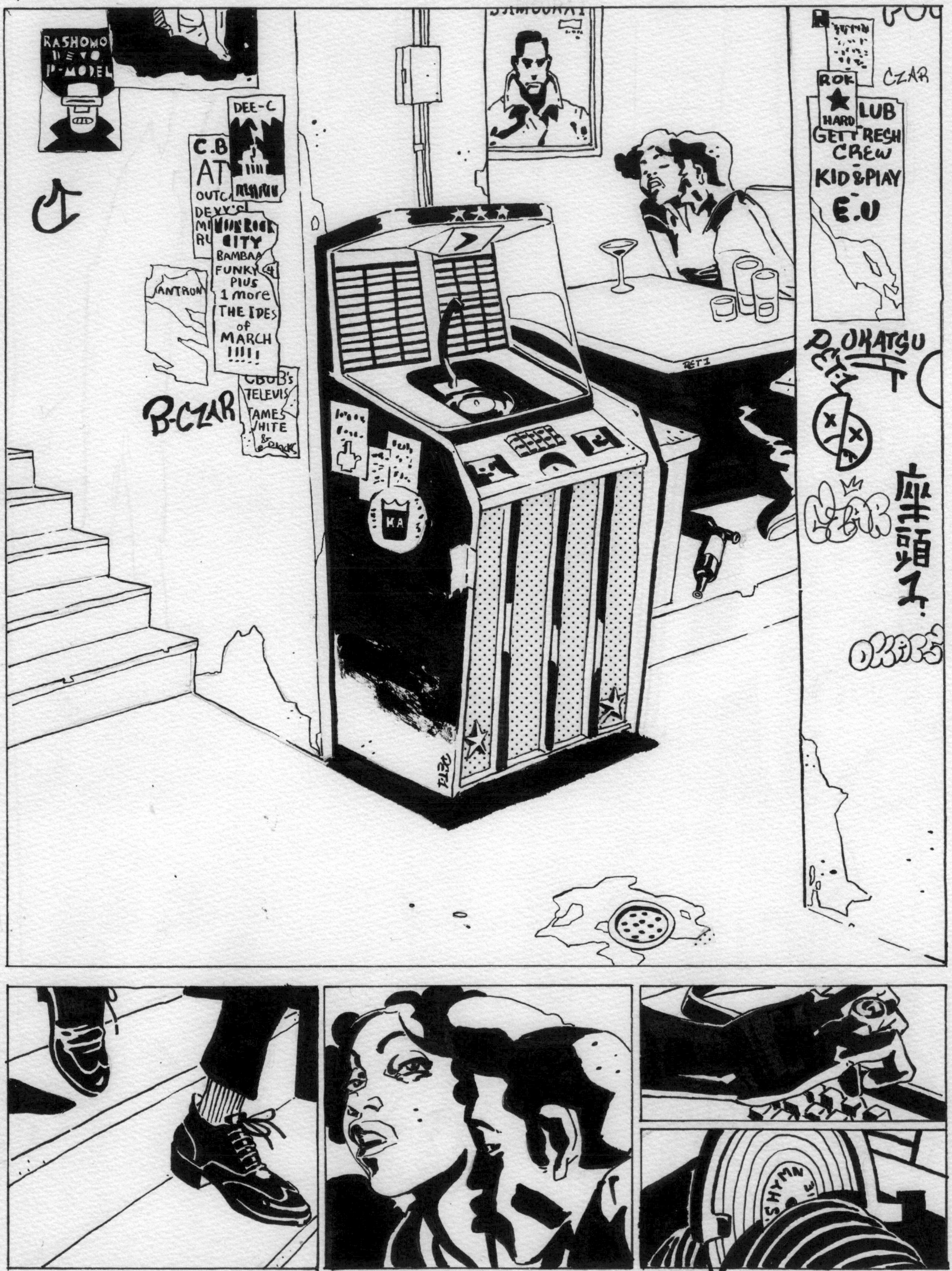
RASHOMO
DEVO
P-MODEL
DEE-C
CITY
BAMBAA
FUNKY
1 more
THE IDES of MARCH
ANTRON
B-CZAR
TELEVIS
CZAR
ROK HARD
LUB
KID & PLAY
E.U
OKATSU


DJ '09
09

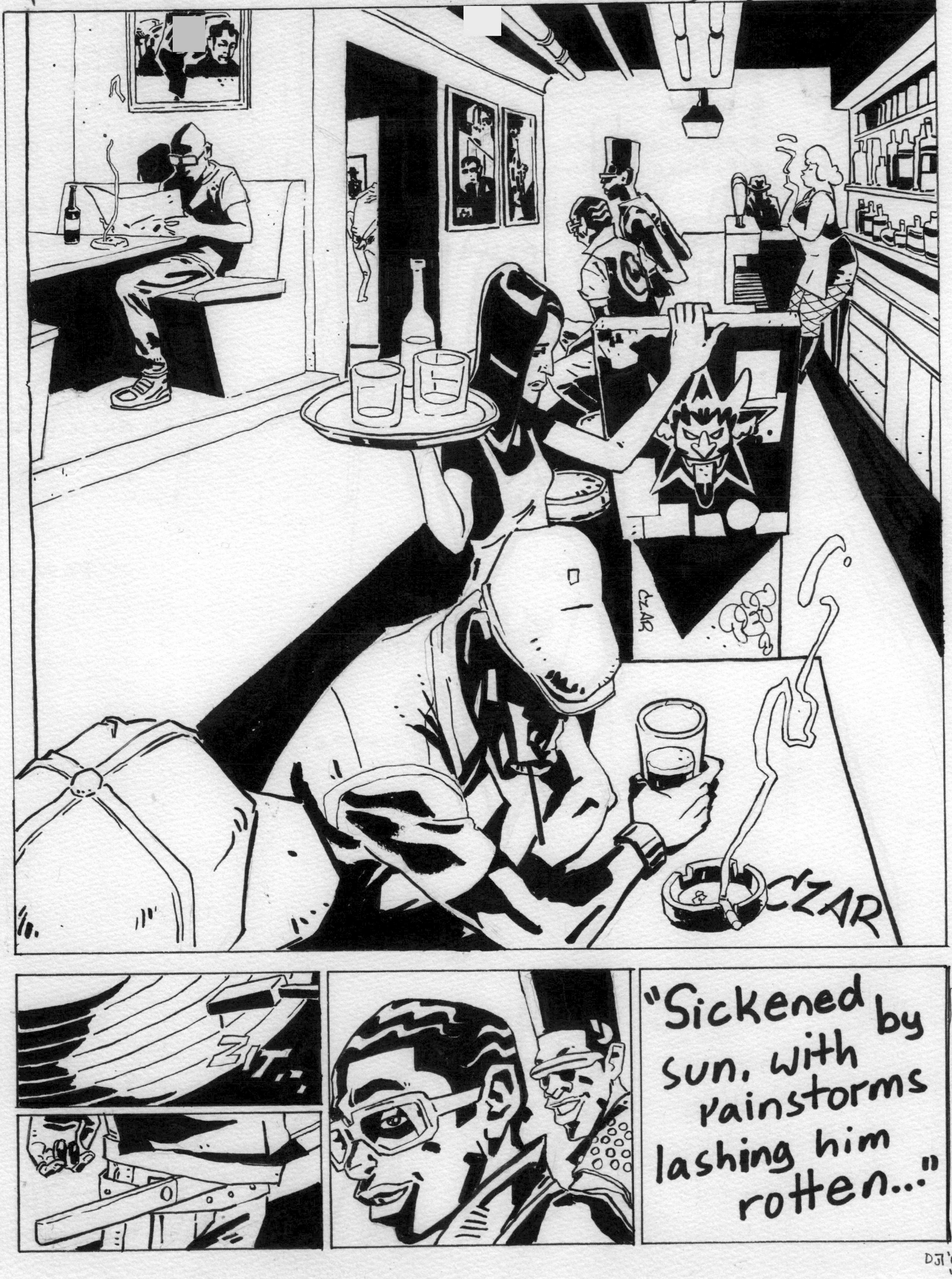
CZAR
CZAR
ZIT..
"Sickened by sun, with rainstorms lashing him rotten..."

DJ '09

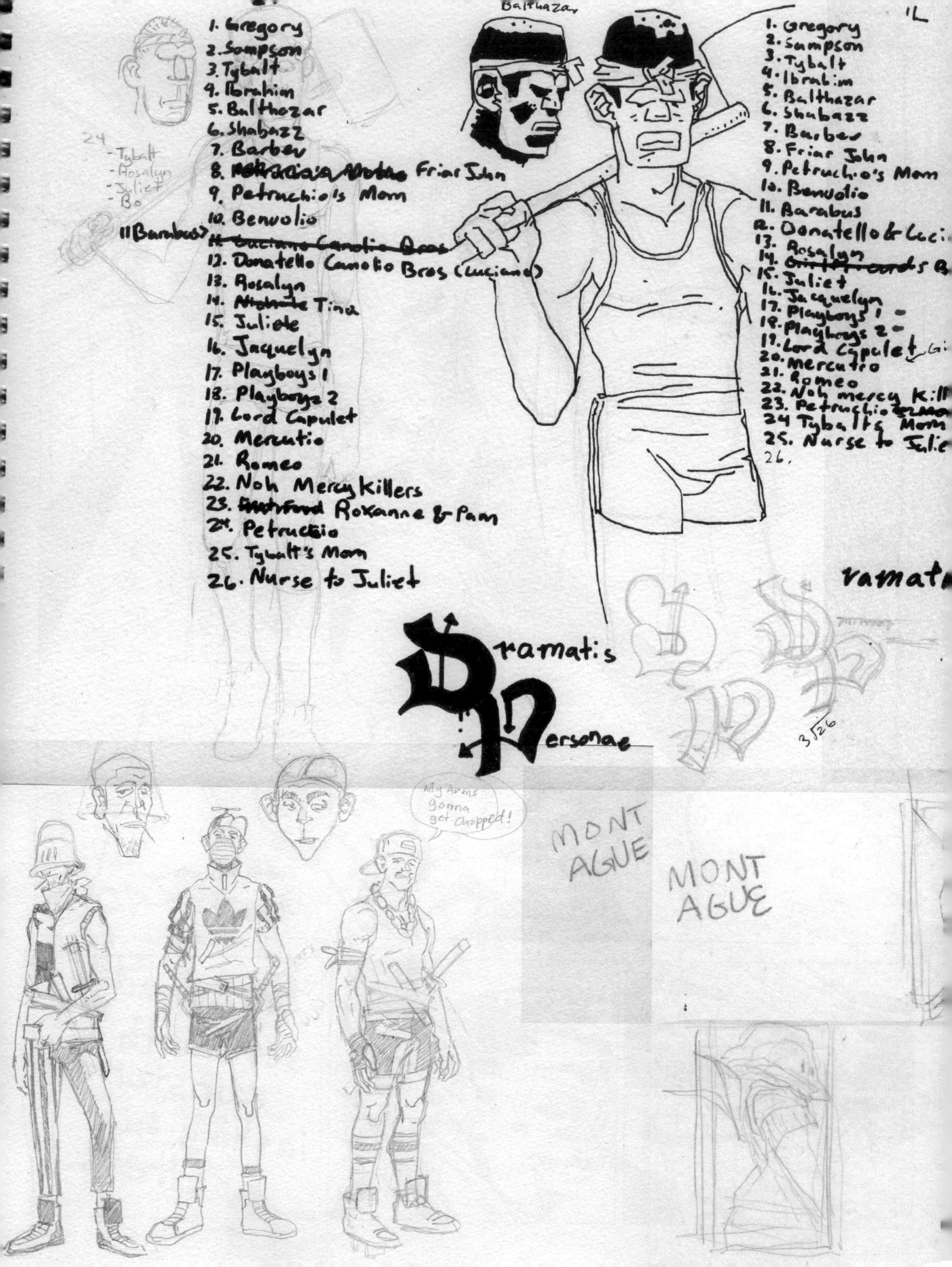
Balthazar
1L
1. Gregory
2. Sampson
3. Tybalt
4. Ibrahim
5. Balthazar
6. Shabazz
7. Barber
8. Friar John
9. Petruchio's Mom
10. Benvolio
11 Barabus
12. Donatello Canolio Bros (Luciano)
13. Rosalyn
14. Tina
15. Juliete
16. Jaquelyn
17. Playboys 1
18. Playboys 2
19. Lord Capulet
20. Mercutio
21. Romeo
22. Noh Mercy Killers
23. Roxanne & Pam
24. Petruchio
25. Tybalt's Mom
26. Nurse to Juliet
24
- Tybalt
- Rosalyn
- Juliet
- Bo
1. Gregory
2. Sampson
3. Tybalt
4. Ibrahim
5. Balthazar
6. Shabazz
7. Barber
8. Friar John
9. Petruchio's Mom
10. Benvolio
11. Barabus
12. Donatello & Luci
13. Rosalyn
14. s B
15. Juliet
16. Jacquelyn
17. Playboys 1 =
18. Playboys 2 =
19. Lord Capulet
20. Mercutio
21. Romeo
22. Noh mercy Kill
23. Petruchio
24 Tybalt's Mom
25. Nurse to Julie
26.
Dramatis Personae
ramati
My Arms gonna get Chopped!
MONT AGUE
MONT AGUE

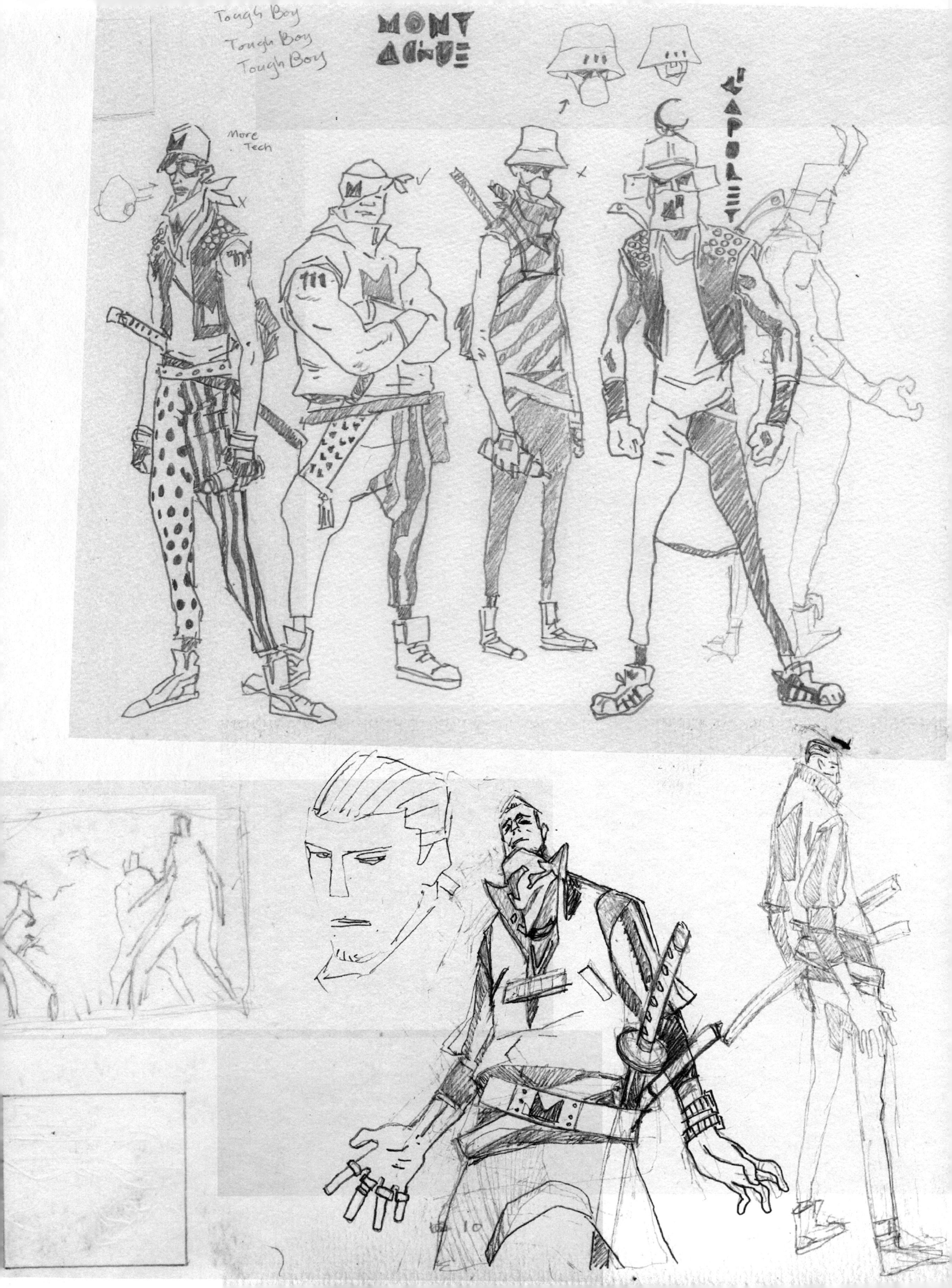
Tough Boy
Tough Boy
Tough Boy
MONT
AGUE
More Tech
CAPULET

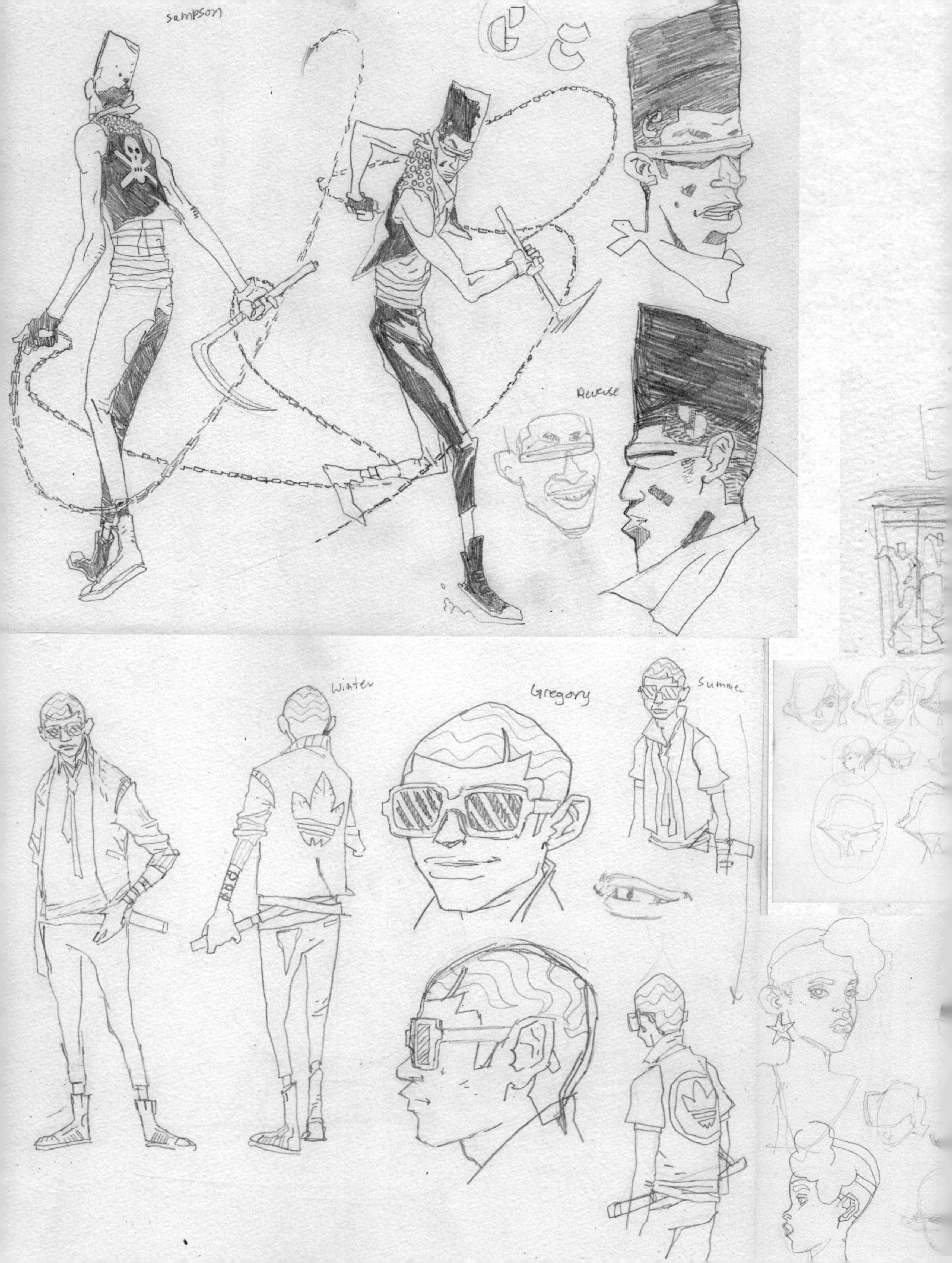
sampson
Revise
Winter
Gregory
Summe

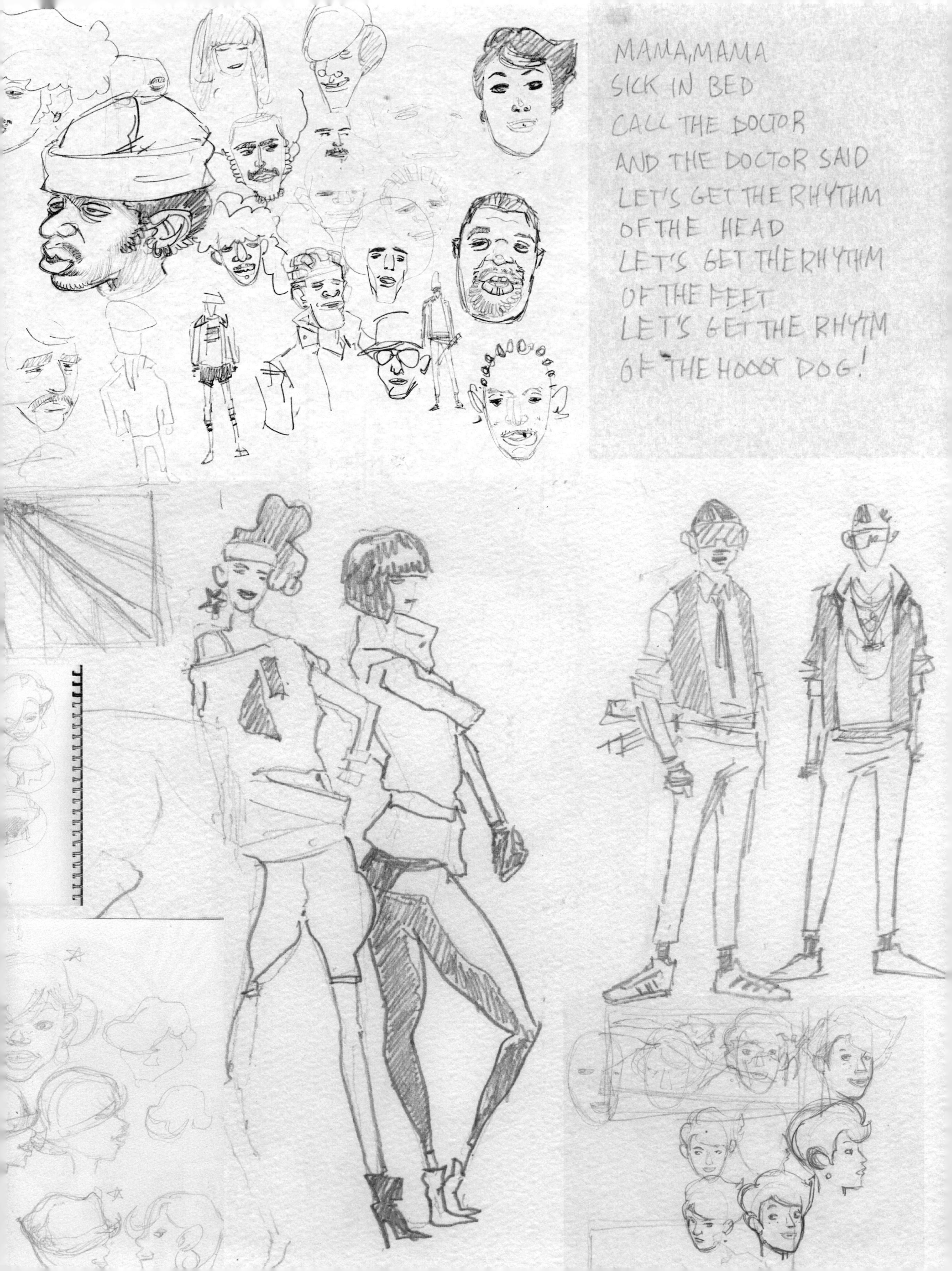
MAMA, MAMA
SICK IN BED
CALL THE DOCTOR
AND THE DOCTOR SAID
LET'S GET THE RHYTHM
OF THE HEAD
LET'S GET THE RHYTHM
OF THE FEET
LET'S GET THE RHYTM
OF THE HOOOT DOG!

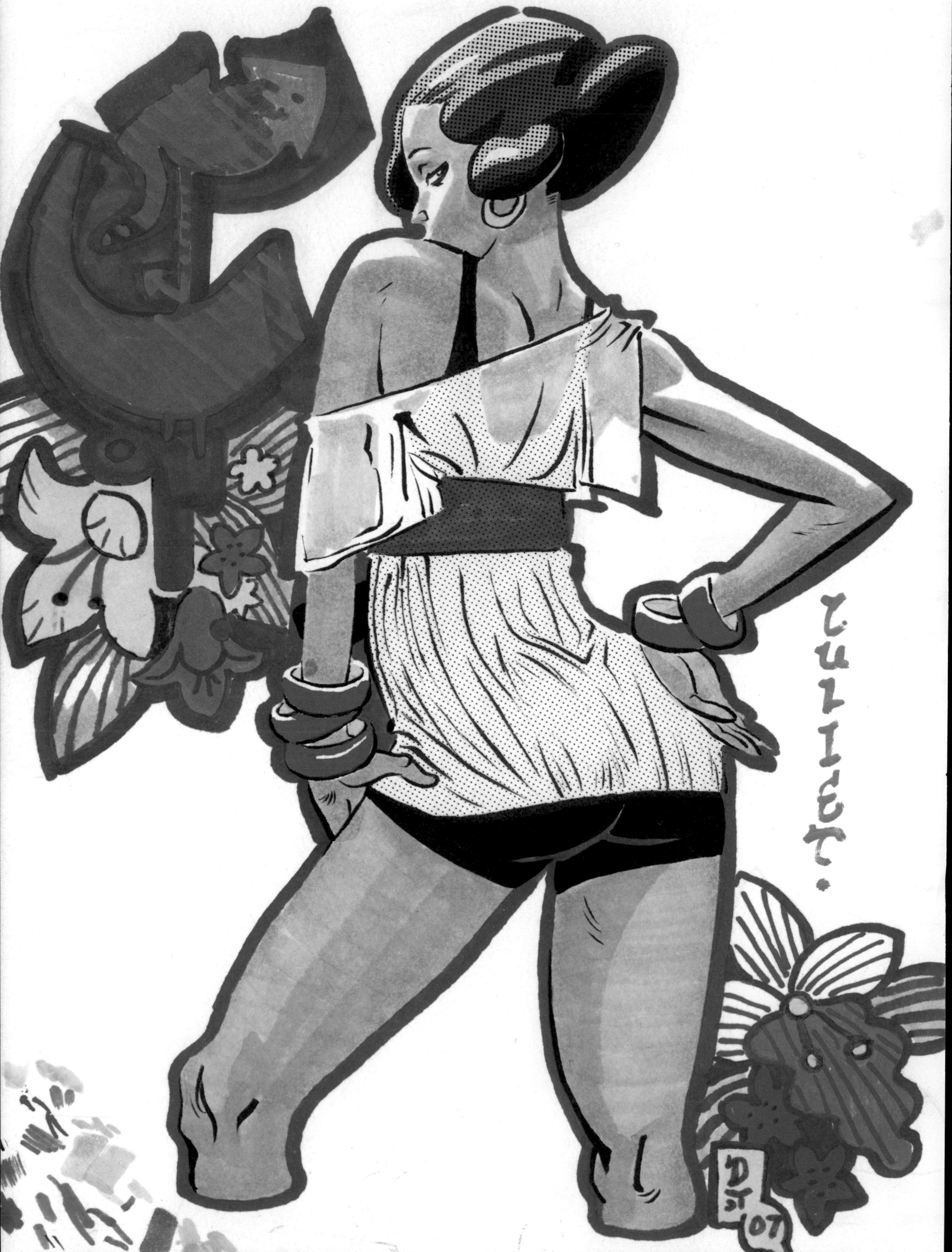
JULIET.